Edited by Michael Parkin
and Michael T. Sumner

Inflation in
the United Kingdom

Manchester University Press

University of Toronto Press

Published by
Manchester University Press
Oxford Road
Manchester M13 9PL

ISBN 0 7190 0695 3

Published in Canada and the United States 1978 by
University of Toronto Press
Toronto and Buffalo

ISBN 0 8020 2321 5

British Library cataloguing in publication data

Inflation in the United Kingdom - (Studies
    in inflation).
    1. Inflation (Finance) - Great Britain.
    I.   Parkin, Michael   II. Sumner, Michael
    Thomas   III. Series
    332. 4'1   HG939. 5

    MUP ISBN-0-7190-0695-3

    UTP ISBN 0-8020-2321-5

Printed in Great Britain
By Unwin Brothers Limited
The Gresham Press Old Woking Surrey England

Contents

Foreword to the series

In July 1971 a group of some twenty economists, econometricans and accountants, financed by the Social Science Research Council, began work at the University of Manchester on a three year research programme on the problem of inflation. The research consists largely of a series of self-contained investigations of various aspects of the inflationary process. In order to ensure that our own work does not develop in isolation from that being carried out elsewhere, it is the policy of the Manchester-SSRC Inflation Programme regularly to invite scholars from other Universities in the United Kingdom and elsewhere to present papers at Manchester. Though our own work, and that of our colleagues at other institutions, consists of self-contained projects, certain common themes continue to emerge as research progresses.

The purpose of this series of volumes is to bring together in a convenient form papers on related aspects of inflation so that other research workers and students will have easy access to a relatively integrated body of material. Though each volume will contain a large proportion of previously unpublished work, previous publication in a learned journal will not disqualify an otherwise relevant paper from being included in this series.

In promoting a wider understanding of the inflationary process original research is vital, but the dissemination of the results of that research is just as vital. It is our hope that this series of volumes will enable the results of our own work at Manchester, and that of our colleagues elsewhere, to reach a wide audience.

Michael Parkin
David Laidler

Preface

This final volume of the University of Manchester's *Studies in Inflation* brings together papers dealing with the determinants of price and wage movements in the United Kingdom. While all the contributions focus on this narrowly defined set of phenomena, they do not form individual parts of a fully integrated model designed to give a comprehensive account of the generation of U.K. inflation. Further, they represent the results of research conducted at various times during the period between 1971 and 1977. Nevertheless, the conclusions which are presented appear to be extremely robust with respect to the time period studied and the time at which the original work was executed.

All the papers which appear here grew out of the weekly meetings of the University of Manchester - Social Science Research Council Inflation Workshop, and they therefore reflect the criticisms, comments and encouragement provided by the members. Two of our colleagues, Malcolm Gray and George Zis, made such outstanding contributions, both to the content of this book and the research programme in general, that we must single them out for special thanks. We have been aided throughout the programme by the industrious and conscientious efforts of Robert Ward, who has handled all our data collection and computing requirements with skill, speed and impressive accuracy. Additionally, Richard Smith, Paul Temple and Kevin Tinsdale have provided research assistance for particular studies.

Excellent secretarial support has been provided by Marg. Gower, Linda Leonard, June Maddocks, Monica Malkus, Betty Newman and Vicki Whelan.

We are grateful to the editors of the *American Economic Review* and *Economica*, and to the Cambridge University Press for permission to reprint with amendments and additions articles previous published by them.

Finally, we acknowledge with thanks the financial support of the Social Science Research Council

Manchester, May 1977   Michael Parkin
                                             Michael T. Sumner

Contributors

John A. Carlson: Professor of Economics, Purdue University, Lafayette, Indiana, U.S.A.

David Laidler: Professor of Economics, University of Western Ontario, London, Canada.

Michael Parkin: Professor of Economics, University of Western Ontario, London, Canada.

Graham W. Smith: Lecturer in Economics, University of Manchester, Manchester, England.

Michael T. Sumner: Senior Lecturer in Economics, University of Manchester, Manchester, England.

1 United Kingdom inflation: an overview and summary

Michael Parkin and Michael T. Sumner

I THE QUESTIONS

Active macroeconomic policy in the post-war years has sought to achieve high and stable growth rates of per capita real income; low and steady unemployment; stable prices; and a balance in external payments while (until the early 1970s) maintaining fixed exchange rates. Judged against these objectives, all governments in all countries must be reckoned as failures; the performance of the United Kingdom has been a spectacular failure and, as such, stands as an important case to analyse both in its own right and for the lessons which it might contain for other countries. The questions examined in this book concern the failure to achieve only one of these objectives, price stability; but this failure has impinged on other facets of Britain's post-war economic problem. Specifically, the book deals with the following questions: what has caused the United Kingdom's post-war inflation; how could it have been prevented; and how may an inflationary future be avoided? These issues can be more appropriately structured if they are divided into three sub-sets of related questions. First, what induces firms to raise their prices and, acting jointly with trade unions, their wage rates? Notice the emphasis on variability. If prices and wages rose year in and year out at a constant rate, there would be no basis for an explanation and not much of a problem. It is the variability of inflation which makes it both a phenomenon of social and economic importance and one which is amenable to explanation using standard techniques of statistical inference. The first set of questions then concerns what might be called the 'proximate determinants' of inflation: why do firms and unions behave in such a way as to raise prices and wages at varying rates, and what are the variables exogenous to each firm and union which cause that variability in price- and wage-setting over time?

The second set of questions concerns government policy. Put directly, what are the effects of monetary and fiscal policy and direct controls on the price and wage setting behaviour of

firms and unions? This set of questions calls for an analysis of
the transmission mechanism from a given policy setting to the
behaviour of prices and wages, operating directly or through the
medium of other variables such as output and employment.

The third set of questions concerns the determinants of
government policy: why at some times and in some places do
governments pursue (or permit) inflation and at other times
engender price stability?

This book deals with all these questions in the context of
post-war Britain; however, its major concern is with the first set.
This uneven emphasis and allocation of attention does not reflect
our judgements as to the relative importance of the three sets
of questions: on the contrary, we believe that inflation cannot be
avoided until they have all been answered fully and clearly. Our
justification for focusing on the first set of questions is that an
enormous intellectual investment is already being lavished on the
second, and that the third constitutes a separate field of study by
virtue of a major difference in the appropriate methods of analysis.
Vast quantities of resources are being devoted to the second set of
questions, in the large scale econometric models of the London
Business School, the National Institute for Economic and Social
Research, Southampton University and the Treasury. In these
studies, highly disaggregated models of the aggregate demand side
of the economy are being developed. However, their treatment of
the aggregate supply side, the division of a change in nominal

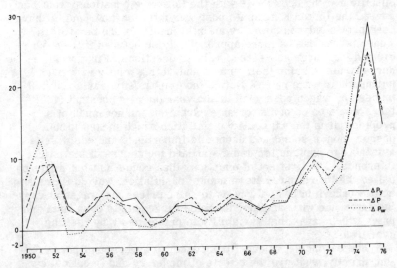

Figure 1.1 Inflation in the United Kingdom, 1950-76

demand between output and employment on the one hand and
prices and wages on the other, is rudimentary and—in some cases—
non-existent, the wage rate, in the Keynesian textbook tradition,
being treated as an exogenous variable

Our justification for de-emphasing the third sub-set of questions is that we suspect those will be more amenable to solution,
not in the context of a time-series study of an individual country
but in that of a cross-section study of several countries. Although
some tentative ideas on the 'political' determinants of inflationary
policies are now being developed,[1] an empirical study on the re-
quisite scale is beyond the scope of this book.

One of the recurring themes in our concentration on the
proximate determinants of inflation is that the unprecedented
experience of the last decade, with which few readers will be un-
familiar, is most appropriately regarded not as a unique event but
as part of a much longer process of evolution, the earlier part of
which may be less familiar. Accordingly, our next task is to provide a brief account of the facts to be explained.

II THE FACTS TO BE EXPLAINED

There is no unique measure of inflation However, if a variety of
alternative measures all tell broadly the same story, then lack of
a unique measure does not constitute a problem. In the case of
post-war inflation in Britain, the main alternative measures,
although differing in detail, do indeed tell broadly the same story.
Figure 1.1 sets out that story as revealed by annual rates of
change in wholesale prices (Δp_w), retail prices (Δp) and the more
comprehensive Gross Domestic Product implicit deflator (Δp_y).
This figure gives a clear picture of the broad trends and cycles
in Britain's inflation rate. The story begins with the Korean War
inflation bubble taking inflation up to the ten per cent region. That
historically high inflation rate was of short duration, so that, by
1954, Britain was virtually free from inflation. This was followed
by a marked cyclical upturn with the inflation rate hitting its peak
in 1956, then falling again to the neighbourhood of zero by the turn
of the decade. The broad trend for the 1950s, if we take into
account the Korean War peak, was clearly strongly negative.
Ignoring the Korean War peak, the trend was virtually flat.

In 1961 the inflation rate began to rise and through the first
seven years of the 1960s went through two marked and quite
regular cycles, peaking in 1961-2 and again in 1965. These cycles,
however, were superimposed upon a slightly, but nevertheless
distinctly, rising trend. Regardless of how it is measured, the
peak inflation rate in 1965 exceeded that of 1961-2 by almost a
full percentage point. Since 1967, the inflation rate has behaved

in a very much more volatile manner. Gradual increases in the rate between 1967 and 1969 were followed by a strong explosive burst which took the rate almost to its Korean War level of ten per cent by the turn of the decade. In 1972 the inflation rate fell, though only very slightly; this lull was followed in 1973-5 by the strongest explosion of all, reaching a peak in the mid-twenties in 1975. During 1976, the rate has fallen again to the mid-teens.

Although Britain's inflation rate has been high, it has been more than matched by increases in money wages. Real wages not only grew in line with productivity growth, which averaged a little over two per cent per annum, but grew fast enough to produce a rise in income from employment as a percentage of GDP from 66 per cent in 1952 to 71 per cent by 1974. That rise in the relative share of income from employment was markedly cyclical and, with the exception of a strong upward movement in 1974, has every appearance of having been on a level trend since 1965.

The movements in money wages (Δw), which, together with price level movements, underlie the movements in relative shares are shown in Figure 1.2, along with an indicator of the level of real economic activity, the unemployment rate (U). Several features of this chart are noteworthy. First, it is apparent that the broad trends of money wage change are similar to those of price changes. There is a slight but unmistakable downward trend from 1951 to 1962. That slight downward trend is followed by an equally slight upward trend to 1969. Thereafter wages explode in two

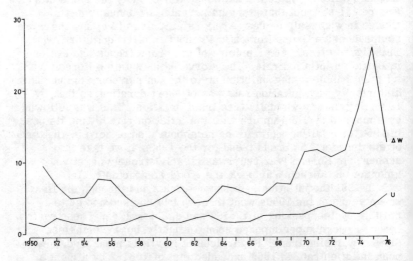

Figure 1.2 Unemployment and wage inflation, 1950-76

stages, rising faster than ten per cent per annum from 1970, with a further jump in 1974-5. Secondly, the behaviour of unemployment and its relation to the rate of wage change is very interesting. A strong inverse relation between money wage change and unemployment is apparent during the period up to 1967; from 1967 to 1971 both unemployment and wage inflation rise together; however, in 1972 and 1973 the inverse relation appears to return but very much displaced, while in 1974, with unemployment virtually constant, wages explode. The inverse relation finally reappears in the last year shown. The third striking feature of Figure 1.2 is the steadily rising trend of unemployment throughout the entire period under review.

Throughout the post-war years, various combinations of fiscal and monetary policy as well as direct wage and price controls ('prices and incomes policy') have been used in attempts to control inflation and the associated problems of unemployment and the balance of payments. In overall terms it is clear that the demand management policies in Britain were conservatively contractionary during the 1950s and generally, with important exceptions, expansionary during the 1960s and 1970s. Wage and price controls were in force during the bulk of the 1960s, during which time the rest of the policy stance was inflationary and the inflation rate itself was rising.

Details of the development of wage and price controls are set out in Table 1.1. There are many features and dimensions of direct controls on wages and prices which could be important in influencing their effects on inflation. We have focused on three aspects of controls in the summary data given in Table 1.1. First we have distinguished between voluntary and statutory controls: presumably the latter have greater weight than the former. Secondly, we have distinguished between controls on the basis of the nature of the enforcing agency: in several cases no agency was set up, but in others elaborate machinery for review of wage and price changes and for policing the behaviour of unions and firms was part and parcel of the programme. Thirdly, programmes have varied in the limits which they have sought to place on wage and price adjustments. Not surprisingly these limits tended to rise with the rate of inflation, the objective typically being to reduce the rate of inflation below its most recent level rather than to reduce it to zero.

This brief review of the movements in prices, wages and unemployment, and even briefer account of demand management policies and wage-price controls, enables us to state in more direct form the questions which this book seeks to answer. Specifically, what are the interrelationships between price and wage movements and how are they each influenced, if at all, by demand management and by prices and incomes policies?

Table 1.1 Wage and price controls in the United Kingdom 1948-76

Period	Wage norms or limits	Statutory (S)/ voluntary (V)/ compulsory (C)	Enforcing agency
1948-50	None	V	TUC
1956	None	V	None
July 1961– March 1962	Zero ('Pay pause')	V	None
April 1962– October 1964	2-3·5% ('Guiding light')	V	National Incomes Commission
December 1964– July 1966	3-3·5% ('Statement of intent')	V	National Board for Prices and Incomes (PIB)
July-December 1966	Zero ('Freeze')	S	PIB
January-June 1967	'Severe restraint'	S	PIB
July 1967– June 1970	Successive relaxation, rising to 4·5% by 1969. Special provisions for low paid and productivity agreements.	S	PIB
November 1972– January 1973	Zero ('Stage I freeze')	S	None
February– October 1973	£1 p.w. plus 4% ('Stage II')	S	Pay Board and Price Commission
November 1973– February 1974	7% plus 'threshold' indexation ('Stage III')	S	Pay Board and Price Commission
March 1974– July 1975	Cost of living increase ('Social contract')	V	None
August 1975– July 1976	£6 p.w.	C	None
August 1976– July 1977	4·5% (subject to maximum absolute amount)	C	None

III ALTERNATIVE ANSWERS

Up to the middle of the 1960s there was a strong consensus on the answers to the above questions. Inflation was seen as the consequence of using monetary and fiscal policy to achieve a very high degree of capacity utilisation and low unemployment, and the cycles in inflation were seen as the result of a 'stop-go' pattern in that monetary and fiscal policy. Little role was ascribed to prices and incomes policies in modifying the course of inflation. However, in the late 1960s, this explanation was increasingly called into question. The principal 'awkward fact' which raised the strongest doubts was the behaviour of inflation and unemployment in the latter part of the 1960s and the 1970s, as displayed in Figure 1.2 above. The failure of the traditional answers naturally led to the formulation of a variety of alternative hypotheses designed to account both for the period prior to 1967 and also capable of explaining the late 1960s and 1970s. The alternative hypotheses advanced to explain what some were calling 'the new inflation' can be classified in a variety of ways, but, for present purposes, the most useful is one which divides the alternatives into 'domestic' and 'international' theories. The principal 'domestic' theories identify the behaviour of money wages as the central economic variable which proximately determines the rate of inflation, and suggest a variety of alternative (but not necessarily mutually exclusive) socio-psychological factors which lead to variation in the degree of 'wage-push'. The international approach, drawing on an intellectual pedigree running back to David Hume, emphasises the capacity of the world monetary system under fixed exchange rates to transmit inflation from one country to another. On this view, inflation is a phenomenon determined at the level of the fixed-exchange-rate world aggregate, imported by countries with tight monetary policies and balance of payments surpluses (such as West Germany) and exported by countries with slack monetary policies and balance of payments deficits (such as the United Kingdom and, in the late 1960s especially, the United States). An individual country's inflation rate may exceed or fall short of the world average rate for prolonged periods because of movements in relative prices associated with differential growth rates. Also, inflation rates may differ, but for shorter periods, because of relatively slack or tight domestic demand management policy leading to changes in the relative prices of internationally tradeable and non-tradeable goods. If the divergence is not reversed, then exchange rate adjustments will eventually be required, thereby validating the relative price differential on a permanent basis. If the divergence continues so long that exchange rates have to adjust frequently or float, then it becomes necessary to treat the individual country's inflation rate as being determined by its own monetary policy and its exchange rate movement relative to that in the rest of the world.

We do not claim to be able to provide final and definite discrimination between these alternative hypotheses. We do claim, however, that it is possible to interpret the main movements in the United Kingdom's inflation as arising from movements in world prices, modified by variations in domestic aggregate demand and associated inflation expectations, and as being amenable to control by control of domestic aggregate demand. Greater freedom in this respect is made possible by the floating exchange rate. Further, we claim that whether or not some movements in wages and/or prices originate in a socio-psychological 'push', direct controls on prices or wages or both are instruments with negligible power in any period longer than the shortest of short runs.

A full account of the work done by the University of Manchester-SSRC research programme bearing on British inflation will not be found here. The international aspects of inflation

and its transmission between countries were the subject of two
earlier volumes in this series (Parkin and Zis, 1976a, b); accordingly, those aspects receive relatively little explicit attention here.
They cannot be ignored in accounting for variations in expected
inflation, but, as noted above, we do not examine here the sources
of variations in aggregate demand nor the specific contribution
of exogenous shocks from the external sector. Similarly, those
aspects of the labour market explored in Laidler and Purdy (1974)
and previous work on incomes policies reported in Parkin and
Sumner (1972) have an obvious bearing on the subject of this book,
but that earlier material is not summarised extensively here.

IV ORGANISATION

The organisation of the rest of the book reflects the questions
posed above and proceeds in the following ways.

First, in Chapter 2 we present a review of the alternative
explanations which have been advanced for British inflation. This,
it is hoped, comprehensively surveys all the alternative views
which can be found. They have been forced into two broad categories: those which emphasise wage-push (and other exogenous
forces) as the originating factors on the one hand; and those which
emphasise aggregate demand (whether emanating originally from
excessive money creation or from excessive budget deficits) on
the other.

Chapter 3 goes on to provide what might be thought of as an
extensive summary of the basic view adopted in this book. It
provides an account of Britain's inflation, the policy debate
surrounding it, and a 'monetarist' perspective on its origins and
on the relationship between inflation and other macroeconomic
indicators.

Chapter 4 is a central chapter dealing with the most contro-
versial aspect of the sources of inflation in Britain, the proximate
determinants of the rate of change of money wages. This examines
the debate concerning the relevance of the Phillips curve, the
augmentation of the Phillips curve by expectations, the factors
determining expectations, and factors influencing the long-run
trade-off (if any) between inflation and unemployment.

The proximate determinants of the price-setting behaviour of
firms are the subject of the next chapter (Chapter 5). This con-
centrates on the question of whether excess demand has a separate
influence on price determination, or whether prices are affected
only by costs so that firms are an entirely passive element in
the inflation transmission mechanism.

Expectations of price change dominate explanations of wage
and price change themselves and therefore are a central feature

of our analysis. Rather than leaving these variables as unobserved
and eliminating them from our empirical studies by some untested
auxiliary hypothesis, we have put a great deal of effort into, and
emphasis on, the direct measurement of expectations of inflation.
In Chapter 6 we deal with the measurement and determination of
price expectations by consumers, and in Chapter 7 with producers'
expectations of wholesale prices and unit costs.

V SUMMARY OF CONCLUSIONS

A summary characterisation of our conclusions is not easy, but
will be attempted here for the convenience of the reader. Britain's
inflationary history up to 1967 can only be understood if one takes
a world view of the inflationary problem. Until that date Britain
was operating on a fixed exchange rate with the rest of the world.
International trade and arbitrage ensured that Britain's inflation
rate could not get too far out of line with the inflation rates prevailing elsewhere. Furthermore, the course of that inflation was
heavily dominated by the inflationary behaviour of the world's
largest economy (the United States), but also influenced by the
other large countries (Germany and Japan and other European
countries). Through the 1950s the rate of inflation in Britain was
falling; through the early 1960s it was rising gently. These trends
match exactly the broad trends in the rest of the world, and are a
reflection of relatively conservative Keynesian policies being
pursued in the United States and Germany throughout the 1950s,
followed by a major change in policy stance in the United States
in the early 1960s which led to a more inflationary era. Britain's
inflation since the late 1960s is to be explained partly by the continued acceleration of world inflation, but also by Britain's own
excessively expansive fiscal and monetary policies and consequent
sterling exchange rate adjustments. For this later period the
British inflation is, to a larger extent than earlier, a domestically
generated phenomenon. The mechanisms which we believe caused
that inflation start with a strong rise in public expenditure in the
late 1960s. We do not know why that event occurred, but we would
identify that as the major source of the inflationary problems of
the 1970s. That increase in expenditure not matched by associated
increases in taxes led to an increase in the overall level of demand
and an increase in the rate of monetary expansion. This excess
demand started to generate rising wages and prices and rising
expectations of inflation. The interaction of these factors, together
with a continued expansion of the money supply, permitted the
inflation rate to accelerate and reach a percentage in the mid-
twenties by 1975. A central part of the transmission process is
an expectations-augmented Phillips curve with a natural unemploy-

ment rate that is independent of the rate of inflation but not, however, independent of certain other key factors which have caused it to rise substantially in recent years.

The inflationary experience of Britain has been somewhat modified by the operation of wage and price controls, but the broad trends have hardly been touched by these policies. As far as we can tell, wage and price controls have had at best transitory, and subsequently negated, effects on the course of British inflation.

Our studies find it unnecessary to invoke labour union militancy, profits-push inflation originating in the behaviour of firms, or any other special factor to account for variations, more particularly the steep increases, in inflation. Undoubtedly labour unions do vary in their degree of militancy, and undoubtedly such things as strike activity vary in a systematic fashion over time; however, our earlier studies could find no evidence and no reasons in theory for the supposition that these factors are anything other than a consequence rather than a cause of the inflationary process in post-war Britain.[2]

The above is an extremely sketchy overview of our conclusions and should not be taken to be a fair and accurate summary of them. Many qualifications and probabilistic conditions should be attached to all the above statements. This can only be done at length and, indeed, is the subject of most of the rest of this book and of the other volumes to which we have referred.

NOTES TO CHAPTER 1

[1]   See in particular Gordon (1975), Parkin (1975b), and Parkin and Swoboda (1977)

[2]   The concept of labour militancy and the problems of isolating its influence on wage determination have been explored by Purdy and Zis (1973, 1974, 1976); Ward and Zis (1974) and Zis (1977) discuss the role of strikes.

2 Alternative explanations of United Kingdom inflation: a survey [1]

Michael Parkin[2]

Up to the middle 1960s there was little disagreement about the causes of British inflation. The mainstream view, following the pioneering work of Phillips (1958), Klein and Ball (1959), Lipsey (1960) and Dicks-Mireaux (1961) was that, in the short run, the rate of inflation varied directly with the excess demand for labour and the rate of increase in import prices and inversely with the rate of productivity growth. Also, the excess demand for labour and the unemployment rate were inversely related, hence there was a trade-off between inflation and unemployment. In the long run, with productivity growing at a steady rate, import prices and domestic prices growing at the same rate as each other,[3] and wage and price inflation linked by productivity growth, the rate of inflation would depend solely on excess demand for labour, or, equivalently, on the unemployment rate. This long-run trade-off between inflation and unemployment, according to Phillips' original estimate, and assuming a productivity growth rate of 2·5 per cent a year, implied a zero inflation rate at just over two per cent unemployment and only a six per cent inflation rate at one per cent unemployment.[4] In addition, some evidence was presented in the Klein-Ball study suggesting that the wage and price restraint policies of the late 1940s had reduced inflation to below what it otherwise would have been given the then prevailing level of unemployment. This result was replicated in subsequent studies by Brechling (1972), Smith (1968), Lipsey and Parkin (1970) and Parkin (1970).[5] These more recent studies also found, however, that *only* the 1940s prices and wages restraint experiments were successful, all the subsequent episodes having no significant impact on the rate of inflation, at least up to 1970.

Although there was, up to the middle 1960s, broad agreement on the causes of inflation, there was not complete unanimity. There was an inconsequential difference of emphasis between those who interpreted the Phillips curve as a manifestation of the working of competitive markets and those who saw it as representing the working-out of a bargaining process.[6] There was also, however, a substantive disagreement concerning whether or not trade unions pushed up money wages independently of the state of demand for labour. The major proponent of the view that they did was Hines. He argued (Hines, 1964) that wage-push via union strength, as measured by the rate of change of the percentage of the labour force unionised, had been more important than the un-employment rate in influencing the course of money wages between 1893 and 1961. Hines' results did not, however, shake the main-stream view and his union strength variable was accepted by many subsequent scholars as what Archibald (1969) called an 'intruder' into their explanations of wage change. However, with union density[7] having almost reached saturation point in the post-war years, the major emphasis in explaining wage (and indirectly price) inflation remained on excess demand (or unemployment). Excess demand was seen as being amenable to direct manipulation by fiscal and monetary policy and, whilst there were (and are) dif-ferences of opinion on the relative importance of these two groups of policy instruments, there were (and are) no doubts about their capacity to influence excess demand.

There were, of course, outstanding questions: the inter-war years continued to defy simple explanation; the loops around the Phillips curve could at best be explained only in *ad hoc* terms; the precise role of excess demand—whether it operated via labour markets only or via both goods and labour markets—was in dispute; the detailed channels whereby monetary impulses fed through to affect excess demand were not well understood.[8] Despite these outstanding problems there was an essentially settled view as to how and why inflation happened, what the trade-offs were, and how it could (and should) be controlled.

During the period since 1966, two groups of events have occurred which have disturbed this settled state. First, our in-flationary experience has been such as to call into serious ques-tion the mainstream explanation of inflation just outlined. Secondly— and partly, though not entirely, in response to this recent inflation experience—there has developed a series of alternative and often conflicting hypotheses to explain the phenomenon. Apparently, we have not yet reached a state of agreement comparable to that of the middle 1960s, differences of opinion being rather fundamental in some cases, especially in their policy implications.

The inflationary events which have occurred since 1966 are first, and most importantly, a worldwide wage and price explosion which took inflation to new post-war heights. Secondly, in the United Kingdom this explosion occurred at the time when the un-employment rate was also moving up to new post-war heights. This simultaneous increase in unemployment and acceleration of inflation ('stagflation' as it became known) was the single most important fact leading to the discrediting of the traditional ex-planation of inflation. As the second half of the 1960s was unfolding,

the use, with varying degrees of severity, of direct controls on
wages and prices led to a clouding of the forces at work since
such direct controls, whilst probably not much affecting the
average rate of inflation, were capable of modifying its timing,
holding it back during short periods of 'freeze' or 'severe restraint' and showing a tendency to 'bulge' during subsequent
periods. However, by the early 1970s, the most ardent defenders
of the traditional explanation were ready to admit that a new
one was needed.

Many, of course, had been dissatisfied with the traditional
explanation even during the period when it seemed to work and it
was from these that new hypotheses came. Dissidents fell into
three groups. First, there were those who regarded the Phillips
hypothesis as a departure from the traditional economic theory
of price and monetary dynamics. This group, led by Friedman
(1968) and Phelps (1968), proposed an augmentation of the Phillips
curve by the so-called 'expectations hypothesis' and the rehabilita-
tion of the role of money as the main exogenous force driving an
inflating economy. This expectations-augmented Phillips hypothesis implies that there is a trade-off between inflation and unemployment in the short run only and that, in the long run, if
unemployment is below its natural rate, inflation will persistently
accelerate. It was subsequently pointed out by Mundell (1971) and
Johnson (1972) that the expectations-excess-demand/monetarist
model, at least in the form usually presented, applies only to a
closed economy, or in the long run, to an open economy with a
floating exchange rate. According to their analyses, in an open
economy with a fixed exchange rate, the rate of inflation will tend
to the world rate and domestic monetary policy will affect only
the country's balance of payments. The no-long-run trade-off
conclusion is not affected by open economy considerations.

Secondly, there were those dissatisfied with the Phillips
hypothesis (and the usually accompanying fixed percentage mark-
up price equation) because of a lack of explicit emphasis on the
institutional details of wage and price determination. Wages in the
United Kingdom are, for the most part, set by a process in which
trade unions and employers bargain with each other. No one would
disagree with this as a description of the wage-setting process, yet
the Phillips theory of wage determination almost completely ignored it and was formulated as if all labour markets were competitive. Attempts to get closer to the institutional details sometimes took the form of explicit theorising about the bargaining
process and sometimes the *ad hoc* introduction of variables into
wage equations with vague references to bargaining as justification.
Additionally, price-setting behaviour treated prices as being
mechanically determined as some constant mark-up over costs
(perhaps with an excess demand adjustment) and ignored the

growing body of microeconomic evidence that firms set their prices in accordance with 'normal' rather than 'actual' unit costs.

The third group was dissatisfied with the traditional explanation of inflation because of its narrow economic nature. Inflation is seen by this group, notably Harrod (1972), Jones (1972), Marris (1972) and Wiles (1973), as essentially a social and political phenomenon, not a narrow economic one.

It is from these three groups of very different dissatisfactions with the Phillips curve theory of inflation that alternative explanations for the late 1960s and 1970s have come. It is interesting to note that those same groupings which were evident in the 1960s are still evident today and are displayed in the recent *American Economic Review* symposium on United Kingdom inflation. In that symposium, Laidler (see Chapter 3) presents what is essentially the development of the Phelps-Friedman analysis of inflation in the framework of a Mundell-Johnson model of an open economy. Miller (1976) and Williamson and Wood (1976) place major emphasis on the role of unions' targets for real income and explain the major movements of wages (the principal origin of price rises) as the outcome of attempts to achieve target real wage growth. These two papers span the second 'union strength' and the third 'socio-political' groups of 1960s dissidents identified above.

An important group of scholars not identified above is the school which is most aptly labelled 'eclectic'. This school sees virtue everywhere it looks and asserts that, whatever extreme views there are, the truth lies somewhere in the centre. A recent example of this group is to be found in the fourth contribution to the AER symposium, namely that by Ball and Burns. Ball and Burns present a discussion of the causes of inflation which allows all facts to show up with some degree of importance. However, in their historical interpretation of United Kingdom inflation, they are in close agreement with Laidler and with the conclusion reached in this book.

The aim of this chapter is to examine and review both the theoretical and empirical development of the three broad groups of hypotheses identified above, to show the relationship between them, revealing points of agreement and points of conflict, and to attempt to reach a considered judgement on the causes of inflation.

The next section (2.I) examines what I have called the 'proximate' determinants of wage and price change. That is, it reviews the theories of and empirical evidence on the influences upon firms and unions in their wage and price setting decisions. In Section 2.II, wage and price setting behaviour is examined as one component of a complete macroeconomic model for both a closed and an open economy. In Section 2.III, an attempt is made to come to grips with 'non-economic' explanations of inflation, while Section 2. IV presents the main conclusions.

I THE PROXIMATE ECONOMIC DETERMINANTS OF WAGE AND PRICE CHANGE

This section examines: (*a*) theories of wage determination; (*b*) theories of price determination; (*c*) the role of foreign prices in the price and wage setting process; (*d*) the problem of making inflation expectations an operational concept as a partial explanation of inflation; and (*e*) the empirical testing of wage and price determination and expectations formation models.

(*a*) Theories of wage determination

(*i*) *The expectations-excess-demand theory of wage determination* was simultaneously advanced by Friedman (1968) and Phelps (1968). The models of these two originators of the hypothesis differ in detail but have identical implications for an economy with no productivity growth. Friedman's hypothesis is that the labour market behaves as if it were competitive and adjusts *real* wages to remove excess demand. Since it is *money* wages and not *real* wages which are set in the markets for labour, those money wages will be adjusted to take account both of excess demand and the expected rate of price change. The coefficient on the expected rate of price change will be unity if the excess demand for labour is homogeneous of degree zero in the money wage and price level.

The Phelps variant of the hypothesis is slightly more general than Friedman's. He argues that competitive firms deciding on a wage offer will first form an expectation of what wage offer other firms are going to make. If they have neither an excess supply nor demand they will simply change their wage by the same percentage as they expect others to change theirs, thereby preserving their relative wage and neither encouraging nor discouraging a net change in their labour force. If they have an excess demand for labour they will raise their wages by more than they expect others to and if they have an excess supply, by less. Thus, the rate of wage change will equal the expected rate of wage change plus an adjustment for excess demand. If the rate of productivity growth is put explicitly into Friedman's model, the two become equivalent. Both accept some version of the Phillips-Lipsey relation between excess demand for labour and unemployment and its rate of change, but their analyses imply that there exists a 'natural' unemployment rate at which excess demand will be zero and inflation will be constant and equal to its expected rate.

A more rigorous derivation of the expectations-augmented Phillips curve model is provided by Mortensen (1970), who analyses the labour supply behaviour of an expected income-maximising worker with incomplete information about wage offers in an atomistic labour market and the optimal wage setting behaviour of an individual firm in the same environment. The outcome of his analysis after aggregation of individual behaviour is a short-run labour supply curve which has all the properties ascribed to the 'Phillips curve'. The major virtues of the Mortensen analysis are twofold. First it provides a rigorous competitive theoretical underpinning for the Phillips curve hypothesis but, secondly, and more importantly, it suggests that the 'natural' unemployment rate is not constant but will vary systematically and inversely with the rate at which workers receive offers from potential employers and directly with the quit rate, the rate at which new workers enter the labour force and the amount of dispersion of wage offers.

A derivation of the expectations-excess-demand hypothesis which is less rigorous than Mortensen's but more general and potentially more useful empirically than that of Mortensen, Phelps or Friedman, has been suggested by Parkin, Sumner and Ward (1976). The basic idea is seen best by considering the simple Friedman framework. The excess demand for labour (X) depends only on the real wage rate W/P, i.e.

$$X = F(W/P) \tag{2.1}$$

or, for simplicity

$$X = \alpha_0 - \frac{1}{\alpha}(w - p) \tag{2.2}$$

where w and p are the natural logarithms of W and P respectively. Now the three variables, excess demand, wages and prices are related to each other over time by

$$\Delta X = -\frac{1}{\alpha}(\Delta w - \Delta p) \tag{2.3}$$

Assume that the wage setting agent, whether it be the employer or a trade-union-employer bargaining process, sets wages with the above process in mind by forming an expectation of price change, Δp^e, so as to eliminate current excess demand. Then, $\Delta X = -X$ and $\Delta p = \Delta p^e$ so that

$$\Delta w = \alpha X + \Delta p^e \tag{2.4}$$

which is Friedman's version of the wage determination process.

The generalisation arises from noting that the excess demand for labour will, in general, depend on more variables than 'the real wage'. First, the real wage means different things to employers and workers. On the demand side it is the ratio of gross-of-tax (including payroll tax) wages to the price of output. On the supply side, it is the ratio of net-of-tax wages to the price of consumer goods. It will also depend on the demand side on technology and on the supply side on demographic variables. To the extent that changes in any of these variables are anticipated, whether correctly or not, they will lead to a change in wages independently of the state of excess demand. If they are correctly anticipated that will be the end of the matter. If they are incorrectly anticipated there will be a subsequent series of adjustments as positive or negative excess demand emerges. The rate of money wage change will be homogeneous of degree one in *all* money prices.

(ii)   The role of trade unions. The fact that most wages are set as the outcome of a bargaining process between unions and employers has led to two separate but related lines of development in the theory of wage change designed to capture the role of unions. One is the specification of explicit bargaining models and the other is the introduction of variables into wage equations which are proxies for bargaining strength or power.

Bargaining models as applied to wage determination in situations in which the standard models of competition and monopoly (or monopolistic competition) do not apply have been usefully surveyed by de Menil (1971). He points out that whilst there are a variety of bargaining models which could be applied to wage determination, the fixed-threat-game models of Nash (1950, 1953), Raiffa (1953) and Bishop (1963), and the non-game theoretic approaches of Zeuthen (1930), Harsanyi (1956), Hicks (1932), Foldes (1964), Cross (1965, 1966),[9] and Coddington (1966, 1968), they all have a common structure. They all predict the maximisation of gains from trade and the sharing of those gains in proportion to the relative marginal disutility that each could, would, but never has to, inflict upon the other. In the wage determination context, it is usually the strike or lockout which is treated as the source of disutility. The wage determined by the bargaining process is always a *relative* wage, and is homogeneous of degree one in all other money wages and prices.

In de Menil's own model based on Nash and in Holt's (1970) analysis bargaining determines the union wage relative to the wage in the non-union sector. In a model by Johnston (1972) the bargaining process determines the money wage relative to the employer's assessment of the 'real claim'. Johnston does not distinguish between absolute and relative wages and prices and does not, therefore, find price change and non-union wage change directly entering his explanation of unionised wage change. His prediction is, nevertheless, that wage change will be homogeneous of degree one in the only other money 'price' in his model, namely the rate of change of the 'real (in monetary terms) claim' and, hence, agrees with all other bargaining analyses.

The most striking thing about the bargaining models is the closeness of some aspects of their predictions to those of the expectations-excess-demand model. They agree that wage change will be homogeneous of degree one in money 'price' changes. If taxes were explicitly introduced into a bargaining model—and Johnston and Timbrell (1973) have introduced them in their empirical implementation of the Johnston model—they should behave in exactly the same way as the expectations hypothesis predicts. Additional non-price-change variables, however, affect wage change in the bargaining models, such as profit per unit of labour and concepts such as 'strike propensity'. It is, though, likely that such variables will be closely related to the state of labour market excess demand and hence give rise to an empirically equivalent model to the expectations-excess-demand model. However, it is clear that separate and independent measurement of bargaining-related variables could show them not to be closely correlated with excess demand and hence an important factor explaining wage change.

The second approach to modelling the role of unions, that of introducing variables into wage equations to capture the effects of 'bargaining strength', originates with the work of Hines (1964) who uses the change in the percentage of the labour force unionised as a proxy for union militancy or bargaining strength. The role of this variable is, however, ambiguous and, as shown by Holt (1970), may arise simply from aggregation rather than being a reflection of militancy. If union-set wages are greater than competitive wages the rate of wage change in the economy as a whole will, in part, depend on the rate of change of the fraction of the labour force receiving the union wage, and this will be a correct addition to the competitive wage determination model rather than, as Archibald (1969) has suggested, an 'intruder'. It is clear, however, that on this interpretation, the unionisation variable represents a force making for a change in the distribution of income and not a change in the rate of inflation.[10]

An additional variable which has been suggested by some as reflecting union militancy and thereby affecting wage change in the union sector is strikes (see Godfrey (1971) and Taylor (1975)). It is apparent from the above brief survey of bargaining theory that such a variable has no place as an explanatory variable for wage change. This point is developed at some length in Purdy and Zis (1974). Further, as Zis (1976) shows, there are sufficient differences amongst the various alternative measures of strikes (number of workers, number of strikes, number of man-days; strikes about wages and strikes about other matters; measures which exclude some strikes for some specific reasons) for it to be possible to 'demonstrate' any desired relationship between unions and strikes, and impossible to undertake rigorous hypothesis testing. Additionally, as Johnston (1972) points out, even if strikes are an appropriate explanatory variable in a wage equation, their predicted sign is ambiguous, at least in his bargaining model.

(b) Models of price determination

There has for a long time been dissatisfaction with the essentially *ad hoc* proposition that '$\dot{p} = \alpha(D - S), q = \min (D, S)$' (Phelps and Winter, 1970), and Phelps and Winter (1970) and Barro (1972) both attempt to provide a rigorous theoretical explanation of price adjustment. The Phelps-Winter paper is technically difficult and has been stripped to its essentials and simplified by Carlson (1972). The analyses differ in that Phelps and Winter, and Carlson, deal with atomistic competition and Barro with monopoly. They are similar in that they both see price-setting decisions as profit (or present value) maximising decisions where there are costs arising both from price adjustment and from maintaining a dis-equilibrium price to be offset against each other. Aggregation of the resulting individual behaviour (not without problems in the Phelps-Winter case), and weak supplementary assumptions, yield the proposition that prices will be adjusted faster the greater the excess demand for goods is, the further they are below their long-run equilibrium, and the faster they are expected to rise.

The expectations-excess-demand model of price dynamics can be derived by applying the Parkin *et al.* analysis of wage determination to that of price determination. Let

$$X_i = G(\frac{C_i}{P}, \frac{P_i}{P}) \tag{2.5}$$

where $G_1 > 0, G_2 < 0$, be the excess-demand function for the ith firm's output, where X_i is excess demand, C_i is unit cost, P_i is the firm's price, P is an average of all other prices and the subscript i refers to the firm. For simplicity suppose that

$$X_i = \beta_0 + \beta_1 c_i - \beta_2 p_i - (\beta_1 - \beta_2)p \tag{2.6}$$

where lower-case letters denote logarithms. Then

$$\Delta X_i = \beta_1 \Delta c_i - \beta_2 \Delta p_i - (\beta_1 - \beta_2)\Delta p \tag{2.7}$$

Assume the ith firm adjusts its price in the light of expectations Δc_i^e and Δp_i^e to make $\Delta X_i = -X_i$. Then,

$$p_i = \frac{1}{\beta_2} X_i + \frac{\beta_1}{\beta_2} \Delta c_i^e + \frac{(\beta_2 - \beta_1)}{\beta_2} \Delta p^e \qquad (2.8)$$

Aggregation over all firms would yield

$$\Delta p = \alpha X + \beta \Delta c^e + (1 - \beta)\Delta p^e \qquad (2.9)$$

Several special cases emerge. If the typical firm believes itself to be in a highly competitive environment, then $\beta_2 \rightarrow \infty$ and $\alpha \rightarrow 0$ and $(1 - \beta) \rightarrow 1$; hence, a pure expectations model, $\Delta p = \Delta p^e$, emerges. If the firm believes itself to be in a highly monopolistic environment then $\beta_1 \rightarrow \beta_2$ (i.e., only the firm's own price affects its demand) and $\beta \rightarrow 1$ and $(1 - \beta) \rightarrow 0$; hence, $\Delta p = \alpha X + \Delta c^e$, a variable mark-up hypothesis emerges. Finally, if expectations are such that $\Delta p^e = \Delta c^e$ then the model becomes $\Delta p = \alpha X + \Delta p^e$, or equivalently, $\Delta p = \alpha X + \Delta c^e$. This version of the price equation is easily extended to allow for taxes and other factors which affect excess demand, in which changes may be anticipated. It should be noted that in all cases price change is homogeneous of degree one in all other money variables, implying no long-run trade-off between price change and excess demand.

The major alternative hypothesis to that presented above is that prices move with normal cost. More specifically, 'prices move with long-run costs and do not change because of variations in demand or cost which are thought to be temporary' (Godley and Nordhaus, 1972). Two features of this hypothesis are worth noting. First, it is not incompatible with the view that inflation is in part caused by excess demand since that variable may affect long-run cost changes through labour market pressure. Secondly, it is not incompatible with profit maximisation in a competitive environment where Δp^e is based on long-run cost movements. It *is* incompatible, however, with a non-competitive analysis, a point which Nordhaus (1972a), who makes a similar point about a different model, seems to miss.[11]

(c) *Foreign and international prices*

The models of both wage and price determination discussed so far ignore any considerations arising from the openness of an economy. Yet all economies buy inputs from other economies and sell output to them. Also, in an environment of fixed exchange rates, a feature of the world, at least until 1971, the prices of internationally traded (or tradeable) goods are going to differ only because of transport costs and tariffs. If these latter are relatively stable then inflation rates of tradeables' prices will tend to be equal between countries.

Several analyses of price and wage determination have incorporated foreign prices as additional, and in some cases primary, explanatory variables. In the price equation, import prices are typically included as part of the calculation of unit costs (whether actual or normal) (see Nordhaus (1972a) and Godley and Nordhaus (1972) for extensive bibliographies). Three Swedish authors, Edgren, Faxén and Odhner (1969), have advanced a wage-determination (and by implication price-determination) model which places all the emphasis on foreign prices.

A more general way of allowing for foreign prices in both the price and wage equation is suggested by Parkin *et al.* (1976). This is to use the method suggested above to derive the expectations-excess-demand hypothesis but to recognise that the relative price of tradeables to non-tradeables will affect both the excess demand for goods and the excess demand for labour. This modification (allowing simultaneously for taxes) is presented in Parkin *et al.* (1976) for the wage equation and in Smith (1976) for the price equation (see also Chapter 5). Wage and price change remain functions of excess demand and are homogeneous of degree one in all money variables, which include foreign price and exchange rate expectations as well as domestic price and tax change expectations.

(d)   *Making expected inflation an operational concept.*

Throughout the preceding sections, whether dealing explicitly with the expectations hypothesis of price and wage change or with the bargaining approach to wages, or with the normal cost-pricing hypothesis, many alternative inflation expectations variables have appeared as postulated direct determinants of the rates of wage and price change. At one level, all models employing expectations variables are empty and can be regarded as tautologies which define the expected rate of inflation. However, there are three possible ways of avoiding that charge and of making the expectations hypothesis operational.

The first is to postulate a subsidiary hypothesis which specifies the determinants of the expected rate of inflation. The most commonly employed such hypothesis has been the error-learning model, which postulates that expectations arc adjusted by some constant proportion of the most recent 'error' or discrepancy between the previously held expectation and actual rate of inflation. This has been criticised by Rose (1972) because it will in general be a sub-optimal forecasting rule. Rose, however, has suggested a possible way of rescuing the basic approach. He shows that any time series (after appropriate non-linear transformation) can be represented as a Box-Jenkins (1970) ARIMA process, and the minimum variance forecaster can be represented as a weighted sum of all past errors. Further, the weights can be obtained from a Box-Jenkins analysis of the relevant series and used to construct an expectations series based on the assumption of optimal single series ARIMA forecasting. Whilst this approach is potentially useful, the major objection to it is that it requires the stochastic structure of the series to be stable. A less restrictive approach, which has been gaining in popularity during the past few years, is the 'rational expectations' hypothesis (see especially Muth (1961), Lucas (1972), Sargent (1973). This hypothesis has, however, made only small inroads into empirical models of United Kingdom inflation (see McCallum, 1975).

The second approach is based on the assumption that inflationary expectations are the same in different markets. It is already apparent that expected inflation may be regarded as influencing actual inflation of both prices and wages. It may be assumed that the same inflation-expectations variable explains both of these in a consistent manner. Additionally, however, the relation between real and financial asset prices should reflect inflation expectations, and *changes* in financial asset interest rates (with the real rate of interest assumed constant) will reflect *changes* in inflation expectations. It may further be assumed that this manifestation of inflation expectations in asset markets is the same as that which influences wages and prices. This set of assumptions has frequently been adopted, and the behaviour of interest rates used as a measure of the expected inflation variable in wage and price equations (see especially Andersen and Carlson (1972), Gordon (1971) and McGuire (1976). It is evident from the foregoing that a large number of subsidiary hypotheses are required to make this procedure possible, none of which is easily tested independently. Further, however, the work of Sargent (1972) suggests that this procedure induces systematic bias in the measure of the expected inflation rate.

The third approach to expectations is direct measurement. This may take one of two forms—quantitative or qualitative. It may also be based on the expectations of a large body of 'average' individuals or of particular specialist groups. Econometric and specialist 'judgemental' forecasters' expectations are widely available from regularly published economic forecasts (e.g., for the United Kingdom, the National Institute of Economic and Social Research). Business economists' expectations have been measured by Livingston for the United States but apparently for no other country. Jonson and Mahoney (1973) have measured economic journalists' expectations in a quasi-quantitative manner for Australia. However, quantitative data tend to be very scarce and, almost of necessity, have to reflect the expectations of 'experts'.

Qualitative information is, however, much more common. Surveys asking householders/consumers and businessmen in general, whether they expect prices to rise, fall or remain unchanged over some specified future period are numerous for the United Kingdom and the United States and many other countries. Data are available recording the percentages in these categories, plus the percentage who 'do not know'. For the United Kingdom, we have a Gallup Poll monthly survey of approximately one thousand individuals' expectations of retail prices dating from 1960, and a CBI survey covering businessmen's expectations of both domestic and export selling prices (as well as a host of other variables) on a tri-annual and subsequent quarterly basis dating from 1958. This richness of qualitative data prompted Carlson and Parkin (1975) (see Chapter 6) to devise a method for converting the qualitative data into a quantitative estimate of the expected rate of inflation. Their method involves making assumptions about the distribution of inflation expectations across the sampled population (a normal distribution being assumed)[12] and about an individual's threshold of perception of inflation (assumed to be constant over time and independent of both the level of prices and the rate of inflation). With these, and some less important assumptions, all of which in principle, given enough information, are testable, they are able to compute a time series for the expected rate of inflation based on a simple transformation of the percentage of the population who believe prices will rise and the percentage who believe they will fall. This method has now been used by Carlson and Parkin (1975) to calculate an expected inflation series for retail prices in the United Kingdom, by Parkin *et al.* (1976) and Smith (1976) (see Chapter 7) for wholesale and export prices of United Kingdom producers, by Knöbl (1974) for retail prices in West Germany, by Danes (1975) for wholesale prices in Australia and by de Menil and Bhalla (1975) for retail prices in the United States. There is, thus, a rich and growing body of directly measured information on inflation expectations, but an equally large amount of unfinished work in testing the as yet untested assumptions needed to obtain these quantitative measures from the qualitative survey data.[13]

(e) *The empirical testing of wage, price and expectations hypotheses*

This survey of empirical work on wage, price and expectations determination will cover primarily work relating to the United Kingdom. It will bring in work on other countries only where it is necessary to a more thorough understanding and evaluation of United Kingdom results.

i) *The determinants of wage change.* A pure excess-demand expectations model has been presented and tested by Parkin *et al.*

(1976) and by Sumner (see Chapter 4). Parkin *et al.* explain percentage variations in weekly wage rates with the hypothesis that

$$\Delta w = \alpha + \beta U + \gamma \Delta p_w^e + \delta \Delta p_f^e + (1 - \gamma - \delta)\Delta p_c^e - (1 - \gamma - \delta)\Delta t_I$$
$$- (\gamma + \delta)\Delta t_p + IP + \epsilon \qquad (2.10)$$

where:

Δw = the actual percent per annum quarterly rate of change of wages

Δp_w^e = the expected percent per annum quarterly rate of change of domestic wholesale prices

Δp_f^e = the expected percent per annum quarterly rate of change of export prices

Δp_c^e = the expected percent per annum quarterly rate of change of retail prices

Δt_I = the expected percent per annum quarterly rate of change of the ratio of take home pay to gross pay

Δt_p = the expected percent per annum quarterly rate of change of employers' payroll taxes

U = the average unemployment rate over the previous year

IP = incomes policy dummy variables

All the expected price variables, Δp_w^e, Δp_f^e, Δp_c^e, are measured using the Carlson-Parkin technique from CBI and Gallup surveys, and expected tax changes are computed as actual tax changes.

They find that the *a priori* restrictions implied by their model cannot be rejected at the conventional significance level and that the restricted version of the model estimates as:

$$\Delta w = 5 \cdot 91 - 2 \cdot 00 U + 0 \cdot 50 \Delta p_w + 0 \cdot 20 \Delta p_f + 0 \cdot 30 \Delta p_c - 0 \cdot 30 \Delta t_I$$
$$[3 \cdot 59] \quad [2 \cdot 47] \quad [2 \cdot 58] \qquad [0 \cdot 89] \qquad [2 \cdot 58] \qquad [2 \cdot 58]$$
$$- 0 \cdot 70 \Delta t_p + 0 \cdot 46 IP \ (1961\text{-}2) - 1 \cdot 06 IP \ (1966\text{-}7) \qquad (2.11)$$
$$[0 \cdot 70] \qquad [0 \cdot 29] \qquad\qquad [0 \cdot 70]$$

$$\bar{R}^2 = 0 \cdot 43 \quad \text{D.W.} = 1 \cdot 69 \quad \text{Data period 1956(2) to 1971(4)}$$

This result is noteworthy for several reasons. First, considering that the dependent variable is a highly noisy quarterly first difference of logarithms, the explanatory power is good. Sargan (1971), explaining the same variable, found uncorrected multiple correlations of $0 \cdot 439$ and $0 \cdot 456$. Second, there is no apparent

problem arising from a possible shift in the unemployment—
excess-demand relation.[14] Third, the domestic wholesale and
retail price expectations are the forces which generated the wage
explosions of 1966 and 1969. Fourth, the apparently poor performance of export prices is probably misleading, there being a high
degree of collinearity between Δp_w^e and Δp_f^e which, whilst not
affecting the size of the parameter estimates, makes it difficult to
assess their separate effects. Their joint effect, however, is
powerful and it is clear that the demand side of the labour market
provides a bigger effect on wage change from expectations (0·70)
than the supply side does (0·30). Fifth, and of crucial importance,
the model, with a long-run productivity growth rate of 2·5 per cent,
implies a natural unemployment rate of 1·7 per cent, a value not
unlike, and certainly not significantly different from, that found by
Phillips in the now much maligned study. The major differences
between the above equation and Phillips' is that his analysis
implied a long-run trade-off whilst the above does not. Finally, as
in *all* previous studies, the role of incomes policy is entirely
negligible (see Parkin and Sumner, 1972).

It may be thought that the above result cannot be correct
because the relation between unemployment and excess demand
shifted some time in the late 1960s. Evidence for the shift has
been adduced from an examination of the relationship between
unemployment (U) and vacancies (V). Since $X \equiv V - U$ then a
stable relationship between V and U and a shift in the V, U, relation implies a shift in the X, U relation. Bowers, Cheshire and
Webb (1970) and Gujarati (1972) suggested that the V, U relation
had shifted in late 1966. Foster (1973) suggested that the shift had
been somewhat more drawn out. Bowers, Cheshire, Webb and
Weeden (1972), following up the original National Institute analysis,
modified the earlier view and suggested that unemployment continued to be a good indicator of excess demand and the shift had
occurred at least in part because of an increase in the ratio of
reported to true vacancies. The Parkin *et al.* results agree with
this view. Experiments designed to find a shift in their wage
equations all failed in that search and it was concluded that,
despite earlier doubts, unemployment remained the best indicator
of excess demand, at least as an explanation of wage rates. According to the above model, the late 1960s wage explosion was proximately caused by expectations. Subsequent research on the wage
equation by Sumner (see Chapter 4) suggests that this earlier conclusion requires modification and that, although not detected by that
earlier study, there was indeed a shift in the natural rate of unemployment which started in the late 1960s. However, rising inflation
expectations remain the major source of inflationary acceleration
during that period.

It may be objected that rising inflation expectations cannot possibly be the source of rising inflation since unemployment was *above* its predicted natural rate all through the period that wages were accelerating and those two facts are inconsistent with the expectations—excess-demand model. They are indeed inconsistent with such a model in a closed or flexible exchange rate economy, since excess demand is necessary to generate an acceleration in inflation and expectations of it. However, in a fixed exchange rate economy both export and domestic prices can rise because of world excess demand, thereby imparting an inflationary impulse on to the domestic economy despite domestic excess supply.

A study by Duck, Parkin, Rose and Zis (1976) lends support to this view. That study finds that a closed economy version of the expectations-augmented Phillips curve applied to the industrially almost closed economy of the Group of Ten in aggregate explains 'world average' wage inflation. It also finds that the world as a whole was experiencing excess demand for labour (was below its calculated natural employment rate) from 1963 to 1970 with a sharp rise in excess demand in 1966 giving rise to the world wage (and price) explosion at a time when the United Kingdom was attempting to swim against the world tide. The Duck *et al.* study of wages provides two types of evidence for the expectations excess demand hypothesis in its strong no-long-run trade-off form: first, the hypothesis holds at a 'world aggregate' level, and second it explains how the United Kingdom could be experiencing accelerating inflation even though it had excess supply.

An additional test of the expectations—excess-demand model has been provided by MacKay and Hart (1974) who, using highly disaggregated regional/industrial data find the hypothesis performing well and again with the predicted no-long-run trade-off result holding up well.

Finally, in an important paper which is the first to use a rational expectations[15] framework, McCallum (1975)[16] shows that we cannot reject the hypothesis that wages respond to excess demand and inflation expectations with the latter variable not being formed on the basis of previous movements in the actual rate of inflation but responding rationally to previous monetary and fiscal policy. Non-rejection of rationality of expectations does not imply a rejection of the adaptive expectations formulations since *both* formulations are apparently consistent with the data. Stronger tests will have to be devised before such discrimination is possible. It is worth noting, however, that if the rational expectations hypothesis turns out to be the winner, then all arguments for stabilisation policy using optimal feedback rules fall to the ground. It should be noted also that the Parkin *et al.* study and that by Sumner (Chapter 4), which use directly observed expectations variables, avoid the problem of specifying a subsidiary hypothesis on the formation of expectations and could therefore, be combined with either 'adaptive' or 'rational' formulations.

There has been little testing of pure bargaining models of wage determination in the United Kingdom, and Johnston and Timbrell (1973) provide what is apparently the only recent example. They test Johnston's (1972) model which is based on the following ideas. A firm seeks to minimise the expected cost of settlement and strike given an initial 'real claim' (not the same as the actual claim but the firm's assessment of what the union would in fact settle for without a strike), an estimate of the relation between the probability of strike and the pre-strike wage offer, and an estimate of the length of strike needed to secure an acceptance of a given wage offer. The decision sequence is that the firm receives a claim from the union Δw^c; it then (in an unspecified manner) discounts that to arrive at its estimate of the real claim Δw^{rc}; it then must make a pre-strike wage offer which will be accepted with probability $(1-a)$ or rejected with probability a; if accepted that is the end of the matter. If rejected the firm must decide what wage offer to make as the strike proceeds; it will make an offer which it believes will end the strike after a period which minimises total costs; if it is wrong it will keep changing its offer until a settlement (or shutdown?) is reached. The formal outcome of Johnston's analysis is the proposition that

$$\Delta w = \Delta w^{rc} + f(i, \pi, \delta, b) \qquad (2.12)$$

where all the derivatives of f are positive and:

Δw^{rc} = percent rate of 'real claim' wage change

i = firm's rate of time discount

π = rate of profit per worker

δ = firm's estimate of union propensity to endure a strike

b = parameter (variable?) relating strike length to costs imposed on firm

The empirical implementation of this model is achieved by assuming that Δw^{rc} depends on inflation expectations, Δp^e, proxied by Δp_{-1} and $(\Delta p_{-1})^2$ and either a 'catch up' variable, C, which measures the extent to which real wages have cumulatively fallen behind an assumed target growth rate, or $\Delta \lambda^c$, a variable measuring a three-year moving average of the proportionate rate of change of the ratio of net to gross wages. The variables, i, π and b are treated as constants and δ is for the most part treated as constant but allowed to depend on the number of strikes in some regressions. An additional variable, n, the fraction of the labour force

settling a wage claim in the period in question is also included.
Thus, the empirical model is specified as

$$\Delta w = g(\Delta p^e, \Delta \lambda^C \text{ or } C, n) \tag{2.13}$$

with no homogeneity restrictions suggested.

A large number of results are presented with alternative
definitions of expectations and 'catch up' variables, and two annual
data samples, 1952-71 and 1959-71, are used. Johnston and
Timbrell's preferred equations for 1959-71 are:

$$\Delta w = -0\cdot910 + 2\cdot79n + 1\cdot050\Delta p_{-1} + 0\cdot432C \tag{2.14}$$
$$[0\cdot65] \quad [2\cdot94] \qquad\quad [1\cdot30]$$

$$\overline{R}^2 = 0\cdot620 \qquad \text{D.W.} = 2\cdot10$$

$$\Delta w = 0\cdot492 + 0\cdot06n + 0\cdot383\Delta p_{-1} - 3\cdot44\Delta\lambda^C \tag{2.15}$$
$$(0\cdot02] \quad [0\cdot82] \qquad\quad [2\cdot27]$$

$$R^2 = 0\cdot714 \qquad \text{D.W.} = 2\cdot13$$

It is clear that n is totally unimportant and that, when the 'catch up'
variable is used, Δp^e (proxied by Δp_{-1}) takes on a coefficient of
unity while the introduction of $\Delta\lambda^C$ takes away the explanatory
power of Δp^e.

Comparing the Johnston-Timbrell results with those for the
expectations—excess-demand model reported above is not easy in
view of the annual/quarterly data differences. However, the
strongest result which emerges is that both models agree that
taxes and inflation expectations are important. Further, their
'catch up' variable may easily be interpreted as a market pressure
or excess demand influence. When real wages have been rising
below trend, if marginal productivity has been on trend, then the
cumulative gap between real wages and trend will capture the
cumulative excess-demand gap. In view of these agreements on
two issues of substance, the short sample of the Johnston-Timbrell
study might lead one to favour the earlier reported expectations
model from an empirical point of view, while not rejecting the rich
institutional detail which is captured in Johnston's theoretical
analysis as an alternative explanation for these findings. Johnston
and Timbrell's own comparison of their model with an expectations-augmented Phillips analysis shows the latter to be highly
unsatisfactory with a poorer fit than the 'bargaining' model and a
perverse slope for the Phillips curve. This is entirely to be
expected and not inconsistent with Parkin *et al*. The main reason
for the result is that the Δp^e variable used by Johnston and

Timbrell badly misestimates the movements in measured inflation expectations as used by the other study. In other words, it fails to shift the short-run Phillips curve far enough to the north-east, leaving some positive partial correlation between Δw and U to be picked up by the coefficient on U.

In a very similar vein to Johnston and Timbrell, Henry, Sawyer and Smith (1976) set out to test the hypothesis that trade unions aim to achieve a rise in money wages consistent with achieving the 'target rate of increase in real net earnings desired by workers' (Henry *et al.*, p. 60). However, they also permit the pressure of demand to have an independent effect on the actual rise in wages. Their basic estimating equation takes the form:

$$\Delta w = \delta_0 + \delta_1 \Delta p_{-1} + \delta_2 \ell n U_{-1} + \delta_3 (\ell n NE_{t-1} - p_{t-1}) + \delta_4 t + \epsilon \quad (2.16)$$

where NE = net earnings and t is a time trend. This equation estimates on quarterly data for 1948(1) − 1974(4) as

$$\delta_0 = -0 \cdot 0059 \quad [0 \cdot 23]$$
$$\delta_1 = -0 \cdot 589 \quad [4 \cdot 33]$$
$$\delta_2 = 0 \cdot 00083 \quad [0 \cdot 12]$$
$$\delta_3 = -0 \cdot 1097 \quad [1 \cdot 99]$$
$$\delta_4 = 0 \cdot 00066 \quad [2 \cdot 13]$$

with $R^2 = 0 \cdot 469$ and D.W. = $1 \cdot 466$. Henry *et al.* conclude that 'these results ... provide confirmation of the view that pressure for money wage increases from workers in order to reach some target for growth in take-home pay has been a decisive influence in the current inflation'. Their paper additionally estimates a Phillips—Lipsey equation, an expectations-augmented Phillips model, a Hines model (see below) and a 'monetarist' model, all of which they show to be inferior to their target take-home pay hypothesis.

Several important criticisms can be levelled against the Henry *et al.* interpretation of their results. First, it is important to note that the only statistically significant variable in their explanation of wage change is the time trend. Wages have been increasing at an increasing rate. This is purely a description of the phenomenon for which an explanation is sought and is in no way itself an explanation. Secondly (cf. the above discussion of Johnston and Timbrell), the nearly significant net real wage may clearly be interpreted as a proxy for the excess demand for labour. When real wages are high there will be an excess supply of labour and wages will rise less quickly than otherwise. The negative coefficient δ_3 is clearly consistent with this interpretation. The significantly less than unit coefficient on the rate of inflation in no way contradicts the 'natural rate hypothesis', which predicts a unit coefficient on the expected rate of inflation, for the lagged inflation rate systematically mismeasures the appropriate expected rate of inflation, being both a bad measure of the expected rate of change of consumer prices and a measure which ignores producer (wholesale) prices (important on the demand side of the market). Thirdly, the use of unemployment with no allowance for a shifting 'natural unemployment rate' clearly mismeasures the excess demand for labour when the model is taken through the early 1970s (see Chapter 4). Finally, the overall soundness of fit of the Henry *et al.* equation is not spectacular and the Durbin—Watson statistic indicates potential first-order autocorrelation.

Taken as a whole, these remarks are sufficient to reject entirely the Henry *et al.* hypothesis. Their own negative results on the expectations-augmented Phillips curve model in no way invalidate the correctly specified version of that model, for they both mismeasure inflation expectations and fail to allow for the shifting nature rate of unemployment.

Models which mix competitive and bargaining hypotheses are perhaps the most common. It has been shown above, following Holt (1969), how this properly brings into the picture the rate of change of the fraction of the labour force receiving a union-determined wage as one of the factors affecting average wage change. In the United Kingdom, Hines (1964, 1968, 1969, 1971) has been the strongest proponent of the view that a similar variable, the rate of change of the fraction of the labour force belonging to trade unions, is a dominant influence on wage change; but he argues that it measures militancy and the capacity of unions to push for money wage increases. In other words, Hines sees the change in union density as a variable explaining the rate of change of the *union* wage and not as an aggregation phenomenon. His own most recently published wage equations, a quarterly model of hourly wage rates for 1949(1) to 1969(4) are:

(OLS) $\Delta w = 6 \cdot 076 - 0 \cdot 918U + 0 \cdot 229\Delta p + 8 \cdot 900\Delta T/T$ (2.17)

$\qquad\qquad\quad [2 \cdot 08] \qquad [2 \cdot 43] \qquad\quad [4 \cdot 62]$

$\quad R^2 = 0 \cdot 656 \quad$ D.W. $= 0 \cdot 98$

(TSLS) $\Delta w = 6 \cdot 234 - 0 \cdot 982U + 0 \cdot 214\Delta p + 8 \cdot 800\Delta T/T$ (2.18)

$\qquad\qquad\quad [7 \cdot 05] \qquad [5 \cdot 19] \qquad\quad [10 \cdot 68]$

$\quad R^2 = 0 \cdot 953 \qquad$ D.W. n.a.

It is clear that the unionisation variable, T (measured here as a

proportionate rate of change $\Delta T/T$), has a large, significant
coefficient.

What does Hines' finding mean and how should the above
result be interpreted ? These questions have been treated very
thoroughly by Purdy and Zis (1973, 1974). They consider two
questions: first the robustness of the Hines finding with respect
to other variables in the model and their measurement, and second,
the question of interpretation. Reviewing the Purdy and Zis
1949-69 results only, those directly comparable with Hines' as
reported above, we find that the estimated coefficients on ΔT (as
used in Hines' original studies and not $\Delta T/T$ as in Hines' more
recent study) are a little over one in the three alternative specifications reported. They always appear with a t-ratio greater than
two but also have an inconclusive Durbin—Watson statistic. The
Purdy-Zis empirical formulation differs from Hines' in that they:
(i) calculate ΔT as the percentage of the potentially unionisable
labour force while Hines has the percentage of the labour force
including nonunionisable armed forces and self-employed; (ii)
calculate the rates of change of wages and prices to be consistent
with each other while Hines arbitrarily uses two different methods
for each; and (iii) use annual data while Hines uses quarterly.
Making these changes still leaves ΔT as a statistically significant
explanatory variable. However, its importance (though not much its
significance) is reduced. Since Hines uses $\Delta T/T$ and Purdy-Zis
ΔT, and since in rough terms $T = 1/2$, the coefficients can be
compared by dividing Purdy-Zis' coefficients by 2. Thus, Hines'
average estimate of the effect of a one per cent change in $\Delta T/T$ is,
in round figures, an eight per cent point change in wages while
Purdy—Zis predict a change of a little over a half per cent points,
a ratio of sixteen to one. Thus, Purdy-Zis find a much smaller
role for unionisation. It is clear from a detailed comparison of all
Hines' and Purdy—Zis' results that the major difference in apparent
importance arises from the different data frequencies used. Hines
publishes one annual equation which has a coefficient on the unionisation variable very close to that of Purdy-Zis (see Hines (1971),
pp. 162-3, table 2). The question then arises as to whether the
quarterly or the annual results are the appropriate ones. There
can, in fact, be no dispute here. The coefficient estimates on $\Delta T/T$
in the quarterly models are of very dubious quality for they are
based on *annual* data with quarterly interpolations. This will have
biased downwards the variance of $\Delta T/T$ and biased upwards both
its coefficient and its t-statistic. Hence, the importance of Hines'
unionisation variable is almost certainly that indicated by the
annual models.

The question of interpretation centres on whether ΔT is measuring militancy and wage-push which is independent of market
forces, or whether it reflects partly a reallocation of the labour

force and partly the passive behaviour of households. As an aggregate measure, if it is a militancy variable, the ΔT definition which measures density of potentially unionisable workers (Purdy-Zis) should perform better than the one which Hines used. We have seen that it does not; hence there is already a suggestion here that the reallocation interpretation is better than the militancy one. However, Purdy and Zis do not leave matters there. They use sectoral data and closed shop considerations to calculate a decomposition of ΔT into ΔT_m and ΔT_e, where ΔT_e is the change in union density arising from labour force reallocation—and, hence, the passive component of the effect of unionisation on wage change—and ΔT_m is the change in density arising from the activities which Hines regards as indicative of militancy. Using these two variables they obtain for 1949-61 the following:[17]

$$\Delta w = 0\cdot335 + 0\cdot162\Delta T_m - 3\cdot870\Delta T_e + 0\cdot604\Delta p + 3\cdot730U^{-1}$$

$$[1\cdot355] \; [0\cdot650] \qquad [1\cdot999] \qquad [0\cdot174] \qquad [2\cdot377] \qquad (2.19)$$

$$\overline{R}^2 = 0.711 \qquad D.W. = 1\cdot730$$

A longer sample going back to 1924 gives the stronger overall result:

$$\Delta w = -0\cdot005 + 0\cdot420\Delta T_m - 0\cdot341\Delta T_e + 0\cdot307\Delta p + 6\cdot410U^{-1}$$

$$[0\cdot322] \; [0\cdot161] \qquad [1\cdot064] \qquad [0\cdot091] \qquad [0\cdot938]$$

$$\overline{R}^2 = 0.922 \qquad D.W. = 1\cdot847$$

It is clear from these results that non-reallocative effects (ΔT_m) might have had a very slight but statistically significant effect on wage change in the inter war years, but had no effect after 1949. The coefficient on ΔT_e which is negative is not paradoxical. Its sign would be positive only if union sector wages were higher than non-union sector wages. In a highly competitive open economy like the United Kingdom it would not be surprising if the rents for unions to extract were small (or zero), and hence there can be no *a priori* presumption that union wages exceed non-union wages. Indeed, if lower-skill industries tended to be unionised and higher-skill industries not, then the reverse is possible. The most likely interpretation is that the union and non-union wages are not significantly different from each other, giving a prediction that the coefficient on ΔT_e would not be significantly different from zero. This indeed appears to be the case. On statistical considerations then ΔT appears as a not very important variable in explaining post-war United Kingdom inflation. Additionally, on *a priori* grounds, its role as an indication of militancy is severely attacked in Purdy and Zis' second paper on the basis of a detailed analysis of the multiple objectives and micro-behaviour of trade unions, and on the grounds that households might join unions for security purposes unconnected with militancy at times when strikes are likely. The over-all tentative conclusion must be that changes in union density, either as a militancy or as an aggregation/allocation variable, has little role to play in the explanation of post war wage inflation in the United Kingdom.

A further variable designed to capture bargaining power is the volume of strikes. This has been found by both Taylor (1975) and Godfrey (1971) to improve the explanatory power of wage-change equations. Conversely, it has been found by Johnston and Timbrell (1973) and Ward and Zis (1974) and Zis (1977) to be of virtually no importance. It is noteworthy that there are no *a priori* reasons to expect *causal* relation—though plenty of reasons to expect a corre- lation—between strikes and wage change, and that the correlations that are found are in quarterly and semi-annual models where seasonality is likely to be important, rather than in annual models.

It is worth summarising the above discussion of wage equa- tions. Bargaining and competitive models yield behavioural predic- tions which are close to each other; the rate of wage change seems to depend on expected inflation rates, expected tax changes and the excess demand for labour; the excess demand for labour and the unemployment rate seem to be sufficiently well related for there to be a short-run trade-off between wage change and unemploy- ment; there appears to be no long-run trade-off however; trade union and strike variables are of dubious *a priori* relevance and of limited empirical assistance in explaining wage change; incomes policies have no significant effects; the wage acceleration of the late 1960s has to be seen in its world context; finally there appears to have been a shift in the natural unemployment rate, more pronounced in the 1970s but beginning in the late 1960s.

(*ii*) *The determinants of price change.* The expectations—excess- demand hypothesis of price change has been tested explicitly for the United Kingdom only by Solow (1969) and Smith (1976) (see Chapter 5). Solow gives a lot of empirical results but the one singled out is

$$\Delta p = -0 \cdot 233 + 0 \cdot 081 \, (u\ell c) + 0 \cdot 002 \mathrm{Cu} + 0 \cdot 809 \Delta p^e \qquad (2.21)$$
$$[4 \cdot 77] \quad [1 \cdot 63] \qquad \qquad [4 \cdot 84] \qquad [8 \cdot 11]$$

$$R^2 = 0 \cdot 844$$

where $\Delta p^e = 0 \cdot 7 \Delta p + 0 \cdot 3 \Delta \ell_{-1}$ and where $u\ell c$ is the rate of change of unit labour cost, and Cu is a capacity utilisation index. To inter- pret this result it is necessary to assume that $u\ell c$ is a good proxy for expected factor price changes. With this assumption, the result is very encouraging for the expectations hypothesis. It is the coefficients on ulc plus Δp^e which should sum to unity and their sum is in fact 0.89. The coefficient on the excess demand proxy, Cu, is small but highly significant. Solow presents a further result in which Cu is dropped, the rate of change of import prices, Δp_m, and a Selwyn Lloyd dummy, LD, are included. This gives

$$\Delta p = 0.004 + 0.582 ulc + 0.098\Delta p_m + 0.180\Delta p^e - 0.017 LD$$
$$[0.98] \quad [10.21] \qquad [2.74] \qquad [1.40] \qquad [3.36]$$

$$R^2 = 0.957 \tag{2.22}$$

Δp^e is constructed as before. Although the coefficients have moved around a good deal, it is likely that the omission of Cu has enhanced the role of ulc. Also, the coefficients on $ulc, \Delta p_m$ and Δp^e should now sum to unity if the expectations hypothesis is correct. They in fact sum to 0.86 which is not very different from one although that equality is not tested.

A thorough testing of the expectations-excess demand hypothesis has been carried out by Duck *et al.* (1976) not for the United Kingdom but for the aggregate 'Group of Ten'. They find that prices on the average across these ten countries have behaved in accordance with

$$\Delta p = -0.100 + 0.184X + \Delta p_1^e \qquad \overline{R}^2 = 0.513 \text{ D.W.} = 2.188$$
$$[0.72] \quad [3.31] \tag{2.23}$$
or

$$\Delta p = -0.012 + 0.132X + \Delta p_2^e \qquad \overline{R}^2 = 0.764 \text{ D.W.} = 2.147$$
$$[0.38] \quad [3.38] \tag{2.24}$$

where Δp_1^e is a forecast from a Box—Jenkins $(0, 2, 1)$ model and Δp_2^e is a forecast from a Box—Jenkins $(2, 2, 3)$ model estimated over the same sample period, and X is the deviation of world industrial production from trend. The unrestricted estimates of the coefficients on Δp_1^e and Δp_2^e are 0.814 and 0.869 respectively and neither is significantly different from unity.

The normal cost hypothesis has recently been extensively tested by Godley and Nordhaus (1972). They report that, using ten alternative specifications—one hundred models—only in *four* cases did the excess demand variable show a t-ratio exceeding two. Further, computing the predicted price change $\Delta \hat{p}$ based on an elaborate normalisation of unit cost changes, they found that

$$\Delta p = 0.001 + 0.625\Delta \hat{p} + 0.0002X \qquad \overline{R}^2 = 0.34 \text{ D.W.} = 1.83$$
$$[1.42] \quad [5.36] \qquad [0.66] \tag{2.25}$$

where X was an excess demand variable based on deviations from trend output.

Ball and Duffy (1972) report some success with excess demand variables in the context of a less thorough normal cost model. The above Godley—Nordhaus result cannot be regarded as satisfactory and as being the last word on United Kingdom price determination. To make sense of their model, the coefficient on $\Delta \hat{p}$ should be unity. Their omission of capital costs and taxes is possibly responsible for this. However, their extensive search for excess-demand effects is impressive and suggests that those which have been found may well be accidents. *A priori,* it would be surprising if *national* excess demand had an independent effect on the prices of manufactured goods, most of which are extensively and freely traded in highly competitive world markets.[18]

A study of price determination in the United States by Laidler (1975, chapter 7) shows a simple expectations—excess-demand model to perform well for that country, again with a coefficient not significantly different from unity on the expected rate of price change. In fact, Laidler estimates that crucial coefficient as 1·003 with a t-statistic of 17·5.[19]

The rejection of excess demand as an explanatory variable is, of course, entirely in line with the competitive version of the expectations hypothesis, does not indicate the presence of a long-run trade-off between inflation and excess demand, and does not indicate the absence of a short-run trade-off through the labour market. Our broad conclusions on price formation have to be that excess demand may well not exert a large independent influence on price change in the United Kingdom, where inflation expectations and normal cost changes (which may well be linked) are the dominant force in making for price change. At the world aggregate level, and in the United States however, excess demand as well as expectations probably play an independent part.

(*iii*) *The formation of expectations.* With various expected inflation variables playing such a crucial role in the explanation of wage and price change, it clearly becomes important to both measure and explain movements in those expectations. This has been started by Carlson and Parkin (1975), who measure the expected rate of change of consumer prices based on a Gallup Poll survey, and test various hypotheses about the determination of changes in expectations. The measurement aspect has already been discussed and we here deal only with the second problem.

The most widely used hypothesis about expectation formation is

$$\Delta p^e = \lambda \Delta p_{-1} + (1 - \lambda)\Delta p^e_{-1} \qquad (2.26)$$

the error learning process. Using the Gallup Poll data for Δp^e and the Retail Price Index for Δp and using monthly data from 1960 to 1971 gives

$$\Delta p^e = 0 \cdot 130 \Delta p_{t-1} + 0 \cdot 870 \Delta p^e_{t-1}$$
$$[2 \cdot 607]$$

$$\overline{R}^2 = 0 \cdot 70 \text{ D.W.} = 2 \cdot 33 \tag{2.27}$$

which is clearly a reasonable model. The *a priori* restriction that the coefficients on Δp_{-1} and Δp^e_{-1} sum to unity (imposed in the above result) is not rejected by the data. However, most of the explanatory power comes from Δp^e_{t-1} not Δp and, in an unconstrained estimation, one could not reject the hypothesis that the process is purely autoregressive in Δp^e, at least as a mechanical statistical proposition. The best hypothesis, however, appears not to be the above, although that is clearly not a bad one, but rather one which specifies a second-order error-learning mechanism (as suggested by Rose (1972)), augmented by a devaluation effect. Such factors as incomes policy, political party in power, large and highly publicised wage changes and indirect tax changes appear to have no discernible effects on expected inflation of retail prices. Parkin *et al.* (1976) and Smith (1976) (see Chapter 7) have applied a similar model to firms' expectations of domestic wholesale and export price change expectations with similar success. The major finding that repeats itself consistently in both these studies is that an error-learning model cannot be rejected, and that exchange-rate changes and only exchange-rate changes modify the process.

The overall conclusion emerging from this review of both theoretical and empirical work on the proximate determinants of wages, prices and inflation expectations are that an excess-demand-expectations model with error-learning expectations and with foreign price/exchange rate variations and tax changes having a direct impact, is probably the best explanation we currently have. Institutional factors such as who fixes wages and prices, whether markets are competitive or not, whether income policies are in operation or not, are of secondary importance at most. The above, however, does not in any sense constitute an explanation of inflation. That requires a comprehensive analysis of the interaction of markets for goods and labour with those for money and other assets. We now turn to that.

II 'COMPLETE' MODELS OF THE INFLATIONARY PROCESS

None of the models discussed in the preceding section determines the rate of inflation. The wage and price equations show how those variables are determined, relative to the expected rate of inflation, by excess demand. The expectations models show how the expected rate of inflation reacts to previous levels of the actual rate and, hence, to past levels of excess demand. It is crucial, therefore, if inflation is to be explained, to analyse the determinants of excess demand and its interactions with inflation.

There is, of course, an enormous literature on this which falls into two groups. First, econometric models have been constructed which explain in varying degrees of aggregation the determinants of demand for and supply of goods and labour, and their interactions with price- and wage-setting equations of the type discussed above. For detailed policy forecasting and simulation purposes they are invaluable; however they cannot be analysed in any simple way and do little to illuminate understanding. They simply are too big and have too many variables and equations for it to be possible to get a clear idea as to how they generate inflation. For that the second approach is useful.

This focuses on highly aggregative, simple models which are amenable to analytical manipulation and solution and which have an essentially simple structure. Laidler has presented three models for a closed economy: one in the spirit of Wicksell's analysis (1975, chapter 5), one built around Hicks' trade cycle model (1975, chapter 6), and one based on a simple 'monetarist' analysis of aggregate demand (1975, chapter 7). The Wicksellian model is of limited interest for present purposes because it omits inflation expectations from the price determination process, and the Hicks' model turns out to be analytically untidy. The monetarist model, however, gives many useful insights and is worth considering in some detail.

The model has the following structure: first, inflation and inflation expectations are determined by

$$\Delta p = \alpha X + \Delta p^e_{-1} \tag{2.28}$$

and

$$\Delta p^e = \lambda \Delta p + (1 - \lambda)\Delta p^e_{-1} \tag{2.29}$$

The 'monetarist' content arises from the demand for money (and implicit demand for goods) function which is

$$m^d = \beta(Y^* + X) + p = m \tag{2.30}$$

where

m^d = nominal money demanded

m = nominal money supply

Y^* = full employment real output

$Y^* + X$ = aggregate demand

and lower-case letters denote logarithms.

These three equations, holding Y^* constant, yield the difference equation:

$$\Delta p = \left(\frac{\alpha(1 - \lambda) + 2\beta}{\alpha + \beta}\right) \Delta p_{-1} - \left(\frac{\beta}{\alpha + \beta}\right) \Delta p_{-2} + \frac{\alpha}{\alpha + \beta} \Delta m$$

$$- \frac{\alpha(1 - \lambda)}{\alpha + \beta} \Delta m_{-1} \qquad (2.31)$$

If Δm is constant, and with α, β positive and $0 < \lambda < 1$, this model will always converge on a stable rate of inflation equal to Δm. However, the convergence will be cyclical if

$$\frac{\alpha}{\beta} < \frac{4\lambda}{(1 - \lambda)^2} \qquad (2.32)$$

A step jump up in the monetary expansion rate which is then maintained will always involve an initial overshoot of the inflation rate and then, if non-cyclical, an approach to Δm from above. However, it is almost inconceivable that the above cycle condition will not be satisfied; hence, an oscillatory approach is much more likely.

It is clear from this discussion that attempts to test monetary hypotheses at the aggregate reduced form level are hazardous. In the light of that discussion it is instructive to consider a recent test which has been performed. Nordhaus (1972b) tests a monetary hypothesis by running the regressions[20]

$$\Delta w = \alpha_1 + \alpha_2 \Delta m + \alpha_3 \Delta y \qquad (2.33)$$

or

$$\Delta w = \alpha_0 + \alpha_1 t + \alpha_2 m + \alpha_3 y \qquad (2.34)$$

for seven countries. Nordhaus' view is that the monetarist hypothesis requires that $\alpha_2 = -\alpha_3 = 1$, and given that interpretation finds the 'monetarist hypothesis is rejected whenever the evidence is sufficient. In no country is the hypothesis accepted'. It is clear from the above discussion that Nordhaus has an inappropriate test of the proposition that 'inflation is always and everywhere a monetary phenomenon resulting from, and accompanied by, a rise in the quantity of money relative to output' (Friedman, 1966). Only if expectations are always correct, $\lambda = 1$, and prices perfectly flexible, $\alpha = \infty$, does equation 2.32 above generate Nordhaus' predictions.

The above model deals with a closed economy. Two types of changes are needed if we are to understand the inflation process in

an open economy. First, the relation between inflation and excess
demand needs augmenting with expectations about both world and
domestic price movements and exchange rate adjustments.
Secondly, the process of money creation has to allow for the interactions between domestic credit expansion, the exchange rate and
the balance of payments.

Very simply models, which retain most of the simplifying
assumptions in the above closed economy models and which show
how these things hang together, have been proposed by Parkin
(1975a) and Laidler (1975, chapter 9). Parkin's analysis is
restricted to a full employment situation and has trade flows only
(no capital flows) linking economies. It analyses the inflation,
balance of payments and exchange-rate movements of a small
economy which takes the rest of the world's inflation rate as given.
Alternative exchange rate regimes are considered. The model
contains excess demand functions (which are entirely full employment relative price/real balance propositions) for traded goods,
non-traded goods and labour; a money market, and a foreign
exchange market. Inflation depends entirely on expectations (a
competitive market prediction) which are always correct.
Asymptotically, such an economy inflates at $\Delta p = \Delta p_f + \Delta \epsilon$, where
Δp = domestic inflation, Δp_f = world inflation in the world currency
unit and $\Delta \epsilon$ = rate of depreciation of exchange rate. For a fixed
exchange rate, $\Delta p = \Delta p_f$, of course, which is the well-known
Johnson—Mundell result. For $\Delta \epsilon$ flexible, the equilibrium movement in the exchange rate is shown to be given by $\Delta \epsilon = \Delta d - \Delta p_f$,
whence $\Delta p = \Delta d$, where Δd is the rate of domestic credit expansion
(and growth is ignored); another well-known result. The novel
result to be found by Parkin is that even with full equilibrium in
domestic labour and non-tradeable-goods markets, a fixed-
exchange-rate economy which increases domestic credit at too fast
a rate for balance of payments equilibrium will in the short run
inflate at a faster rate than the rest of the world. The historical
length of the short run is of course an empirical matter.

Laidler's model is more general than Parkin's in that it
allows for unemployment (although like Parkin's it does not have
capital movements). It considers only a fixed-exchange-rate
economy. Inflation is defined as a weighted average of the inflation
rates of domestic non-tradeables and tradeables. The price of the
latter is exogenous and determined in world markets, while
domestic non-tradeables prices respond to excess demand for
them and to their expected rate of inflation, which, in turn, is
determined by an error-learning process. There is a conventional
open economy money supply and the demand for real money
depends only on real aggregate demand. The balance of payments
is determined by excess demand and relative prices. The model
produces an equilibrium domestic rate of inflation which equals

the world rate and which is stable if some very weak conditions are satisfied. Thus, the equilibrium properties of the model are entirely standard. The disequilibrium behaviour of the model is very interesting. The impact effect of a rise in the domestic credit expansion rate is to raise the level of excess demand. However, this is followed in the next period by an equal and opposite effect. The effects on domestic inflation are of course of the same sign as the excess demand effects on impact, but have to be modified and become ambiguous for subsequent effects because of induced expectations movements.

Another well-known open economy model is that of Edgren, Faxén and Odhner (1969). That model is usually presented as if it were different from the monetary approach to inflation in an open economy. However, for a fixed-exchange-rate country (the case for which the model was developed) it has the same predictions as the monetary model. For a flexible-exchange-rate economy, the Swedish result collapses and again parallels the results of monetary analysis. To see these results, consider the following simple version of the Swedish model. The economy produces two goods: a tradeable (or exposed good) with price P_T, a non-tradeable (or sheltered good) with price P_N. The economy has a fixed exchange rate and a competitive (or administered as if competitive) labour market. Output per head grows at Δq_T in the tradeable sector and Δq_N in the non-tradeable sector. Inflation of wages in the tradeable sector will be

$$\Delta w_T = \Delta p_T + \Delta q_T \tag{2.35}$$

where both Δp_T and Δq_T are exogenous. Competitive labour markets will ensure that $\Delta w_N = \Delta w_T$, hence average wage inflation:

$$\Delta w = \alpha \Delta w_T + (1 - \alpha)\Delta w_N = \Delta p_T + \Delta q_T \tag{2.36}$$

That is, the rate of wage inflation depends entirely on the world-determined rate of inflation of tradeables' prices and the productivity growth rate in the tradeable sector.

This model has implications for price inflation since

$$\Delta p_N = \Delta w_N - \Delta q_N \tag{2.37}$$

and

$$\Delta p = \alpha \Delta p_T + (1 - \alpha)\Delta p_N \tag{2.38}$$

where α = the weight on traded goods in the domestic price index. This shows that the domestic rate of inflation equals the foreign rate, Δp_T, plus an adjustment (essentially a relative price term) to allow for productivity differentials. This is of course entirely in line with the monetary approach which predicts that $\Delta p = \Delta p_T$ in terms of the above notation. The additional productivity term showing how relative prices are moving is not present in the usual monetary analysis which, by implication, assumes $\Delta q_T = \Delta q_N$.

We saw, in our closed economy discussion of the reduced form relation between inflation and monetary expansion, that no simple relationship should be found if money is the inflation-generating agent. The above open economy models suggest that for such (i.e., all) economies, simple reduced form tests will be even less instructive. From Laidler's open economy model it is apparent that a cyclical response of Δp to a steady expansion of domestic credit is possible. However, the inflation rate and the monetary expansion rate both converge on the world rate of inflation. The precise time relation of Δp to Δm will be most complex and almost impossible to capture with any distributed lag response between the two variables. Push sources of inflation in the fixed-exchange-rate case have not yet been thoroughly analysed. However, some limited things may be said. If Δp goes ahead of that of the rest of the world because of push and if the exchange rate is rigidly fixed, then a balance of payments deficit and slowdown of Δm will follow. This will put deflationary pressure on the domestic economy, which will depress output and/or the inflation rate. Conversely, if non-monetary forces are operating in a way so as to depress the domestic rate of inflation below the world rate (e.g., a 'successful' incomes policy) then, again with a rigid exchange rate, the balance of payments will move into surplus, and the money supply will expand more quickly than the inflation rate thereby putting demand pressure on the economy, which will eventually bring its inflation rate up to world level.

A much less hazardous method of attempting to discriminate between monetary and push hypotheses would involve a detailed structural analysis of the inflation process. The models so far discussed contain three central ingredients. First, a set of relations which explain how prices and wages respond to excess demand and inflation expectations; secondly, a process for generating expectations; and thirdly, a process whereby excess demand is generated by monetary (and more generally fiscal) policy. We have, in Section 2.1 undertaken an extensive and comprehensive review of the first two components of a complete model and found considerable support for an error-learning expectations—augmented excess demand hypothesis. The above discussion of the generation of excess demand has been limited to very simple propositions which could be analysed in the context of a complete model. However, there is, in addition, a vast literature—larger for the United States than any other country, but vast enough even for the United Kingdom—which explains the linkages between monetary and fiscal variables on the one side and total spending (and therefore excess demand) on the other. It is not the purpose of this paper to review that extensive literature. It is necessary only to draw attention to the fact that no serious scholar denies that fiscal variables—taxes and government spending levels—have quick and fairly predictable effects on total spending. Also, no serious scholar denies that monetary variables—in the form of both interest rate and real balance effects—have important effects on demand. However, these effects are distributed over time and, in the short run, difficult to predict. Nevertheless, the path of excess demand is influenced by the previous paths of fiscal and monetary instruments.

A fourth part of a structural model of inflation (not present in the above model) has received little attention: this is the process whereby monetary and fiscal instruments are determined. There are two ways of proceeding here. One is to undertake a thorough historical analysis of the determinants of monetary policy such as, for example, that undertaken by Friedman and Schwartz (1963) for the United States. They have done enough to convince Tobin at least that some 'monetary changes were clearly independent of contemporary or immediately preceding economic events ... and have put to rout the neo-Keynesian, if he exists, who regards monetary events as mere epiphenomena, postcripts added as afterthoughts to the nonmonetary factors that completely determine income, employment and even prices' (Tobin (1965), p. 81). There is no study comparable to that of Friedman and Schwartz for recent American history or for the United Kingdom. It is apparent, however, that the world monetary expansion of the late 1960s was heavily influenced by the social and political objectives of the American government on the social security, space and Vietnam fronts. It is also clear that the United Kingdom's late 1960s and 1970s monetary expansion has arisen as a result of pursuing a fixed exchange rate while the United States was flooding Europe with money and by pursuing policy designed to keep interest rates relatively low, especially in the housing sector, while at the same time increasing the fraction of resources commanded by the public sector.

The second method of studying the determinants of monetary and fiscal policy is to use the Theil optimum control analysis to study the reaction functions of the government and central bank in the setting of policy instruments. Such studies for the United Kingdom suggest that monetary policy in the form of the level of interest rates becomes tight primarily because of foreign exchange reserve losses and slack when reserves are accumulating, and is influenced little by the unemployment and inflation rates. (See Pissarides, 1972).

The above analysis and argument seems to suggest that an error-learning expectations-augmented excess-demand model explains the movement of prices and wages rather convincingly, and that the course of excess demand is determined by monetary and fiscal policy. The converse proposition, that prices are determined by push forces which lead to validating changes in monetary and fiscal policy, does not seem to be nearly so convincing.

Before accepting this view let us finally turn to a consideration of some non-economic explanations of inflation.

III NON-ECONOMIC EXPLANATIONS

Non-economic explanations of inflation as advanced by Jones (1972), Marris (1972) and others have not, of course, been presented within the framework which has been adopted in the preceding sections. These non-economic explanations typically start off with a hypothesis about the proximate determinants of price and wage change, and if money is introduced into the argument at all, it appears as a consequence rather than as a cause of inflation. An excellent example of this approach can be seen in Anthony Barber's speech introducing the wage—price controls of November 1972: 'Certainly the effect of our measures on prices ought to be reflected in due course in the figures for money supply ... ' (Hansard, vol. 845, col. 850). It seems useful however, in this section, to examine the non-economic hypotheses in the context of the framework developed above. Within this framework there are two basic ways of approaching inflation from a non-economic point of view. One possibility is that non-economic forces are acting as proximate determinants of price and wage change. That is, the individual firms and unions responsible for setting wages and prices may be doing so in direct response to socio-political forces. Alternatively, non-economic factors may be thought of as operating in conjunction with the expectations-augmented excess-demand monetary model as outlined above. The non-economic forces are then seen as determinants of the behaviour of the money supply and the direction of monetary policy. There has not been a great amount of empirical work done on either of these questions but more exists on the first than the second. We now review this work.

Perhaps the most commonly advanced non-economic hypothesis about inflation is that it is caused by a struggle either between the major classes or between groups of workers for increased relative shares in the national income. The hypothesis usually runs in terms of each individual group having a desired income in relation either to the average or to some leading group. Taking all desired incomes together more than exhausts what is available. The usual proposition about the determination of actual wages is that they are equal to desired wages. This means that the current level of wages will always exceed the previous level by some amount depending upon the extent to which desired income exceeds actual income. With exogenous productivity growth, this implies that the rate of price change will be faster the greater the rate of change of 'frustration' is, and the faster wages have recently been inflating. This model could be made compatible with the monetary discussion in preceding sections by a passive monetary expansion and a flexible exchange rate policy.

There are two kinds of problem with a model like this. First, it is difficult, if not impossible, to give objective quantitative meaning to the concept of dissatisfaction with relative shares. Second, even if it were possible to give meaning to such a concept, it seems highly unlikely that the variable would behave in a manner that contained some systematic cyclical component and, through various phases, long trends sometimes in an upward and sometimes in a downward direction. It would require the belief that in the period from 1951 to 1959 people were increasingly happy with their relative shares but from 1959 to the present day increasingly unhappy. It would also require a belief that there have been quite systematic cycles superimposed upon these two decade-long trends.

None of this is to deny that in a period when inflation is accelerating there is a great deal of frustration, anger and various types of social and industrial conflict. These, however, are easily accounted for by the expectations—excess-demand hypothesis in terms of unfulfilled expectations. The faster inflation is accelerating the greater the degree of disappointment of expectations and therefore the greater the degree to which social unrest will be manifest. Excellent discussion of this and other related topics appear in Laidler (1975, chapter 1). On this view, strikes and unrest are caused by, and not causes of, inflation.

A close neighbour of the above hypothesis is one which asserts that inflation is caused by frustration concerning not relative shares but real income growth; the rate of change of wages will be faster the greater the degree of frustration is with recent real income experience. This would imply a rate of inflation that was countercyclical in relation to the real cycle. That is, when productivity growth and real income growth were at their slowest, frustration would be at its greatest and wages would be pushed up fastest, hence driving up prices even faster. With real income growth accelerating, frustration would be reduced and inflation would thereby fall off. This, of course, is counter to our general observations about the relationship between price changes and demand and real output changes. Hence, the hypothesis seems to be of little empirical value. More formal tests of the hypothesis by Nordhaus (1972b) show this to be so for a simple frustrations hypothesis and an excess-demand Phillips-type relation augmented by 'frustrations'. In fact, it is the worst hypothesis tried for all the seven countries featuring in the Nordhaus study.

A further hypothesis, which is not obviously non-economic but at least has some non-economic content, is that wages and prices inflate faster the greater is the degree of security felt about the pursuit by the government of full employment policies. There is a sense in which this is the same hypothesis as the expectations—excess-demand analysis of the preceding two sections. In that case, if the government were pursuing employment policies that kept the unemployment rate below its natural rate the rate of inflation would accelerate without limit. However, it is often suggested that wage-setting behaviour will be modified in such a situation as workers and their wage negotiators become increasingly confident about the pursuit of full employment policies. In its extreme form it is presented as a model in which the demand function for labour services is perfectly inelastic with respect to money wages. At the simplest level there is an obvious fallacy of composition at work here. It may be the case for the economy as a whole that the demand for labour is invariant with respect to the money wage because of the validating monetary and fiscal policy pursued by the authorities. However, for any individual group of workers it is clear that the demand for their services is not independent of their money wage given the level of money prices. No matter how large or influential a particular group of workers, it seems almost inconceivable that they would negotiate a money wage increase of any arbitrary value in the knowledge that everyone else would be almost immediately falling into line with them. It is certainly inconceivable if they did so behave that they would inconvenience themselves and other people by having strikes in the process of achieving such a money wage, since no real wage change could be achieved.

Perhaps the most pessimistic view of the determinants of inflation is that of Wiles (1973). He regards inflation as being determined by the rate at which wages rise and regards that as simply a number plucked out of the air by trade union negotiators.

It is not uncommon in the non-economic approach to inflation to emphasise the sectoral linkages between different parts of the labour market. The central idea is that there is in some sense a leading sector which achieves a particular rate of change of wages, and rigid linkages between that sector and the rest of the economy ensure that whatever rate of wage rise the leading sector obtains spreads itself through fairly automatically and fairly quickly to the rest of the economy. The non-economic approach to inflation does not have a monopoly on this idea. It is possible to view the most classically generated monetary inflation as proceeding in just such a way. If there is a monetary injection raising the overall level of demand this will be felt by some sector, or sectors, before the rest of the economy. The long run need not be a long historical period but simply the period during which the

economy is returning to its equilibrium relative prices. Unless
there are substantial changes in taste and/or technology and/or
relative monopoly power, which coincidentally occur at the same
time as the rapid monetary expansion, relative prices will not
change except in the short-run transition process and so inflation
will, as it were, have spread from the leading sector through to the
rest of the economy. The fixed-exchange-rate open economy
analysis which emphasises the role of the export sector is a model
of this type. It is a model in which the export sector is the leading
sector, excess demand is first manifest in that sector and via competitive forces spreads inflation to the rest of the economy.

In summary, these non-economic socio-political hypotheses
about the determination of wage change and price change do not
appear to offer a convincing alternative to, or even augment, the
main economic explanation considered in the two preceding
sections. Let us now, however, turn to the consideration of the
role of socio-political factors as determinants of the rate of
monetary expansion. Here there appears to be much more scope
for such forces to be at work.

At the level of the domestic economy the interest-rate and
exchange-rate policies pursued for political purposes certainly
seem to have important monetary and inflationary implications.
It is common practice throughout the liberal democracies of the
western world (although not universal practice) for governments
to pursue interest-rate policies both in support of cheap mortgages
for house buyers and to make the financing of government budget
deficits relatively painless. Pursued too far and for too long, such
policies will unquestionably generate a rate of monetary expansion
sufficient to produce accelerating inflation. Secondly, the choice of
exchange-rate policy, usually for national pride and prestige
reasons, has led to exchange rates in many countries being fixed,
and fixed at levels which were too low for the maintenance of
steady prices. Such an anti-inflation economy as West Germany,
by pursuing fixed exchange rates for too long through the 1960s,
has inevitably shared in the inflation that everyone else has been
suffering from. Additionally, at the domestic level, the pursuit of
full employment with no reference to what that means in terms of
price stability can be a source of accelerating inflation. If the
national political attitudes regard some particular value of the
unemployment rate as the value to be aimed for and if policy is
geared to achieving that rate, then, unless by a happy accident it
happens to be the equilibrium or natural rate, either persistent
inflation or deflation, and typically the former, will follow. Why
some countries regard 4 per cent unemployment as acceptable
while others regard even 2 per cent as an outrage is not at all
clear. However, it does not seem likely that it is a simple narrow
economic matter.

At the international level, there are further political and social considerations to take into account. The particular international monetary system adopted by the world will inevitably have implications for the behaviour of national and world money supplies. A world of perfectly flexible exchange rates, with each country pursuing anti-inflationary domestic monetary policies, would yield stable prices everywhere and exchange rates that, whilst flexible, would not move very much. A world of rigid fixed exchange rates with a central monetary authority for the world determining the rate of world monetary expansion and keeping that monetary expansion rate roughly in line with productivity growth would likewise produce a world of stable prices. However, an international monetary system which has fixed exchange rates but which might be moved from time to time in the event of 'fundamental disequilibrium' arising, and with nobody in particular *controlling* the world monetary expansion rate, and in which that monetary expansion rate is being determined by the *ad hoc* monetary policies of a large number of independent countries all pursuing various interest rate and unemployment targets, is likely to produce monetary expansion that is excessive and leads to a worldwide inflation. Why such a monetary system is adopted and how the world may move from such a system to a more firmly based one is a serious unsolved political problem.

Thus, I do not want to deny the importance of political factors in determining inflation. The thrust of the analysis and material surveyed in the preceding sections, however, suggest that it is simply not possible to ignore the monetary, excess-demand and expectations processess that generate inflation. Socio-political forces, whatever they are, or however they work, probably work through their consequences for the behaviour of the monetary expansion rate of an economy.

IV CONCLUSIONS

This survey has consciously directed its attention at the causes of inflation and said little about policies for controlling inflation. It has also concentrated primarily on what we know and said little about what we do not know. This concluding section briefly summarises the main conclusions on the causes of inflation, examines the major outstanding questions and then, in fairly brief terms, considers the policy implications of the present state of knowledge and ignorance.

Our conclusion on the causes of inflation is very simple to state. Inflation is probably caused by both competitive and monopolistic price and wage setters responding to excess demand and their own expectations of the rate of inflation. Those expectations are probably generated by an error-learning process which, taken together with price- and wage-setting behaviour, implies that wages and prices will be determined by the whole time path of excess demand. Excess demand itself is generated by monetary and fiscal policy and with complex time lags linking changes in monetary policy to changes in excess demand. Institutional factors and socio-political factors do not appear to be important determinants of wage- and price-setting behaviour. However, political arrangements, and other socio-political objectives, are undoubtedly among the major determinants of excessive monetary expansion.

Our major gaps of knowledge concern the ways in which political and social forces which influence monetary expansion are themselves determined. Additionally, in terms of the details of the inflationary process, we need to know a great deal more than we currently do about the formation of, and manipulation of, expectations. We also know little about the determinants of the equilibrium unemployment rate and the factors which might be manipulated to lower that rate. A detailed analysis of the interaction of fiscal and monetary policy to reduce inflation with the least cost in terms of underemployed resources has not been as fully analysed as it might be. The precise way in which the international monetary system and alternative international monetary systems generate world monetary expansion needs much closer analysis. The precise relationships between monetary expansion and excess demand and the detailed time lags involved in that relationship are also not well understood.

The policy implications of this state of knowledge and ignorance seem to be very straightforward. First, sharp movements in the rate of monetary expansion clearly are capable of setting up large cyclical movements in the inflation rate. It therefore seems appropriate, especially in view of the imprecise knowledge of the time lags involved, to pursue monetary policies which are steady. This would mean increasing the money supply at roughly the same percentage rate each year. If the money supply is currently growing at a rate faster than that desired, with inflation also continuing on a path which is faster than desired, then steady monetary policy could be conceived of as slowing down the rate of monetary expansion but at a steady rate. Second, if inflation is to be avoided, the unemployment rate must not be set by some political mores with no relation to the underlying equilibrium unemployment rate. If pursuing a steady monetary expansion policy or a steady deceleration of the monetary expansion rate produces an unemployment rate that is unacceptably high, then measures which affect the relationship between unemployment and excess demand are the sorts of measure that have to be introduced. We do not know enough about these but can conjecture that improvements in the efficiency of the labour market as an allocative and reallocative device raising the state of information on both sides could presumably help; also, reducing regional differentials could presumably help. There is no evidence at all either from the studies of the determinants of inflation or from more direct studies that wage and price controls materially affect the rate of inflation. All the evidence goes in the opposite direction, and indeed it is not impossible that direct controls on wages and prices would worsen the equilibrium unemployment rate, thereby worsening the short-run trade-off between inflation and unemployment. The above policy of steady monetary expansion and the acceptance of an equilibrium unemployment rate can only be pursued with a flexible exchange rate or with all other countries pursuing the same policies at the same time in synchronised fashion. In view of the difficulty of obtaining international co-ordination it seems much more sensible. therefore to make exchange-rate flexibility an integral part of an anti-inflation programme, at least in the immediate future.

NOTES TO CHAPTER 2

[1]   This is a revised and updated version of the author's 'The causes of inflation: recent contributions and current controversies', originally published in *Current Economic Problems,* edited by Michael Parkin and A. R. Nobay, Cambridge University Press, 1975, pp. 243-74.

[2]   I am grateful to my colleagues in the Manchester Inflation Workshop and especially to Malcolm Gray, William Peters, Michael Sumner, Graham Smith, Martin Timbrell and George Zis for their extensive discussion and comment on an earlier draft, and to Robert Ward and Caroline Joll who have provided excellent research assistance.

[3]   This is the long-run equilibrium condition with constant terms of trade and has to be modified if the terms of trade are secularly changing. Purely monetary effects, i.e., different domestic and foreign inflation rates not connected with changes in the terms of trade, would be adjusted for by exchange-rate changes so that, in terms of domestic currency, import and domestic prices would inflate at the same rate.

[4]   The Phillips estimate of the Phillips curve was

$$\Delta w = -0 \cdot 9 + 9 \cdot 638 U^{-1 \cdot 394}$$

with

$$\Delta p = \Delta w - \Delta q$$

$$\Delta q = 2 \cdot 5$$

this implies $\Delta p = -3 \cdot 4 + 9 \cdot 638 U^{-1 \cdot 394}$

hence

$$\Delta p = 0 \text{ when } U = 2 \cdot 111$$
$$\Delta p = 6 \cdot 2 \text{ when } U = 1 \cdot 000$$

where $\Delta w, \Delta p$ and Δq are the annual percentage rates of change of wages, prices and productivity respectively.

5   It was also confirmed in too many studies to cite individually, in Parkin and Sumner, eds, (1972)

6   See for example Eckstein and Wilson (1962) and Perry (1966).

7   The term used by Purdy and Zis (1973) for the percentage of the labour force belonging to a trade union.

8   This is not intended to be an exhaustive statement of outstanding questions as of the middle 1960s. Rather it is intended to indicate that those questions were of secondary importance and did not lead to sharp divisions of opinion between economists.

9   Cross' analysis is richer than the others cited in that it deals with the dynamics of learning in the face of imcomplete knowledge.

10   Specifically, the average wage index in an economy is given by $W = TW_T + (1 - T)W_C$ where W_T = union wage, W_C = competitive wage, W = wage index and T = the proportion of labour force receiving union wage. The percentage rate of wage change on the average wage will be $\Delta w = a\Delta T + b\Delta w_T + (1 - b)\Delta w_C$ where

$$a = \frac{W_T - W_C}{W} \text{ and } b = \frac{W_T T}{W}$$

It is clear that if the union differential is constant so that $\Delta w = \Delta w_C$ then the rate of wage change in the economy as a whole will be given by $\Delta w = a\Delta T + \Delta w_C$. It is worth noting that if this rationalisation for T is correct (i) it should appear in wage equations as an *absolute* and not proportional rate of change; (ii) its coefficient should be a *variable*, $(W_T - W_C)/W$, or, the coefficient on the composite variable, $\Delta T(W_T - W_C)/W$, should be unity, and (iii) the same variable should appear in the price equation with equal but opposite sign.

11   Nordhaus (1971) points out that a model which few seem to care for, 'mark-up pricing' is optimal only for competitive industries—precisely those industries for which its advocates believe it does *not* apply. The same is true of the model espoused by Godley and Nordhaus (1972).

12   For an early analysis of qualitative data which contains some of the ideas used by Carlson and Parkin, see Theil (1966), chapter 11.

13   Carlson (1975) has now done work with United States data to check the assumption that expectations are normally distributed across the population This assumption, in fact, does not accord well with the facts. How important this may turn out to be is, however, at this stage, an open question.

14   Extending the data period beyond 1971, as we do in Chapter 4, changes this finding substantially. Indeed, with the alternative specification of the wage equation developed there, a shift in the natural unemployment rate is detectable in the late 1960s.

15   See Muth (1961), Lucas (1972), Sargent (1973).

16   See also McCallum (1974).

17   Data problems prevent the $\Delta T_m, \Delta T_C$ split being updated.

18   This is true, of course, only for a fixed-exchange-rate world. With flexible exchange rates maintaining balance of payments equilibrium, domestic excess demand would be expected to affect domestic prices of internationally traded goods.

19   Laidler's model is not sufficiently strongly specified to allow discrimi nation between a direct effect from excess demand on prices and an indirec

effect via factor costs. The time lags employed suggest the latter interpretation.

[20]   The dependent variable is wage rather than price inflation, and
Nordhaus makes the transition to wage inflation by assuming a stable rate
of productivity growth and that marginal product is equal to the real wage.

3 United Kingdom inflation and its background: a monetarist perspective[1]

David Laidler[2]

I INTRODUCTION

From 1953 to 1969 the British inflation rate never exceeded five per cent and the unemployment rate rose above three per cent of the labour force in only one quarter (1963 first quarter). In 1975 the inflation rate reached a peak of over 30% per cent in the second quarter, unemployment reached five per cent of the labour force, and at the end of the year was still rising rapidly. The contention of this paper is that Britain's difficulties in the 1970s arise from ill-designed policies based upon long and widely held misconceptions about how the economy works. The basic error committed has been to neglect to control the money supply while pursuing an unrealistically low unemployment target, primarily by fiscal means.[3] Monetary expansion, largely a by-product of 'full employment' fiscal policies, has been responsible for the high British inflation rate of the early 1970s.

Figure 3.1 portrays the time series behaviour of inflation (Δp), unemployment (u) and two measures of the rate of monetary expansion (Δm_1 and Δm_3) over the period 1953-75.[4] To argue that variations in the rate of monetary expansion are the main cause of variations in the inflation rate by no means implies that there should be any simple correlation between the two series, as has been shown elsewhere (Laidler, (1975, chapter 7), Gray and Parkin, (1976), Laidler and Parkin (1975)). Nevertheless, results presented there for the United States economy do suggest that marked changes in the monetary expansion rate have a discernible impact on the inflation rate with about a two-year time lag, and the data charted in Figure 3.1 are consistent with the claim that a roughly similar relationship governs the behaviour of British data. The pattern is particularly marked from 1968 onwards, but it is possible to discern a similar, though much less clear-cut, relationship for earlier years as well.[5] The transmission mechanism between monetary expansion and the inflation rate that underlies this interpretation of the evidence involves the initial impact of monetary changes falling on real aggregate demand—for which the unemploy-

ment rate may be regarded as a proxy—and thence influencing the
inflation rate. Inspection of Figure 3.1 shows that such a 'Philiips
curve' relationship is clearly present in the pre-1967 data, vanish-
es between 1967 and 1971, and begins to re-establish itself, although
at much higher levels of inflation and unemployment, thereafter.[6]

Two interrelated questions are prompted by the data charted
in Figure 3.1. First, the pursuit of high employment with fiscal
policy was just as much a characteristic of British policy before
1967 as after: why did a policy that apparently succeeded for
nearly two decades fail so badly in the 1970s? Second, why did the
'Phillips curve' disappear between 1967 and 1971? The answers
offered to these questions in the next few pages may be summarised as follows. A fixed exchange rate and a low inflation rate in
the world economy lay at the root of the apparent success of
Keynesian policies in Britain before 1967. These policies led to
the devaluation of 1967, which coincided with the beginning of the
Vietnam War inflation that ultimately destroyed the Bretton Woods
system. The way in which these changes impinged upon Britain
accounts for the temporary disappearance of the Phillips curve
after 1967. However this phenomenon was interpreted by those in
control of British policy as confirming a belief, widely held in the
1950s, but temporarily unfashionable in the 1960s, that inflation was
to be explained in terms of 'wage-push' factors, many of them
noneconomic. As a direct result of this misreading of the evidence,

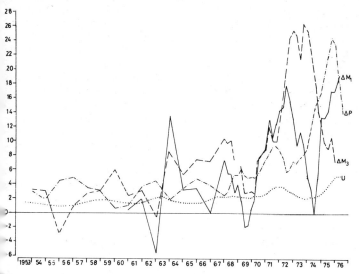

Figure 3.1 Inflation, unemployment and monetary expansion,
1953-76

in 1972 fiscal policy accommodated by monetary expansion and a flexible exchange rate was combined with wage and price controls in an attempt simultaneously to reduce unemployment, increase real growth and reduce the inflation rate. The current condition of the British economy is the direct consequence of this policy, but because this diagnosis is not widely accepted in Britain, there is now a grave danger that the errors of 1972-3 may be repeated.

II RELATIVE INFLATION IN AN OPEN ECONOMY

A version of the 'natural unemployment rate' hypothesis is an important implicit component of this paper's basic thesis. My first task is to show how this hypothesis can be reconciled with the behaviour of the economy over the 1953-67 period. The expectations-augmented Phillips curve in terms of which this hypothesis is usually formulated may be written:

$$\Delta p = g(U) + \Delta p^e \qquad g' < 0 \tag{3.1}$$

where u is the unemployment rate, Δp is the inflation rate and Δp^e the expected inflation rate. It is common to postulate that expectations of inflation are formed according to a first-order error-learning scheme applied to the actual inflation rate, but this hypothesis ignores the fact that data on the past path of inflation are not usually the only information readily available and relevant to forecasting its future time path; where such extra information is available, economic agents are likely to make use of it.[7] In a fixed-exchange-rate open economy the time path of the price level in the rest of the world is of vital importance. It does not take much sophistication to know that, if a fixed exchange rate is to be maintained, domestic inflation cannot for ever deviate from that ruling in the world economy. If agents expect the exchange rate to be maintained, then they will also expect the domestic inflation rate to converge on that ruling abroad. There are many specific hypotheses about the formation of inflationary expectations in an open economy compatible with this rather general set of propositions, but one, admittedly *ad hoc*, model that I have experimented with elsewhere with considerable success has expectations about domestic inflation being revised according to a weighted average of the deviations of domestic and world inflation from the previously expected rate of inflation.[8] Thus, with $\Delta \pi$ as the world rate of inflation, the change in the expected inflation rate is written as:

$$\Delta p^e - \Delta p^e_{-1} = d[v(\Delta p_{-1} - \Delta p^e_{-1}) + (1 - v)(\Delta \pi_{-1} - \Delta p^e_{-1})$$

$$0 < d, v < 1 \tag{3.2}$$

Combining this expression with equation (3.1) and solving for a situation in which $\Delta p = \Delta p_{-1}$ and $u = u_{-1}$ yields:

$$\Delta p = \frac{1}{1 - v}\, g(U) + \Delta\pi_{-1} \qquad (3.3)$$

Equation 3.3 *appears* to show that a 'long-run' trade-off between inflation and unemployment is implicit in this approach to modelling the Phillips curve for an open economy, that a lower unemployment rate may be maintained for ever at the cost of a higher but not accelerating inflation rate.[9] However, this result can hold only as long as the exchange rate is held constant and is expected to remain constant. The correct long-run implication of equation 3.3 is that, if an open economy maintains a lower than 'natural' unemployment rate, this will result in a higher inflation rate than that ruling in the rest of the world and hence in a secularly worsening balance of payments situation. Equation 3.3 is not, therefore, a steady state for it can be sustained only so long as foreign exchange reserves permit.

In Britain, over the period 1953-67, too low an unemployment target was set, the country experienced an inflation rate higher on average than that ruling in the rest of the world, and that higher inflation rate was associated with a secular deterioration in the balance of payments.[10] Apparently successful 'Keynesian' full employment policies thus culminated in the devaluation of November 1967. Data illustrating this argument are charted in Figure 3.2.

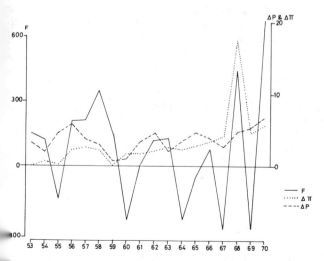

Figure 3.2 Inflation and the current account balance, 1953-70

Devaluation was bound to produce a short-term step-up in the
inflation rate as British prices adjusted to the new exchange rate,
and the lower level of real income implicit in it, even if the inflation rate ruling in the rest of world had remained constant. But,
as Figure 3.2 also shows, in 1967 the world inflation rate was
already accelerating. This acceleration is usually explained as
being the result of United States policies toward financing the
Vietnam War.[11] Devaluation and the simultaneous step-up in the
world inflation rate largely account for the acceleration of British
inflation after 1967.

Figure 3.2 shows that the balance of payments did not respond
immediately to the 1967 devaluation. Whether this was due to slow-
ness of quantities of imports and exports to respond to relative
price changes, or to the fact that British monetary policy continued
to be expansionary after devaluation, is not of central importance.[12]
The problem did lead, in 1968, to the IMF requiring a policy of
monetary stringency as a condition of aid, a policy which was adopted and which, it has already been argued, had its effect in 1970-2,
at first solely on unemployment and only subsequently on the rate
of inflation.

III DEVALUATION AND DEPRECIATION

The experience of 1967-71 was widely misinterpreted in Britain,
by professional economists and 'informed opinion' alike. In the
1960s the Phillips curve, in its original form unaugmented by
inflationary expectations, had gained acceptance among both groups
as a valid hypothesis about the relationship between wage inflation
and unemployment. For example, at least two of the three operational large-scale forecasting models in terms of which so much
discussion of policy took place had, until the late 1960s, treated
price inflation as largely depending upon a wage inflation rate
determined by some form of Phillips curve. By 1971 the Phillips
curve had been dropped from these models leaving money wage
inflation as a exogenous variable in all three of them.[13] This
change was proximately caused by the failure of the non-expecta-
tions-augmented version of the curve to deal with post-1967 data,
but also reflected renewed and increasing acceptance of the position, popular in the 1950s, that wage, and hence price inflation was
the result of wage-push factors of mainly domestic origin.[14] The
alternative view that the accelerating inflation of 1967-71 was
largely imported, with an overlay attributable to the 1967 devaluation, found few supporters in 1971.

Crucial to reinforcing the belief that inflation was a matter of
domestically originating wage-push was the so-called 'wage
explosion' of 1969-71. Between 1966 and 1969 the rate of increase

Table 3.1 Average annual percentage rates of change of prices, hourly wages, real hourly wages.

(a) Five-year periods, 1956-71

Period	Prices	Wages	Real wages
1956-61	2·29	4·38	2·09
1957-62	2·40	4·25	1·95
1958-63	2·21	4·22	2·01
1959-64	2·75	4·68	1·93
1960-65	3·48	5·09	1·61
1961-66	3·57	5·15	1·58
1962-67	3·23	5·04	1·81
1963-68	3·76	5·61	1·85
1964-69	4·16	5·63	1·47
1965-70	4·51	6·38	1·86
1966-71	5·50	7·58	2·08

(b) Year on year changes, 1966-71

Period	Prices	Wages	Real wages
1966-67	2·5	3·9	1·4
1967-68	4·6	6·6	2·0
1968-69	5·2	5·2	0·0
1969-70	6·2	9·8	3·6
1970-71	9·0	12·3	3·3

of hourly wage rates averaged 5·2 per cent per annum; between 1969 and 1971 it averaged 11·1 per cent per annum, and that at a time when unemployment averaged about 2·7 per cent of the labour force, an unusually high figure by past standards.[15] In retrospect this episode is not difficult to explain. As Table 3.1a shows, the rate of growth of real wage rates over the 1966-7 to 1970-1 period was similar to rates achieved in the late 1950s and early 1960s. The growth of real wage rates was unusually slow in the mid-1960s.

Moreover, as Table 3.1b shows, price inflation began to accelerate immediately after 1967 and money wage inflation did not immediately accelerate so rapidly. Some of this wage lag was due to the effect of wage and price controls which had strong short-term effects on wages, in 1966-7, and also according to some studies in 1968 (Parkin and Sumner (1972), chapters 1, 4, 10). Some of it was perhaps due to lags in the adaptation of expectations to an accelerating and largely imported price inflation. On this interpretation the 'wage explosion' simply represents a 'catch up' whose underlying causes were strong enough, for a while, to offset the effects of monetary stringency and rising unemployment.[16]

However, this interpretation was very much a minority view at the time. The Proceedings of the Conference on 'The Current Inflation' held at the London School of Economics on 22 February 1971 (Johnson and Nobay, 1971) give considerable inslight into the state of contemporary opinion. As Johnson put it in his Introduction to the Proceedings, 'the prevailing mood of the Conference seemed to be to dismiss a change in external influences in favour of a change in internal influences, as a primal causal factor in the current inflation'. The internal influences in question all centred on the idea of exogenous wage-push.[17] By the end of 1971, those in a position to influence British policy were united in the view that the inflation rate was not susceptible to any policy relevent extent to influence by variations in the level of aggregate demand.[18] Thus, when in that winter, and with a little journalistic licence (see Brittan (1975), pp. 70-2) unemployment reached the magic number of one million, the scene was set for the implementation of an economic policy which, though coherent enough in terms of this new prevailing orthodoxy, was, from a 'monetarist' viewpoint, inherently contradictory. The strategy, crystallised in Mr Barber's 1972 budget, involved using fiscal policy to stimulate aggregate demand, and letting monetary expansion take up the resulting public sector deficit lest high interest rates should interfere with real expansion or discomfort owner-occupiers.[19] Initially an attempt was made to get voluntary controls on wages and prices accepted, but by November 1972 statutory controls were introduced to deal with inflation.[2] Exchange-rate flexibility was adopted, explicitly to ensure that balance of payments problems did not, as they were judged to have done in the past, jeopardise the pursuit of full employment and growth.

The government were showered with praise for their policy. The National Institute did criticise the budget, it is true, but for not being expansionary enough (*Review*, May 1972). *The Economist,* though noting that the public sector borrowing requirement might lead to monetary expansion, and putting little faith in informal and voluntary wage and price controls, nevertheless concluded that 'Within the context of a budget that ignored [getting to grips with wage inflation] Mr Barber produced something very close to the best economic strategy that a now very professional Chancellor could' (25 March 1972, p. 13). By November, when statutory controls were introduced, *The Economist* welcomed them with the comment that 'It has been obvious for at least the past two years that Britain can avoid South American style inflation only by enforcing a statutory incomes policy' (11 November 1972). No possibility of conflict between rapid expansion of aggregate demand and a policy of wage and price controls was noted, not just because inflation was regarded as independent of the level of aggregate demand in the economy, but because expansion of real output and consumption were actually regarded as necessary prerequisites for the success of controls.

An increase in output could be relied on to reduce unit labour costs and hence lead to a short-term slackening off of price inflation; in the longer term an expansion of real consumption would enable the living standards of the labour force to be raised, hence fulfilling the very expectations of rising real incomes the frustration of which, in conditions of slow growth, was supposed to be the main cause of inflation. As the *National Institute Economic Review* for August 1972 put it, 'The present situation in the British economy permits a rapid expansion of output for the next two or three years and requires, in the short period at any rate, a sharp increase in consumption. It is the most favourable possible situation for the introduction of [incomes] policies ... ' (p. 6). In November, it returned to the same theme: 'The prospects for success of Phase II [of the newly introduced policy] are themselves dependent on the growth of the economy and *on our forecast* some additional stimulus is likely to be needed if the Chancellor's target [of five per cent growth] is to be achieved. There certainly seems little need for actually *cutting* public expenditure plans for 1973' (p. 6).[21]

Mr Barber's 'go for growth' policy of 1972-3 was qualitatively similar to Mr Maudling's 1963-4 'dash for growth', and based on similar intellectual foundations. The Maudling policy quickly foundered on balance of payments problems. In 1972, the adoption of exchange-rate flexibility against the background of the crumbling Bretton Woods system ensured that the consequence of Mr Barber's policy would instead be a falling exchange rate and accelerating domestic inflation. However, the adoption of exchange-rate flexibility was, in particular, singled out for praise, a typical reaction being that of *The Economist,* which referred to 'an extraordinary conversion [of the Government] to the sensible doctrine that the right way to meet any balance of payments deficit will be to set sterling floating' (25 March, 1972, p. 11).

Given only the existence of a stable aggregate demand for money function in the United Kingdom—and there was abundant evidence of this by 1972—there was no conceivable way in which the

Conservative Government's policy could have succeeded in achieving the goals of price stability and rapid growth at a high level of employment.[22] In 1972 the money supply was already expanding rapidly, largely as a result of a favourable balance of payments, but also as a result of the implementation of the Competition and Credit Control 'reforms' which had left the banking system with substantial excess reserves. The large public sector borrowing requirement (about four per cent of GDP) implicit in the 1972 budget, coupled with a commitment to hold down interest rates, implied a strong, domestically originating, stimulus to monetary expansion. Under a fixed exchange rate this would have been bound to wipe out the existing surplus and run the balance of payments into deficit, exactly as had happened in 1964, but in 1972 the commitment was to let the exchange rate go in such circumstances.

The possible outcome of the Conservative Government's policy lay between two not very distant extremes. On the one hand, wage and price controls would be ineffective from the outset, domestically originating monetary expansion would lead first to an intensification of an already incipient expansion of real output and thence to inflation and a falling exchange rate. On the other hand, controls might have some initial success. In this case monetary expansion, not being directly absorbed by rising domestic prices, would spill over into the foreign sector, driving the exchange rate even further down than it would fall if controls were ineffective. The result in this case would be an increasingly distorted relative price structure in the economy which eventually would force the abandonment of controls. In either case the inflation rate was bound to accelerate and sterling bound to depreciate. The inevitable duly began to happen in 1972. The monetary expansion rate continued to rise, unemployment started to fall rapidly, inflation to accelerate, slowly at first, the balance of payments went into deficit and the exchange rate began to fall, reaching a level 10 per cent below its trade-weighted average Smithsonian parity with other currencies by the end of 1972 and 18 per cent below by the end of 1973.

IV THE DENIAL OF RESPONSIBILITY

The conventional and widely accepted interpretation of the 1972-3 boom in Britain is that a correctly conceived policy, reasonably well implemented, foundered as a result of imported inflationary pressures beyond the control of the British authorities. As *The Economist* explained the matter at the time: 'Rising import prices and devaluation robbed Mr Heath of success in stages 1 and 2 [of his incomes policy] and threaten his growth strategy through the impact of high interest rates and monetary restraint to defend sterling' (6 October, 1973, p. 87). *The Economist* did not consider the possibility that 'devaluation' might have been the consequence of the government's 'strategy' and nor do any of the other proponents of the foregoing interpretation of the events of 1972-3.

Cost accounting exercises do indeed show that, over this period, rising import prices 'contributed' more to domestic inflation than did changes in money wages, profits, or indirect taxes. Such exercises, interesting though they are for the evidence they generate about the behaviour of relative prices, are in Britain often interpreted as saying something about the proximate causes of inflation. A clear statement of the approach to the analysis of inflation that leads to such an interpretation was given by Mr G. D. N. Worswick, the director of the National Institute for Economic and Social Research, to the House of Commons Public Expenditure sub-committee. 'The principal [factors determining the movement of prices] are the level of wages and costs. The secondary one is profit margins. ... Thirdly there is the intervention by government by taxes or subsidies to raise or lower the market price from the factor cost price. Fourthly there is the import cost. In the last two or three years there has been a worldwide increase in the rate of inflation. ... But who is causing it and how we interact with each other is complicated. We suffer from the worldwide rise in commodity prices. ... The position we started with with the freeing of the exchange rate allowed it to fall rather in comparison with our competitors, which adds to the import prices. To blame that on the incomes policy introduced in 1972 would be, in a certain sense perverse' (House of Commons (1974), para. 115, p. 38). The Treasury's evidence to the same committee (paras. 462-9, pp. 135-7) shows that their approach to the analysis of inflation is the same as that of Worswick and *The Economist,* though they did not there apply the analysis specifically to the 1972-3 period.[23]

It is above all the behaviour of the unemployment rate during the 1972-3 boom that has led so many to believe that inflation since 1972 could not have its source in domestic monetary and fiscal policies and hence must be 'imported'. As Figure 3.1 shows, inflation began to accelerate when the level of unemployment was high by historical standards, and even at the peak of the boom it stood above two per cent, a rate higher than the *average* for the 1953-67 period. This is treated as *prima facie* evidence that there existed considerable spare capacity in the economy throughout 1972-3.[24] Nevertheless, it is not difficult to reconcile the existence of a 'high' unemployment rate with a demand-induced explanation of accelerating inflation.

First, and least important, the mechanics of a expectations-augmented Phillips curve, when expectations are based on some kind of error-learning mechanism, predict that when unemployment is falling, inflation will accelerate before the natural unemployment rate is reached. There is evidence that such an expectations scheme fits British data rather well.[25] Second, if as many believe, wages and prices respond more rapidly to excess demand than to excess supply, then an expansion of demand that is accompanied by an increase in the dispersion of demand pressure across micro-markets will lead to inflation rising above its expected rate *before* the natural unemployment rate is reached. There is evidence that the 1972-3 boom was accompanied by just such an increase in dis-persion of demand both between industries and between regions.[26] Finally, the 'natural' unemployment rate of the British economy was, by 1972, well above the level that had prevailed on the 1950s and 1960s. As Figure 3.1 shows, unemployment rose secularly throughout the period 1953-75 but this tendency was particularly marked after about 1966.

This increase in the natural unemployment rate was widely discussed in Britain in the late 1960s and early 1970s, the pheno-menon usually being referred to as a shift in the vacancy-unem-ployment relationship. It seems to have had a number of sources. The low birth rate of the inter-war years coupled with the high post-war birth rate meant that, by the late 1960s, older workers reaching retirement age and young, relatively inexperienced work-ers made up an unusually high proportion of the labour force. Moreover, there is some evidence to suggest that until the late 1960s labour hoarding by firms involved the existence of a certain amount of hidden unemployment. This unemployment be-came visible partly as a result of a 'shake out' of labour during the rather deep 1970-1 recession but also as a result of a consid-erable improvement in unemployment compensation that was brought about in the mid-1960s. Further, there is evidence to suggest that the latter factor contributed to an increase in search unemployment.[27]

Nevertheless the behaviour of unemployment over the 1972-3 period simply confirmed those who held it in their belief that inflation was not the result of domestic policies. The National Institute went so far as to interpret the behaviour of the balance of payments—which had gone from a current account surplus of £0·07 billion in 1972 to a deficit of £1·47 billion, or over two per cent of GDP, in 1973 despite an 18 per cent fall in the exchange rate over the two previous years—as providing evidence *against* the presence of general excess demand in the economy.[28] However, even if the deterioration of the balance of payments and the decline in the exchange rate were not attributed to the conduct of domestic policy by the authorities and their advisers, these factors certainly began to influence the conduct of policy at some time in 1973. Although the miners' strike, the three-day week and the February election marked the final collapse of the Conservative Government policy in early 1974, that policy had been changing for a few months previously. Although expansionary policies were not blamed for th

behaviour of the balance of payments and the exchange rate, contractionary policies were nevertheless implemented in order to
deal with these problems.

V THE DISINTEGRATION OF THE BUDGETARY PROCESS

We have seen that monetary policy became sharply contractionary
in 1973, and continued in that vein throughout 1974. This change
roughly coincides with a large increase in the ratio of sales of
public sector debt to the non-bank public to total public sector
borrowing. This ratio averaged 35 per cent over the last three
quarters of 1972 and 55 per cent in 1973. Whether the reversal of
the monetary aspect of economic policy was deliberate or acciden-
tal is hard to say, for it has been and remains the constant claim of
all political parties that they would not resort to a tight money
policy in order to combat inflation, but this turn-around was shortly
followed by an attempt to reverse fiscal policy as well. The borrowing requirement of the public sector for 1973-4 generated by the
March 1973 budget was just under £4·5 billion or about seven per
cent of GDP. A supplementary budget introduced in December 1973
sought to reduce the borrowing requirement substantially for
1974-5, and at the beginning of March 1974 it was forecast to be
£3·4 billion. Although some observers were worried that the reversal was being implemented a bit too rapidly for comfort, particularly as far as the rate of monetary expansion was concerned,
it nevertheless appeared that, in the winter of 1973-4, some kind of
rough and ready sanity was being restored to the conduct of macroeconomic policy in Britain despite prevailing economic orthodoxy.
In fact the very opposite was happening.

Budgets are usually an annual affair in Britain, but the December 1973 budget was the first of a series of five in a sixteen-month
period. Even the most orthodox 'Keynesian' might find such zeal
for fine tuning excessive, and suspect that all was not well with the
conduct of policy during these months. However, the actual aggregate outcome of these budgets bore so little resemblance to the
government's expressed intentions at the time of their introduction
that the only reasonable conclusion must be that 1974 saw the dis-
integration of the machinery of macroeconomic policy-making in
Britain. During the fiscal year 1974-5, the public sector intended
to borrow just under five per cent of GDP but in fact ended up
borrowing about ten per cent; public sector borrowing for 1975-6
ran a little above this level, and about one-quarter of this borrowing again was not forecast. This unintentionally high expansionary
fiscal policy ran against a continued tight monetary policy, and the
unemployment statistics for 1974-6 are eloquent testimony of
which policy tool proved the more powerful.

At this stage there can be no definitive account of what went
wrong with the budgetary process in 1974-6, but two broad factors
seem to have contributed to the debacle, the first political and the
second technical. The Labour Government, elected in early 1974,
replaced statutory wage controls with a voluntary programme
known first as the 'Social compact' and later as the 'Social contract'. Its essence was that the Trade Unions agreed to limit their
demand for increased wages to the rate of inflation, while the
government in turn agreed to maintain, for a while, the price control programme of their predecessors, to freeze certain key
prices such as rents, and to subsidise certain basic foodstuffs.
Since it was never specified whether the rate of inflation to which
wage demands were to be limited was the past rate, the current
rate, or the expected rate, it was not even necessary for anyone to
resort to subterfuge in order to achieve whatever wage increases
market conditions indicated.

General wage inflation coupled with price restraint in the
public sector involved nationalised industries in increasing deficits;
food subsidies had to be paid; and a rent freeze in an economy
where about one-third of households occupy already subsidised
publicly-owned housing ensured a further open-ended commitment
to public expenditure. One cannot lay the 'Social contract' at the
door of professional economists, either inside or outside government service.[29] They are more culpable of whatever it was that
went wrong with official and unofficial forecasts of inflation and
unemployment rates in 1974-5. Public expenditure planning in
Britain is carried out in real terms. Government departments are
automatically granted funds to cover inflation-induced cost increases. There was, until 1976, no current purchasing power cash
budget to constrain their expenditure. Such a modus operandi
means that errors in forecasting the inflation rate and relative
prices play havoc with government finances. At the same time,
the whole thrust of British government forecasting is geared to
predicting real income and unemployment. Forecasts of the inflation rate are ancilliary to this goal, so that it is not too surprising that such forecasts are relatively unreliable. The major
part of the error in forecasting public sector borrowing in 1974-5
seems to have arisen from underestimates of the effects of inflation on public sector costs.[30]

Even though public sector borrowing climbed steadily in
1974-5, and was doing the same in 1975-6, a relatively low rate of
monetary expansion was nevertheless maintained until the end of
1975. Although the current account of the balance of payments
remained in heavy, though decreasing, deficit throughout the period
the exchange rate nevertheless remained stable between the end of
1973 until mid-1975, when it fell abruptly to an effective devaluatio
of about 30 per cent below its Smithsonian parity. The explanation
of these facts is straightforward. First, the ratio of sales of public

sector debt to the non-bank public to total public sector borrowing remained high throughout 1974 and 1975. Moreover, the oil price increase of 1973 led to large capital inflows into Britain, first as oil producers invested surplus funds in London and secondly as the increase in the prospective value of North Sea oil attracted development capital. In addition to this the public sector actively raised funds in foreign markets over this period.

The effects of the exchange rate being thus supported by capital inflows and public sector borrowing were to permit real domestic expenditure to remain substantially above domestic output and to ensure that the inflation rate was somewhat lower than it otherwise would have been. Policies to reduce the level of public sector borrowing must form a key part of any strategy that is to restore long-run stability to the British economy, and the period of exchange-rate stability during 1974-5 might have played a valuable role in smoothing out the inflation rate a little while such policies were implemented. However, this breathing space was wasted; all that was accomplished by the delay in the decline of the exchange rate was to transfer to late 1975 and 1976 some inflationary pressure that would otherwise have been felt earlier. In 1974-6 rising unemployment, generated by, but not attributed to, monetary policy inhibited the authorities from any serious attempts to tighten up on the fiscal side, though given the breakdown in the machinery of policy implementation already described, it is far from clear that they could have succeeded in this endeavour if they had tried.

VI FUTURE PROSPECTS

The behaviour of the British economy during 1976 created a confusing picture. At the beginning of the year the public sector was borrowing close to 12 per cent of GDP, much of this to finance transfers and subsidies. Increasingly this borrowing requirement had to be met domestically. At the same time unemployment, though rather low by international standards, was still high enough to create a major political problem. The government was undertaking all manner of piecemeal job saving and creating schemes to deal with it and these were, of course, adding further to public expenditure. Inflation still seemed to be regarded in official circles as mainly a cost-push phenomenon, and recently introduced wage controls were regarded as being successful in reducing inflation. I would argue, however, that it was the unemployment generated by the tight monetary policies set in motion in 1973 that was the major cause of the sharp reduction in the inflation rate that began after mid-1975.

One hopeful aspect of the situation as it stood at the beginning of 1976 was that far more attention was being paid to the behaviour of the money supply than in the past.[31] Indeed in late 1975 the government publicly committed itself not to permit renewed rapid monetary growth and in September 1976 began to announce targets for the rate of monetary expansion. The question remains, however, as to how durable that commitment will prove to be when confronted with other policy goals. The key to maintaining a reasonable monetary expansion rate in Britain during 1976 and thereafter lay in a reduction of public sector borrowing. Unfortunately, although attempts to cut public expenditure and borrowing were made in the first half of the year, these were largely cosmetic in nature. Outside Britain this was widely perceived to be their true nature, and the exchange rate fell rapidly from the second quarter of the year onward, while the monetary expansion rate did indeed show at least a short-term tendency to accelerate in the middle of the year. The fall in the exchange rate continued despite the granting of short-term standby credits to Britain by a consortium of industrial countries at mid-year and despite the opening of negotiations for a $3·9 billion line of credit from the IMF in the second half of the year. The latter negotiations were accompanied by further cuts in public expenditure and by tax increases designed to reduce public sector borrowing, but like the measures taken earlier in the year, these too were, rightly or wrongly, quite widely regarded outside Britain as being insufficient to bring the rate of monetary expansion under control in the long run: 1977 will show whether this judgment was accurate or not.

The main difficulty faced by the authorities in getting to grips with their expenditure and borrowing during 1976 seems to have been political rather than economic, but the political difficulties in question had deep roots in the same faulty economics that, I have argued, underlay so much of earlier policy. It has been mentioned in the previous paragraph that the voluntary wage control programme instituted in 1975 was, during 1976, given credit for the substantial reduction in the inflation rate that took place over the previous twelve months. This programme required the co-operation of a trade union movement strongly opposed to large-scale cuts in public expenditure, particularly on social services and in areas where expenditure cuts might be expected to have direct effects on employment.

Given that the authorities believed that the wage restraint programme underlay the fall in the inflation rate, one can understand their reluctance to antagonise the trade union movement upon whose goodwill the future success of the programme was perceived to depend.[32] To attribute the fall in the inflation rate to the influence of previously restrictive monetary policy, as I have done, is to imply that the government's reluctance to cut their expenditure and borrowing during 1976 was based upon false premises, that they could indeed have brought their borrowing requirement under control during that year without thereby setting in motion another round of 'cost-push' inflation. This is not to say that had they done so there would not have been grave political difficulties, not least *within* the Labour party, and an increase in industrial unrest, but it is to argue that the inflation rate would not have behaved any differently.

As things stood at the end of 1976, the government was committed to attaining targets for the domestic credit expansion rate and the rate of monetary expansion, and had obtained overseas credits which ought to prevent the exchange rate deteriorating far in the short run. However, even after the public expenditure cuts of 1976 the projected public sector borrowing requirement for 1977 is still not far short of nine per cent of GDP and, given the past record of forecasting of that requirement, one wonders how accurate this projection will turn out to be. Thus there is considerable doubt that the authorities will be able to meet their monetary policy targets and prevent sterling from depreciating further during 1977-8. If they cannot, 1976 will prove to have seen the lower turning point in a series of ever more explosive inflationary cycles in the British economy, rather than to have witnessed the implementation of measures whereby a serious inflationary problem was finally brought under control. It is early as yet to make any firm predictions about which of these alternatives is going to come about—for so much depends upon the actual outcome for public sector borrowing—but this writer is no more optimistic about the future of the British economy at the end of 1976 than he was at the beginning.

NOTES TO CHAPTER 3

[1]   This chaper is a slightly amended version of 'Inflation in Britain: a monetarist perspective', *The American Economic Review,* vol. 66, September 1976, pp. 485-500. The paper draws heavily on the work of the University of Manchester-SSRC Inflation Workshop, of which the author, with Michael Parkin, was joint director. An earlier version of this paper was given at the University of Western Ontario money workshop and the University of Chicago money workshop. Extremely valuable criticism was received on these occasions. I am particularly grateful to Michael Parkin, Douglas Purvis, Milton Friedman and Robert Lucas for their comments, but nevertheless exonerate them of all responsibility for the contents of this version.
[2]   With the permission of the author and the editors of *The American Economic Review* we have made some editorial changes in this paper to achieve a greater measure of integration between this chapter and the rest of the book. At the same time however, we have left it as a coherent whole which stands alone and may be read independently.

3   The view that the quantity of money is unimportant is an article of faith in British Keynesian economics, receiving its most famous statement in the Radcliffe Report (1959). It is still influential. See, for example, the evidence of Wynne Godley and Lord Kahn to the House of Commons Public Expenditure Committee in 1974 (House of Commons (1974), paras. 25-6, p. 18 and paras. 269-70, pp. 90-1 respectively).

There has, however, always existed a minority of economists in Britain who have taken the opposite position on this matter. See, for example, the evidence of Professors (now Lord) Robbins and Paish to the Radcliffe Committee, Walters (1969) and Johnson (1972). So-called 'monetarist' views however, have never, as far as one can tell, had any influence on policy. The reader who wishes to assess the extent to which the author of this paper is being wise after the event is referred to Laidler (1975), chapters 4 and 10, written in late 1970 and early 1972 respectively.

4   Two measures of monetary expansion are presented here because it is often asserted that the two series in question tell markedly different stories. However, such differences are much more apparent on a quarter-by-quarter basis than they are over a longer time period. The long-term qualitative behaviour of the series is very much the same. My own preference has always been to pay rather more attention to the broader money supply series, but nothing crucial hinges on this.

Note that with the introduction of the Competition and Credit Control reforms in late 1971 the banking system became much freer to produce near monies bearing interest at competitive rates. Such assets are included in M_3 but excluded from M_1. Thus the sharp downturn in the rate of expansion of M_1 at the beginning of 1972 reflects not a turn-around in monetary policy but a substitution out of demand deposits into various types of time deposits suddenly available on more favourable terms. By the same token, the continued acceleration of M_3 growth through 1972 certainly owes something to this same effect and overstates the expansiveness of monetary policy. At the end of 1973, changes in the reserve requirements against interest-bearing liabilities made it much less attractive for the banks to emit these. The rather rapid expansion of M_1 in 1974 at least partly reflects a shift towards non-interest-bearing deposits rather than renewed monetary expansion, while the data on M_3 overstate the tightness of policy for similar reasons. Nevertheless, with greater flexibility of interest rates on near-money, one would expect the turning point in the M_1 series to come a little before that in M_3 when monetary policy is changed. For example, as policy tightens up, short-term interest rates rise, and a substitution out of demand deposits into interest bearing bank liabilities involves the growth rate of M_1 turning down while that of M_3 is temporarily sustained.

Finally note that for the period over which quarterly data are plotted the monetary expansion rates are annual logarithmic first differences of end-quarter data; these changes are centred on the end of the second quarter of the one-year period over which they are measured, and, as is well known, such measures tend to shift turning points backwards in time when these are sharp. These considerations are important in assessing just when, in 1973, monetary policy began to tighten up. My own inclination is to argue that the process began gently early in the year, being associated with the authorities beginning to meet a much larger fraction of government borrowing by securities sales to the non-bank public, and became severe in the final quarter.

5   I would not argue for long with anyone who found the evidence of the influence of money on inflation for the pre-1967 period presented in Figure 3.1 unconvincing. Rather I would refer him to the studies of Artis and Nobay (1969) and Bank of England (1970 a and b) which use data from this earlier period and do find evidence consistent with the view that changes in the quantity of money influenced certain variables, including money income and hence the inflation rate with a 'long and variable' time lag. However, the results these studies generated were certainly much less clear-cut than those produced by similar studies done for the United States economy. Dr Goodhart, the author of one of the Bank of England's studies, expressed a similar view of the results generated by these studies in 1974 (House of Commons (1974), para. 346, pp. 111-12). The extent to which these results reflect the fact that the British economy in the 1950s and 1960s was so stable that there was little systematic variation in income and prices to explain, and the extent to which they reflect the fact that the interaction of money and prices in a rather open fixed-exchange-rate economy where an interest-rate stabilisation policy is being pursued is more complicated than in a relatively closed economy, is too complex a question to enter into here. For a simple formal analysis of the interaction of money and inflation in a fixed-exchange-rate open economy model, see Laidler (1975), chapter 9.

6   An extensive analysis of the relationship between wage change and unemployment is presented in Chapter 4 of this book.

7   For a full discussion of the measurement of and a testing of alternative hypotheses concerning the formation of inflation expectations, see Chapters 6 and 7.

8   See Cross and Laidler (1976) and Laidler (1976).

9   It is worth noting that, for some countries, Cross and Laidler (1976) found that v was not different from zero, implying that there is no difference in slope between the long- and short-run inflation unemployment trade-offs in those countries; Britain, however, was not one of them, v taking a value of about one-half for that country.

10   But the unemployment target was perhaps not set very far above the natural rate. Sumner estimates the natural rate to have been 2·5 per cent over the 1953-67 period, while the actual rate averaged 1·54 per cent. This estimate is subject to a wide margin of error and certainly looks low, but is not obviously inconsistent with Phillips' (1958) estimate that a 2·5 per cent unemployment rate was compatible with price stability in post-war Britain, since the expected inflation rate was surely slightly positive over the relevant period.

11   British economists do not always attribute the worldwide inflation of the late 1960s and 1970s to this cause. Thus Phelps-Brown (1975), while admitting that monetary expansion might have been a permissive factor, puts the acceleration of inflation on a worldwide scale down to wage-push factors based upon rising real income expectations. Such expectations are transmitted across national boundaries by the motor car and television, these playing the same role as the bicycle, the popular press, and the cinema in the period 1899-1914. He views the Paris students' revolt of 1968 as a crucial event that 'sparked a prairie fire of strike action that spread across Europe'. Lord Kahn, on the other hand, believes that the breakdown of wage and price controls in Holland in the early 1960s was the source of accelerating worldwide inflation. As he told the House of Commons Expenditure Committee, 'In fact it was really from the Netherlands in the second half of the 60s that the infection of wage inflation started and

spread to most of the main industrial countries' (House of Commons (1974), para. 233, p. 82).

12   For a detailed analysis of this question, see Jonson and Kierzkowski (1975).

13   The three models to which I refer here are those of the Treasury, the National Institute of Economic and Social Research, and the London Business School respectively. All three treated the wage inflation rate as an exogenous variable, forecast on a judgemental basis, in 1970 (see House of Commons (1974), para. 456, p. 134, and Johnson and Nobay (1971), chapters 1 and 2, with respect to these three models). It is not clear from the above sources that money wages were ever treated as anything but an exogenous variable in the Treasury model in the 1960s, but Phillips curves were definitely incorporated in the other two.

14   A typical and comprehensive statement of this point of view in the literature of the 1950s is to be found in Kahn's evidence to the Radcliffe Committee. See *Memoranda of Evidence*, vol. 3, pp. 141-4.

15   See also on this matter Perry (1975).

16   Note that an article in the *National Institute Review* for February 1971 (reprinted in Johnson and Nobay (1971) contained evidence to show that inflationary expectations were systematically influencing wage behaviour, though not with a unit coefficient; moreover the relevance of the 'Nordic' model of imported inflation (Edgren, Faxén and Ohdner, 1969) to the contemporary British situation was considered and recognised. However, these ingredients were not developed into an analysis of the type offered here.

17   The following quotations are typical. Professor J. R. Ball of the London Business School: 'My own favourite candidate is ... the frustration hypothesis ... wage earners seek to realise some real wage objectives the frustration of which eventually causes the Phillips curve to shift', though he did note that this hypothesis needed to be squared with the existence of inflation in a number of countries (Johnson and Nobay (1971), pp. 47-48). Mr Leslie Dicks-Mireaux of the Bank of England: 'I would not argue that there is an overriding external factor common to the recent inflation; indeed we must probably look to factors closer to home not all of which perhaps are economic' (*ibid.*, p. 184). Mr Ralph Turvey, former Deputy Chairman of the Prices and Incomes Board: 'It is a question of relative deprivation and the perception of social justice which is the key to understanding what has happened' (*ibid.*, p. 200). Sir Fred Catherwood, Director General of the National Economic Development Office: 'We are in a position where a key factor of production, which is labour, can be withdrawn and it pays to pay a premium all the time to keep [labour] in full supply. This to me is the major cause of wage inflation' (*ibid.*, p. 189). For other recent British statements of hypotheses linking causes of inflation to the institutional structure of the labour market and other, non-economic, factors, see, for example, Jones (1972), Hicks (1974), chapter 3, and Wiles (1973). It is one of the oddities of British debates at the turn of the decade that, although the inflationary problems of the time were proclaimed as being something new, requiring equally novel explanations, the explanations that were then actually advanced bore so much resemblance to those which Lord Kahn put to the Radcliffe Committee more than a decade earlier as explanations of the mild inflation in the 1950s. Moreover, these explanations owe a great deal to the analysis of labour market institutions developed by Hicks in the *Theory of Wages* (1932) and further developed by him in the 1950s (Hicks, 1955).

[18] The sharp fall in the inflation rate that was associated with the high unemployment rate ruling in 1971, as the 'Phillips curve' began to re-establish itself, did not have any effect on those who held this view. Indeed it was still the view of the Treasury as late as 1974 that no policy-relevant trade-off between inflation and unemployment existed (see House of Commons (1974), paras. 465-6, p. 136). In 1974, Miss Patricia Brown of the Treasury explained the fall-off in the inflation rate in 1971-2 in the following terms. 'Looking at the rate of growth of the Retail Price Index for the second quarter 1970 to the second quarter 1971, and then the second quarter 1972, there is a very sharp difference in the rate of growth of food prices ... the prices of services provided by nationalised industries ... direct to consumers ... went up by $17\frac{1}{2}$ per cent over the first twelve-month period and only $7\frac{1}{2}$ per cent in the second twelve-month period. I think that these two factors probably largely account for the slowing down in the Retail Price Index as a whole' (House of Commons (1974), para. 69, p. 137). Perhaps the reader will agree that there is more than a little confusion here between describing what happened to the components of the index, on the one hand, and explaining the behaviour of its overall value, on the other.
[19] The year 1971 did of course see the advent of new regulations for the banking system that at least paid lip service to enabling the authorities to exert greater control over monetary aggregates. Whatever the purpose of 'Competition and credit control', from the very outset the authorities made it clear that steps would always be taken to protect the level of mortgage interest rates under the new regime (Bank of England *Quarterly Bulletin* June 1971, para. 15, p. 192). I believe that the desire of all parties to placate owner-occupiers (over 50 per cent of all households) played an important role in the political process that underlay Britain's failure to get to grips with her inflationary problems in the early 1970s.
[20] Note that by 1972 there existed a large body of evidence that suggested that, with the exception of the 1948-9 episode, wage and price controls had had no systematic influence on inflation. See Parkin and Sumner, eds. (1972), chapter 1, for a survey of this evidence, and note particularly that by then, the initial finding of Lipsey and Parkin (1970), that controls did reduce the rate of inflation in conditions of high demand, had been discredited.
[21] The recipe of high employment and rapid growth as a cure for inflation has, of course, been a long-standing theme in post-war British economics. Mr Thomas (now Lord) Balogh's evidence to the Radcliffe Committee dealt with it in some detail (see *Memoranda* ..., vol. 3, pp. 40-1). In fairness to Balogh, however, it should be noted that in 1958 his call was for an expansion of *investment* to stimulate long-term *growth* as a pre-requisite for a voluntary incomes policy. The 1972 budget concentrated almost entirely upon generating an expansion of *consumption* while the incomes policy that eventually went with it was *statutory*. There was more than a little confusion between long-term growth of productive capacity on the one hand, and short-term expansion up to a level of output that fully utilised existing capacity on the other, underlying economic policy in 1972-3. More than a vestige of the views under discussion here is to be found in a recent paper by Lord Kahn (1976) who argues that low employment reduces inflationary pressures by making the Trade Unions more willing to co-operate with wage and price controls.
[22] Quite apart from the early studies of Brown (1939) and Khusro (1952), and Paish's evidence to the Radcliffe Committee, ignored by them in their Report (*Memoranda*, vol. 3, pp. 182-8, *Minutes of Evidence*, pp. 693-700),

there were in print by early 1972 studies by Kavanagh and Walters (1966), Fisher (1968), the Bank of England (1970a), and Laidler and Parkin (1970) all of which confirmed the existence of a stable demand for money function. There also existed at least three studies that seemed to show that monetary policy variations were associated, albeit weakly, with fluctuations in nominal income with a long and variable time lag (Artis and Nobay (1969), Bank of England (1970 a and b)). None of these studies had any influence on policy, apparently because the relationships which they produced were not sufficiently well determined to be useful in short-term forecasting exercises. For the Treasury's view on this see House of Commons (1974), paras. 477-84, pp. 138-9. Recent work by Artis and Lewis (1976) suggests that competition and credit control did not render the demand for money function unstable after 1971.

23   In its 17 November 1973 issue, *The Economist* produced data purporting to show that domestically generated inflation in Britain over the previous year had been lower than in any other OECD country, attributed this to the success of wage and price controls, and headlined the article 'The miracle that Ted [Heath] pulled off, and nobody saw him do it'. On 27 July 1974 (p. 85), *The Economist* again argued that 'Mr Heath's success in holding [wages] back with his counter-inflation policy begun in the autumn of 1972 is striking. But as wage increases slowed down, import prices took off.' For an example of a similar cost-accounting exercise masquerading as an explanation of inflation in a learned journal, see Allen (1975). Hicks (1975) takes a position somewhat similar to Worwick. He argues that Britain's problem in the 1970s is imported inflation, that the rises in commodity prices that took place in world markets in the 1970s were largely independent of the inflationary policies pursued in industrialised countries, hence were an exogenous source of inflation in those countries, and were not to be counteracted with monetary policy. Even so, his own calculations show that the British import price index, which showed an increase from 100 in 1970 to 226 by the end of 1974 would, if recalculated in terms of Deutschemarks have reached a value of 148 over the same period. In short, 78 percentage points of the change in the index may be attributed to the behaviour of exchange rates.

24   The National Institute devoted pages 24-33 of its November 1973 *Review* to the question of whether or not the economy was 'overheated', and concluded that there was no reason to suppose that it was. Though not stated in such terms, the conclusion was that the natural unemployment rate had not shifted since the 1960s and that the economy was operating well above that natural rate in mid-1973. There is no space here to enter into a critique of the means whereby the National Institute reached this conclusion; suffice it to say that I did not then, nor do now, find the relevant arguments convincing, but certainly recognise that this matter is crucial to the interpretation of the 1972-3 boom that I am advancing here.

25   See equations 3.1-3.3 above, although that formulation of the curve is more relevant to a fixed-exchange-rate regime. Note also that Carlson and Parkin (1975) show that a species of adaptive expectations explains survey data on British inflationary expectations rather well (see Chapters 6 and 7).

26   See *NIER*, November 1973, pp. 28-9 for a discussion of the dispersion of aggregate demand in 1973.

27   On demographic factors, see Foster (1974); on labour hoarding see Taylor (1972), and on the role of the level of unemployment benefits see

Maki and Spindler (1975). Brittan (1975) contains a useful summary of the evidence on these matters.

28   See NIER, November 1973, p. 30. The case put there rests on the volume of imports and exports having grown at the same pace during the boom, whereas it is argued that, had there existed domestic excess demand, the volume of imports should have increased more than that of exports. The Institute did not consider the behaviour of the exchange rate relevant to interpretation of this evidence, but did not explain why.

29   However, in August 1974 the National Institute, though doubting that the 'Social contract' would achieve all its aims, was nevertheless arguing that it should be given a year to run as a prelude however to a new round of statutory controls (p. 6). In response to a Select Committee question about the desirability of statutory wage and price controls, Sir Kenneth Berrill, then Chief Economic Advisor at the Treasury, is recorded as having said, with more than a little irony, 'I do not think I am able to answer that because the present view of the Government, and, therefore, of the Treasury, is that a voluntary incomes policy will work' (House of Commons (1975), para 496, p. 141).

30   See House of Commons (1975) for an account of these and other factors affecting public sector borrowing. I base my account of the role of the inflation rate in official forecasting on the Treasury's evidence to the House of Commons Public Expenditure Commitee (see House of Commons (1974), paras. 426-33, pp. 127-30 and paras. 455-63, pp. 134-5).

31   It is fair to record that this seems to be the view of *The Economist,* which now pays much more attention to the role of monetary factors in generating inflation than it did even as late as 1974. See for example 24 January 1976, pp. 11, 71-2, where it is noted that Mr Denis Healey will keep tighter screws on money and demand than any of his post-war predecessors during [1976]. So far so better.'

32   Indeed in 1976 some commentators were still arguing that a lower unemployment rate would result in a further reduction in the inflation rate (see, for example, Kahn (1976)), but this line of argument was far less prevalent in 1976 than it had been for years earlier.

APPENDIX 3.1 DATA DEFINITIONS AND SOURCES

Δm_1 Annual first differences of the natural logarithm of narrow money. 1960-7 observations are annual, thereafter quarterly. Basic data are for end period stocks. Rates of change are centred at end of interval. Source: *International Financial Statistics,* various issues.

Δm_3 As Δm_1, but basic data are for money plus quasi-money. Source: 1960-75 *International Financial Statistics,* various issues; 1953-1960 *Bank of England Statistical Abstract.*

Note that the Bank of England data include government deposits with Commercial Banks and the *IFS* data exclude them. This minor inconsistency between the series is probably of little importance when estimating percentage rates of change.

Δp Annual first difference of the natural logarithm of of the retail price index. 1953-67, basic data are annual averages centred in mid-year

1967-75, data are quarterly averages centred in mid-quarter. Rates of change are centred at end of interval. Source: *NIER*, various issues.

U — Period averages of the percentage of the labour force unemployed, Great Britain. 1953-67, annual averages. 1968-75, quarterly averages, seasonally adjusted. Source: *NIER*, various issues.

$\Delta\pi$ — Annual first differences of natural logarithm of a GNP-weighted average of various domestic price indices for nineteen countries other than the United Kingdom, converted at the current exchange rate. Source: Cross and Laidler (1976), where the derivation of the series is described in detail.

F — Balance of payments on current account, including invisibles. Source: *NIER*, various issues.

Rate of change of money wages: logarithmic first difference at annual rates of average hourly wage rates in all industries. Source: *NIER*, various issues.

4 Wage determination

Michael T. Sumner

I INTRODUCTION

Few areas of scientific enquiry have aroused more controversy
than the subject of this chapter, or display such an intimate con-
nection between policy issues and academic disagreement. The
central dispute for at least two decades has concerned the role of
excess demand in the inflationary process, but over the period the
focus of the debate has shifted several times.[1]
Phillips' (1958) seminal contribution inspired a host of positive investigations into the form of the relation between unemployment and wage inflation, particularly its sensitivity to policy
influences[2] and to other alleged determinants of the wage bargain.
These positive developments were accompanied by normative
reflections on the appropriate target of demand management, thus
establishing a link between welfare economics and macro policy
and calling into question arbitrary definitions of full employment.[3]
A persistent underlying theme was the difficulty of accommodating
'intruders' (profits, trade-union pushfulness etc.) within Phillips'
framework, and the absence of an alternative theory; but it was the
correction by Friedman (1966, 1968) and Phelps (1965, 1967, 1968),
of an error in Phillips' own use of price theory which produced the
next major change of focus, in search of a trade-off which vanished
in the long run, when expectations were fully adjusted to experience.
The resulting 'natural rate' hypothesis severely limits the significance of demand management. At best, an active policy could
facilitate the transition between equilibria when the natural rate
changed. In a world characterised by imperfect information, a
more realistic role would be the cost-minimising correction of
past mistakes in the choice of the target unemployment rate.
In the current intellectual climate the outstanding issue is not
the limitations on the role of demand management, but whether any
role exists at all. The simultaneous increase in unemployment and
inflation between the 1960s and 1970s was enough to convince many
casual observers that any Phillips-type relationship, whether
partial or otherwise, had vanished. At a less informal level, recent

econometric studies (e.g. Henry *et al.*, 1976) have also failed to isolate such a relationship. However, these studies have implicitly adopted the maintained hypothesis of a constant relationship between wage inflation and unemployment, despite the assertion by Gujarati (1972) and the more convincing argument presented by Maki and Spindler (1975) that at least part of the rise in unemployment is attributable to a relative increase in unemployment benefit rather than a change in the level of excess demand.[4] This latter argument suggests a shift in the natural unemployment rate beginning in the mid-1960s, at a time when wage-price controls became a regular feature of economic life. The simultaneous appearance of two essentially new and contrary influences on wage behaviour raises obvious questions about the separability of their individual effects, a consideration ignored in all existing literature.

The issues that require examination in this chapter will now be apparent. The procedure adopted is to undertake a preliminary exploration using the basic model of wage determination developed by Parkin *et al.* (1976): this investigation is unable to reject the natural rate hypothesis and provides estimates of recent changes in that rate. Then, the behaviour of unemployment is examined in order to provide a means of disentangling, in the final substantive section, the separate influence of wage-price controls and changes in social security legislation on wage determination.

II SOME PRELIMINARY ESTIMATION

The foundation for the empirical work reported in this section is the wage equation first used by Parkin *et al.* (1976). Since the results of the latter study influenced the procedure adopted in this extension, those results are first summarised.

The object was to explain variations in the (quarter-on-quarter) rate of change of weekly wage rates, a less comprehensive measure of the price of labour than that used in the present annual study. The determinants of wage inflation can be divided into four groups. First, excess demand for labour was proxied by unemployment; attempts to incorporate the ratio of unemployment benefit to net earnings were made, but these proved unsuccessful. Secondly, the inflation expectations of firms concerning both domestic and foreign markets, and those of consumers were entered in accordance with a generalisation of the Phelps-Friedman hypothesis. Thirdly, the argument that price expectations are a determinant of wage inflation can be extended to incorporate expected changes in the taxes levied on both employers and employees; in the absence of genuine anticipatory data of the type used for price expectations, actual tax changes were used as a proxy. Finally, conventional zero-one dummy variables were entered to isolate any direct effects of the pay pause in 1961-2 and the freeze and severe restraint in 1966-7.

Four major conclusions emerged from that study of the period 1956-71. The hypothesis that the sum of the coefficients on the inflation anticipations was unity could not be rejected; hence the results were consistent with the natural-rate hypothesis. Secondly, the estimated natural rate of unemployment was surprisingly low: assuming an annual increase in output per head of 2·5 per cent, the unemployment rate required for equilibrium (i.e. constant) inflation was 1·7 per cent. As noted above, an attempt to allow the natural rate to vary with changes in the relationship between unemployment benefit and net earnings produced negative results. Thirdly, the wage-price controls recognised in this model exerted a derisory impact on wage inflation, despite their statutory form. The pay pause always registered a perverse effect; the freeze of 1966 and the period of severe restraint in 1967 had the predicted effect of reducing wage inflation, but by an amount which was numerically small and always insignificant. Finally, the fiscal variables made little contribution to the explanation of wage inflation: the rate of change of the employer's social security contribution entered the unconstrained regressions with the correct sign, but this point estimate was smaller (in absolute value) than anticipated, and was insignificant; the corresponding variable on the supply side of the labour market was not even correctly signed. In subsequent experiments, the fiscal variables were constrained to enter the wage equation with zero weight for successively longer initial periods, in an attempt to determine whether the substantial increases in effective personal tax rates during the later 1960s exceeded some psychological threshold which distorted the results for the full sample period; but no evidence for such an effect emerged.

The performance of the fiscal variables was the only respect in which the results were inconsistent with the model, and hence requires some consideration. The most direct explanation would be that the participants in wage negotiations simply do not form expectations about tax changes, regarding them rather as a random variable with zero mean. More plausibly, in view of the time profiles of the effective tax rates, the attempt to proxy anticipated by actual tax changes may have introduced sufficient measurement error to obscure their role in wage determination.

Other studies which incorporate a relation between wage- and tax-changes have yielded more positive conclusions,[5] so it is worth digressing to establish how much could legitimately be inferred from this partial relation. The problem of interpretation is more subtle than many students of the wage equation have appreciated. The coefficient of (say) an income tax variable in a wage equation provides an estimate only of the direct effect of a tax change on wages; to this direct effect must be added any indirect effect operating through other arguments of the wage equation, and particularly through the excess demand for labour. To analyse the total effect of a tax change on inflation therefore requires a fully specified model, not an isolated structural equation.

The indirect effects of taxation through excess demand provide an alternative explanation for the failure of the fiscal variables. The model is based on the assumption that the supply of and demand for labour are functions only of the relevant real wage: inability to sell planned output at expected prices pushes firms off their labour demand curve, on the lines suggested by Patinkin (1956, chapter 13) and Barro and Grossman (1976). If, however, the effect of taxation in reducing demand is anticipated by firms, but prices do not respond immediately, the labour demand function would be modified, and the predicted direct effect of personal tax changes becomes ambiguous.

Whatever the correct explanation, our earlier results strongly suggest that tax changes can be ignored, at least for the United Kingdom. In addition, the model specified in the present chapter departs from the earlier formulation in three other respects: the actual rate of change of output per man is included as a proxy for its expectation, in preference to constraining the latter to be constant; the assumption of equal expected rates of domestic and foreign inflation, in sterling terms, is imposed; [6] and wage-price controls are ignored in the light of the earlier results. With these modifications incorporated, the wage equation becomes

$$\Delta w = \alpha_0 + \alpha_1 X + \alpha_2 \Delta p_C^e + \alpha_3 \Delta p_w^e + \alpha_4 \Delta q \qquad (4.1)$$

where

Δw = percentage rate of change of average wage/salary

X = excess demand for labour

Δp_C^e = expected rate of inflation held by consumers [7]

Δp_w^e = expected rate of inflation held by firms [8]

Δq = percentage rate of change of output per head

The major question posed by this formulation concerns the nature of the trade-off between excess demand and wage inflation; if the hypothesis $\alpha_2 + \alpha_3 = 1$ cannot be rejected, then no trade-off exists in the long run when expectations are fulfilled. Given an estimate of productivity growth, the level of the proxy for excess demand consistent with stable inflation can then be calculated. However, it is clear from the results reported by Coutts *et al.* (1976a) that when the data period is extended beyond 1971, the unemployment rate performs badly as a proxy for excess demand, appearing with a perversely signed coefficient. The apparent disappearance of the short-run trade-off would seem to render questions about the long-run trade-off irrelevant.

In the face of this problem there are two possible strategies. The first is to abandon the expectations-augmented excess-demand hypothesis in favour of an explicit alternative. This line of reasoning has proved popular in the recent past, but if it is to carry conviction it must include an explanation for the disappearance of the augmented Phillips curve. The 'explanations' currently available typically appeal to an unexplained and unmeasurable increase in the militancy or bargaining power of labour, and so scarcely advance understanding; implausibility appears as an additional ingredient in one version of this story (Bispham, 1975), which attributes the rise in labour's militancy to delayed recognition of the implications of the 1944 White Paper on Employment Policy. The alternative strategy is to account for the failure not of the augmented excess-demand hypothesis, but of unemployment as a proxy for excess demand. That is the direction followed in this chapter; but as an initial step, the nature of the shift in the relationship between wage inflation and unemployment is explored.

The first question to be considered is whether the breakdown of the relationship estimated by Parkin *et al.* (1976) consists of a once-for-all shift or a continuing movement. The question was answered by adding a variety of alternative dummy variables to the specification (4.1). It was found that a single intercept shift for the period 1969-74 was sufficient to re-establish the previously estimated relationship; however, a large residual in 1972 distorted the entire regression plane, so an additional dummy was incorporated to avoid biasing estimates of the natural unemployment rate. With these modifications the estimated wage equation for the period 1952-74 (*t*-ratios in brackets) is

$$\Delta w = \begin{array}{c} 4 \cdot 9054 \\ [6 \cdot 37] \end{array} - \begin{array}{c} 1 \cdot 4157U \\ [2 \cdot 42] \end{array} + \begin{array}{c} 0 \cdot 5183 \ \Delta p_w^e \\ [8 \cdot 38] \end{array} + \begin{array}{c} 0 \cdot 2436 \ \Delta p_c^e \\ [1 \cdot 21] \end{array} +$$

$$\begin{array}{cc} 0 \cdot 4627 \ \Delta q & + \ 2 \cdot 7478 \ D_1 \ + \ 3 \cdot 0240 \ D_2 \\ [2 \cdot 72] & [3 \cdot 53] & [2 \cdot 63] \end{array} \qquad (4.2)$$

$$R^2 + 0 \cdot 9558 \qquad \text{D.W.} = 2 \cdot 0915$$

where

   $U = $ unemployment rate

   $D_1 = 1$ in 1969-74, 0 otherwise

   $D_2 = 1$ in 1972, 0 otherwise

All the coefficients are significant with the exception of that on consumer price expectations, which are treated as constant for more than half of the estimation period. The sum of the anticipa-

tions coefficients is insignificantly different from unity, so the
equation is re-estimated with the restriction imposed, as

$$\Delta w = 4\cdot6925 - 1\cdot8303U + 0\cdot5057 \ \Delta p_w^e + (1 - 0\cdot5057) \ \Delta p_c^e$$
$$\quad \ [6\cdot11] \qquad [3\cdot63] \qquad \ [8.11]$$

$$+ \ \ 0\cdot4360 \ \Delta q \ + 2\cdot3643 \ D_1 \ + 3\cdot6479 \ D_2$$
$$\quad \ \ [2\cdot53] \qquad \quad [3\cdot21] \qquad \ \ [3\cdot42] \qquad\qquad\qquad (4.3)$$

$$R^2 \ \text{(adjusted)} = 0\cdot9510 \qquad \text{D.W.} = 2\cdot1286$$

An F-test does not reject the restriction,[9] and so this form of the
equation is used to calculate the natural unemployment rate, at
which money wages rise at the rate of growth of output per head,
given zero anticipated inflation.

During the sample period the mean rate of growth of output
per head was a little greater than two per cent per annum. The
calculated natural unemployment rate was $1\cdot9$ per cent up to 1968;
this is close to the estimate derived from the earlier equation
when the same assumption about productivity growth is made.
After 1968, the natural unemployment rate rose to $3\cdot2$ per cent, wit
an unexplained aberration in 1972.[10]

To summarise, the estimates reported above indicate that the
short-run trade-off between wage inflation and unemployment
shifted upwards in the late 1960s, but is now re-established at a
higher level. Apart from the puzzling behaviour of wages in 1972,
there is no evidence of a continuing shift, which would have render
ed the trade-off useless for policy purposes. There is a substantia
difference between the short- and long-run trade-offs: the latter is
vertical, as predicted by the natural rate hypothesis; the former
implies that for constant inflation expectations, the rate of wage
inflation is reduced by almost two percentage points for a one percentage point increase in unemployment. In qualitative terms, the
expectations-augmented excess-demand model is not rejected, pro
vided allowance is made for a change in the natural rate of unemployment, a phenomenon not encountered in our earlier study. Thu
the search for new models to account for the experience of the las
decade seems decidedly premature.

The characterisation of the shift in the short-run Phillips
curve, and particularly discrimination between once-for-all and
continuing movements, is an important part of the investigation. It
is equally important, however, to provide an explanation of the shif
The very large residual in 1972 also invites further examination.
At this stage, though, further exploration of wage behaviour directl
does not seem a useful strategy, for the reason indicated in the
introduction: regular recourse to wage-price controls coincided
with a potentially important change in social policy. Moreover, th

directly measured price expectations data begin only shortly
before these developments, so there is a serious risk of compound-
ing the influence of three separate factors. Accordingly, the behaviour of unemployment is investigated in the next section, in an
attempt to isolate the variations attributable to changes in the
excess demand for labour.

III THE BEHAVIOUR OF UNEMPLOYMENT

In most macro-econometric models the labour market is linked to
the product market by invoking Okun's Law (Okun, 1962), which
makes the unemployment rate dependent solely on the rate of
growth of output. More recent work by Maki and Spindler (1975)
indicates that in periods when the relative rewards for work and
leisure are changed by social policy, Okun's Law must be augmented by an additional variable operating on labour supply. Specifically, they estimate that in the United Kingdom the elasticity of
unemployment with respect to the ratio of unemployment benefit to
net-of-tax earnings was 0·62 in the period 1952-72.

This result has obvious implications for the argument about
the source of the breakdown in the partial Phillips relation, since it
suggests that at least part of the explanation is a shift in the level
of unemployment at a given level of excess demand. For our repre-
sentative worker, the average ratio of unemployment benefit to net
earnings was 77 per cent higher in the period 1966-74 than it had
been in 1952-65. It would not be surprising if a change of this
magnitude produced effects quite different from those previously
observed.

In view of widespread misunderstanding it should be added that
the relationship isolated by Maki and Spindler does not require
voluntary quits in response to a rise in the benefit-earnings ratio.
Indeed, payment of unemployment benefit to a worker who quits
voluntarily may not begin for up to six weeks. An increase in the
benefit-earnings ratio may be presumed to operate mainly by
changing the incentive to remain unemployed after being dismissed.
Macro studies, however, are incapable of discriminating among
alternative hypotheses regarding the mechanism involved, and
hence require supplementation at the micro level.

The results reported by Maki and Spindler raise an important
question on which they do not comment. Their Durbin-Watson
statistic is so close to the lower bound for rejection of the null
hypothesis of random disturbances as to suggest mis-specification,
one form of which would be the omission of an explanatory variable.
A possible candidate for that role is indicated by the expectations-
augmented excess-demand model of wage inflation. Suppose wage
bargains are struck on the basis of incorrect expectations of (say)

productivity growth; then the wage equation of the last section implies that the resulting discrepancy between actual and equilibrium real (and money) wages will persist indefinitely unless unemployment responds to that discrepancy. Thus consistency requires a feedback mechanism from the difference between the actual and equilibrium real wage to unemployment: a real wage above the equilibrium level would raise unemployment by inducing substitution between factors[11] or between domestic and foreign sources of supply of final goods.

The further extension of Okun's Law, to allow a relative price influence to operate not only on the supply side of the labour market, through the benefit-earnings ratio, but also on the demand side, requires the inclusion of the product wage and the marginal product of labour in the unemployment equation. The marginal product of labour is proxied by output per head, Q; the relationship between these two variables is log-linear for a general class of production functions which includes the Cobb-Douglas and CES forms. The absolute ratio of the coefficients of the average product and the real wage, θ, will depend partly on the nature of the production function; in addition, because variations in labour productivity contain a substantial transitory component, θ will depend on the proportion of productivity change recognised as permanent.

These considerations suggest a log-linear formulation. The unemployment function is therefore specified as

$$ln\ U = \beta_0 + \beta_1\ ln\ Y_{-i} + \beta_2 t + \beta_3\ ln\ (B/E)_{-j} +$$
$$\beta_4\ ln(W/P_w)_{-k} + \beta_5\ ln\ Q_{-\ell} \qquad (4.4)$$

where Y = GDP at constant prices

t = time trend

B/E = ratio of unemployment benefit to net-of-tax earnings

W/P_w = product wage

and i, j, k and ℓ represent lags to be determined empirically. The equation was estimated with lags which gave the best fit as

$$ln\ U = 91 \cdot 2123 - 8 \cdot 8431\ ln\ Y_{-1} + 0 \cdot 0537 t +$$
$$[4 \cdot 13] \qquad [3 \cdot 97] \qquad [0 \cdot 69]$$

$$1 \cdot 1056\ ln(B/E)_{-1} + 6 \cdot 5757\ ln(W/P_w)_{-2} - 2 \cdot 8002\ ln\ Q_{-2}$$
$$[3 \cdot 48] \qquad\qquad [3 \cdot 55] \qquad\qquad\qquad [1 \cdot 35] \qquad (4.5$$

$$R^2 = 0 \cdot 8135 \qquad D.W. = 2 \cdot 0667$$

Not surprisingly, the estimates display some evidence of collinearity in the insignificance of the time trend and output per head taken individually. The more important feature, however, is that the addition of the real wage and output per head removes the serial correlation found when a formulation analogous to Maki and Spindler's was estimated. The benefit-earnings ratio plays a significant role in the equation, with an elasticity considerably higher than that reported by Maki and Spindler; the one-year lag is consistent with the suggestion that an increase in the ratio raises unemployment by increasing the incentive to remain unemployed, rather than by inducing voluntary quits. The implicit restriction imposed in 4. 5, that the coefficients on the money wage and the wholesale price level are opposite in sign and equal in absolute magnitude, is not rejected when these variables are entered separately.[12] The ratio of $|\beta_5|/\beta_4$ is $\hat{\theta} = 0 \cdot 426$; this ratio is used later in the estimation of the wage equation, where the rate of change of the marginal product of labour is proxied by the rate of change of the average product. After allowance is made for the trend component of the composite variable

$$\left[\theta \ \ell n \ Q_{-2} - \ell n \ (W/P_w)_{-2}\right]$$

the estimated growth rate of GDP consistent with a constant level of employment is 2·55 per cent per annum.

The principal reason for estimating an unemployment equation was not for the intrinsic interest of the exercise, but to derive a

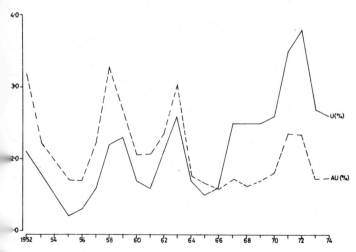

Figure 4.1 Measured unemployment and adjusted unemployment, 1952-74

series for unemployment purged of the effects of social policy. An adjusted unemployment series, denoted by AU, was generated holding the benefit-earnings ratio constant at its average level; hence the means of the new series and of the unadjusted unemployment rate coincide, to facilitate comparison. As is clear from Figure 4.1, however, the two series have little else in common. The marked upward trend of the official measured unemployment series is reversed in the adjusted series. The two indicators do not even coincide in their dating of peaks and troughs, let alone in their ranking of successive expansions and contractions. The most striking feature of the comparison is the major discrepancy between the two indices in their ranking of the 1971-2 recession; the difference is sufficiently dramatic to require little comment.

The obvious question raised by this comparison is whether the adjusted unemployment series, which eliminates variations in voluntary unemployment, is any more successful than the official series in accounting for variations in wage inflation.

IV WAGE-PRICE CONTROLS, THE WAGE EXPLOSION, AND STRUCTURAL STABILITY

The derivation of the adjusted unemployment series does not solve all the problems discussed above. In particular, the major divergence between the two unemployment series coincides with the use of wage-price controls as a regular, rather than exceptional, instrument of policy. The method of avoiding the potential problem of collinearity adopted here is to estimate the wage equation up to 1965, a period in which relatively little use was made of controls, and then to use this equation to predict wage inflation up to 1974. This method has the additional advantage of not prejudging the periods in which controls succeeded in reducing wage increases. It also allows more flexibility than the use of dummy variables; for example, controls may alter the timing rather than the average level of wage increases, but to test this hypothesis using dummy variables would require extensive experimentation.

The forecasting criterion provides a severe test of the wage equation. The average rate of increase of wages and salaries in the period of fit was 5·6 per cent; in the prediction period it was 9·8 per cent. Hence, 'success' requires prediction of the wage explosion, usually regarded as indicating a fundamental change in the structure of wage determination.

The one major problem remaining is that to terminate the estimation period in 1965 means that the inflation anticipations series, which run from 1963 and 1964 for firms and households respectively, cannot be used in fitting the wage equation. It is therefore necessary to use actual price changes as a proxy. This

Table 4.1 Wage equations estimated for period 1952-65

Equation	Intercept	AU	Δp_w	Δq	$\Delta p_w + \hat{\theta}\Delta q$	Δp_c	D62	R^2	D.W.
4·6	6·3668 [6·43]	−0·9470 [2·67]			0·5142 [4·04]		−1·0300 [1·44]	0·7757	1·4797
4·7	6·4882 [4·45]	−1·0323 [2·67]	0·3352 [1·33]	0·1152 [0·52]		0·2260 [0·67]	−1·4006 [1·65]	0·8020	1·4850
4·8	4·7823 [4·22]	−0·8782 [1·82]			0·4586 [1·59]	0·5414 —	−1·5506 [1·47]	0·5929	1·1279

constraint is not disturbing in the case of firms, since their expectations do indeed appear to display perfect foresight, at any rate on the annual basis used here;[13] but all the available evidence indicates that consumers responded sluggishly to the acceleration of inflation. An alternative assumption is that in the fit period the expected inflation rate held by consumers was constant, and equal t the average actual inflation rate. To credit consumers with being right on average seems far more plausible than the supposition tha they were right in each individual year; but presumably the truth lies between the extremes of constancy and complete flexibility.

There is also a minor problem, in that the period of fit includes some controls episodes. The most important example was probably the pay-pause of 1961-2, for which allowance is made in the form of a dummy variable for 1962.

Apart from this modification, all the equations fitted were in the general form of equation 4.1, with the excess demand for labour measured by AU, and the expected rate of inflation held by firms proxied by the actual rate of change of wholesale prices. The anticipated rate of inflation held by consumers was represented either by a constant (in equation 4.6), or by the actual rate of change of consumer prices; the latter formulation was estimated both freely (equation 4.7), and subject to the restriction that the sum of the price coefficients was unity (equation 4.8). The coefficient on the rate of change of output per head was freely estimated in equation 4.7, but constrained to equal the product of θ and the coefficient on the rate of change of wholesale prices in the other two cases. All three equations were fitted for the period 1952-65.

The results are reported in Table 4.1. The common features of these regressions are reasonable but not impressive fits, Dubin-Watson statistics between the upper- and lower-bounds, significant and consistent estimates of the effect of adjusted unemployment, and a relatively large and correctly signed, though insignificant, coefficient on the incomes policy dummy. The interpretation of equation 4.6 in the forecasting exercise to be reported below is that the intercept includes the product of consumer price anticipations and the associated coefficient. Assuming no money illusion, that coefficient is 0.4858, i.e. $(1 - 0.5142)$, and assuming that consumers were not fooled by inflation over the period as a whole, the average rate of inflation expected by consumers was 3.006 per cent; hence the adjusted intercept, net of this price component, is 4.9065.

The remaining two equations use the actual rate of change of consumer prices as a proxy for the corresponding expectation. When the model is freely estimated, in equation 4.7, only the intercept and the coefficient on adjusted unemployment are significant; however, the F-test that the remaining four coefficients are zero is strongly rejected.[14] The hypothesis that the sum of the price

Table 4.2 Predicted wage inflation (%), 1966-74

Year	Δw	Equation 4·6	Equation 4·7	Equation 4·8			
		FE (E)	FE (A)	FE (A)	t	FE (E)	t
1966	5·68	-1·78	-1·07	-1·28	2·43	-1·77	4·02
1967	5·64	-0·91	-0·77	-0·80	2·26	-1·06	1·15
1968	7·00	-3·14	-0·67	-1·56	3·88	-3·31	2·94
1969	6·98	-1·88	-0·45	-1·32	2·60	-2·00	2·47
1970	11·35	1·22	3·02	1·66	2·97	1·26	3·48
1971	11·68	-0·75	2·56	0·04	0·06	-0·76	3·60
1972	10·75	1·56	3·23	1·73	6·32	1·50	5·39
1973	11·46	-0·15	2·19	-0·08	0·22	0·02	0·02
1974	17·51	-1·58	2·40	-3·33	1·74	-0·76	0·18
Mean forecast error		-0·82	1·16	-0·55		-0·76	

Notes to Table 4.2

1. Δw is the actual rate of wage inflation.
2. FE denotes forecast error, defined as actual minus predicted rate of wage change.
3. FE (A) uses actual price changes, FE (E) expected price changes, to generate the predictions.
4. t is the (absolute value of the) ratio of the forecast error to its standard error.

coefficients is unity is rejected by the narrowest of margins.[15] In view of the known defects of proxying expected by actual consumer price changes over this period, and the indecisive nature of the t-test, the restrictions on the sum of the price coefficients and on the coefficient of changes in output per head were nevertheless imposed, in equation 4. 8, and were not rejected by the F-test.[16]

The crucial test of these equations is not their statistical properties within the period of fit, but their predictive power in the nine remaining years. In making these predictions, it is possible either to continue using actual price changes, or to switch to the directly measured anticipations series; this choice affected the details of the results but not their general character. Examples using both assumptions are tabulated below.

The results of the prediction tests are summarised in Table 4. 2. To put these results in perspective, forecasts were made on the same basis but with U substituted for AU. Using the unconstrained estimates, the forecast error averaged 2·8 percentage points; when the constraints were imposed, despite strong rejection by the t and F-tests, the average error was reduced but remained positive. A natural inference would be that wage-price controls, which operated in some form throughout the forecast period except in the period 1970 - November 1972, were strongly perverse in their effects, or were swamped by some unexplained factor. The predictions obtained using adjusted unemployment lead to very different conclusions. The mean forecast errors are all small in absolute value, and provided money illusion is excluded they are al negative. All four sets of predictions indicate the success of controls in holding down wage inflation in 1966-9, and the t-ratios, where calculable, are significant in at least three of these cases. In the formulations which embody the homogeneity postulate the controls of 1974 also register some success, though little effect is visible in 1973. Some evidence of catch-up appears in 1970, and of anticipation in 1972; but in none of the cases which allow for the 'gear change' is 1972 a problem in the sense noted in Section 4. II. The magnitudes of the annual forecast errors vary according to th equation used, but the mean errors all lie within a narrow range.

Three general conclusions are apparent. First, to project the money illusion which seems to characterise relatively quiescent periods into episodes of more rapid and more variable inflation ensures that implausible predictions will be generated. Secondly, there is no need to invoke a dramatic change in the structure of th inflationary process to explain the behaviour of wages in the recer past, provided the homogeneity postulate is imposed and unemploy ment is adjusted for variations induced by changes in social policy Equations which lack either of these characteristics underpredict the wage inflation rate on average, despite the additional factor of governmental efforts to contain wage increases; if the forecasting model incorporates homogeneity and proxies excess demand for labour by adjusted unemployment, the wage explosion is easily explained. Finally, the pattern of forecast errors strongly suggests that previous estimates of the effectiveness of wage-price controls should be revised. The new results are consistent with a perceptible and statistically significant impact of controls in the years of operation; the magnitude of this impact seems too variable to be captured by any simple combination of dummy variables. To judge the controls solely by their impact effect would, however, be misleading, since there is some evidence of partial catch-up in the aftermath of controls, and also some evidence that protracted discussions on pay restraint, as in 1972, exert an announcement effect on wage inflation. Hence, one consequence of controls is to rephase wage increases. The highest estimate of the overall success of more than six years of controls, on the assumption that the predictions would otherwise have been unbiased, is an average reduction in the rate of wage inflation of 0·8 percentage points per annum over the nine-year forecast period. Whether this degree of success is sufficient to offset the allocative consequences of controls must remain an open question.

The final topic to be examined is the level of the natural unemployment rate, and its sensitivity to variations in the benefit-earnings ratio. The implications of equations 4.6 and 4.8 are so similar that consideration is confined to the former.

Point estimates of the adjusted unemployment rate, AU, consistent with equal growth of money wages and output per head at a zero rate of price inflation can be readily obtained; for equation 4.6, for instance, the critical adjusted unemployment rate is 3·41 per cent. Since AU was standardised at the mean benefit-earnings ratio for the full sample period, this corresponds to the average natural unemployment rate. The variations in that rate implied by the unemployment equation are shown for bench-mark years in Table 4.3. The estimates are high, and pose a serious problem of social choice which requires fuller consideration than is feasible within the confines of this chapter.

Table 4.3 Natural unemployment rate

Period	Benefit/earnings ratio (%)	Natural unemployment rate (%)
1952-54	36·37	2·4
1962-64	43·12	2·9
1972-74	70·83	5·1

The estimates are also higher than those reported in Section 4. II above. Moreover, the discrepancy appears to be particularly marked towards the end of the period. The natural rate averaged over the period 1969-74, excluding 1972, is 4·8 per cent, compared with 3·2 per cent reported in Section 4. II. However, part of this discrepancy is illusory, because the dummy variable used to capture the effects of changes in social policy in Section 4. II also picks up the effects of incomes policy, which is not allowed for in the calculation of Table 4. 3. If the forecast errors recorded in Table 4. 2 are attributed to controls, the natural rate in the presence of those controls is reduced to 3·9 per cent. Thus, the estimated profile of the natural rate differs from the crude estimate reported earlier, but by a constant amount.

This adjustment does not alter the fact that the two sets of estimates differ, and that the level of the natural rate under present social arrangements is higher than might have been hoped. Three caveats are, however, in order. Firstly, the point estimate of the natural rate depends on a large number of other point estimates and on quantitative assumptions about productivity growth; while the formal calculation of a standard error does not appear possible, there is no doubt that a substantial degree of uncertainty surrounds the point estimate. The divergence of the two sets of estimates merely reinforces the point. Secondly, the natural rate of unemployment is affected by variables other than the benefit-earnings ratio; these are unlikely to have remained constant throughout the sample period. Finally, the estimates reported here probably represent only impact effects, in the sense that the adoption of the natural rate would ultimately affect the product wage and the average product of labour, and hence through equation 4. 5 the unemployment rate consistent with given social policy and a given rate of growth of GDP. In other words, the natural rate is determined by the entire system, not by two particular equations in isolation.

The estimates obtained here therefore invite further analysis on several fronts. In the meantime, however, there is no point in disguising the stark choice offered by the currently available state of knowledge.

V CONCLUSIONS

This chapter has demonstrated that the influence of excess demand for labour, appropriately measured, on wage inflation has not disappeared, and that special factors need not be adduced on an *ad hoc* basis to account for wage changes over the last decade. This relationship permits the inflation rate to be altered by the traditional tools of demand management in the short run, but does not

offer a permanent trade-off between inflation and unemployment.
To reduce the inflation rate through demand management, or even
to maintain it at its present level, is expensive; but, given the
limited effects of direct controls, quite apart from their allocative
repercussions, the alternative would ultimately be worse.

The survival of a hypothesis, in the sense of non-rejection,
does not of course mean that the hypothesis is correct. Other
hypotheses may be formulated which explain the data used in this
chapter more satisfactorily, on any of several possible criteria.
As yet, no such hypothesis has been offered, except for the ascien-
tific conjecture that the present differs from the past for reasons
which are not yet known, and which therefore may, or may not,
operate in the future. Advocates of this view are in no position to
reject the natural rate hypothesis, however unpalatable they may
find it.

NOTES TO CHAPTER 4

[1]   See Chapter 2 for a fuller survey.
[2]   There is an extensive literature on wage-price controls and on regional
policy as methods of shifting the Phillips curve inwards. The former is
surveyed by Parkin *et al.* (1972).
[3]   The most sophisticated example of this literature is Phelps (1972).
[4]   In addition, the lag structure imposed by Henry *et al.* is extremely
restrictive: the only influence of unemployment on the wage change of
quarter *t* permitted by their procedure is that exercised in the preceeding
quarter.
[5]   See, for example, Gordon (1971) on the United States and Bruce (1975)
on Canada.
[6]   The regression of the expected rate of change of export prices on the
expected rate of change of domestic wholesale prices, using annualised data
from the CBI surveys, yields an intercept which is insignificantly different
from zero, a slope coefficient which is insignificantly different from unity,
a high coefficient of determination and a Durbin-Watson statistic which does
not reject the null hypothesis of random disturbances.
[7]   Assumed constant until 1964, thereafter measured by transformation of
the Gallup Poll surveys; for further discussion see Chapter 6.
[8]   Measured by actual rate of change of wholesale prices until 1963, thereafter by transformation of the CBI surveys; for further discussion see
Chapter 7.
[9]   The calculated F-ratio is $1 \cdot 72$, the critical value of F $(1, 16)$ is $4 \cdot 49$ at
the five per cent level.
[10]   The natural unemployment rate in 1972 was about $5 \cdot 2$ per cent. This
puzzle is resolved in Section 4. IV.
[11]   The standard non-substitution theorem will be invalidated by the
existence of tradeable capital goods.
[12]   The calculated F-ratio is $3 \cdot 26$, the critical value of F $(1, 16)$ is $4 \cdot 49$ at
the five per cent level.

¹³   The regression of the expected on the actual rate of change of domestic
wholesale prices yields an intercept which is insignificantly different from
zero and a slope coefficient which is insignificantly different from unity.
¹⁴   The calculated F-ratio is $5 \cdot 28$, the critical value of F $(4, 8)$ is $3 \cdot 84$ at
the five per cent level. These results are not dependent on the inclusion of
D62.
¹⁵   The calculated t-ratio is $2 \cdot 310$, the critical value of t (8) is $2 \cdot 306$ at the
five per cent level.
¹⁶   The calculated F-ratio is $4 \cdot 22$, the critical value of F $(2, 8)$ is $4 \cdot 46$ at
the five per cent level.

APPENDIX 4.1 DEFINITIONS AND DATA SOURCES

All rates of change are defined as: $\Delta z = (\ln Z / \ln Z_{-1}) \cdot 100$, unless otherwise stated.

1. W = wages and salaries ÷ employees in employment. Sources:
             British Labour Statistics Historical Abstract (BLSHA);
             British Labour Statistics Yearbook 1969 (BLSYB); Monthly
             Digest of Statistics (MDS); Economic Trends (ET)

2. P_w = wholesale output prices index, all manufactured products, home
             sales. Sources: *The British Economy, Key Statistics, 1900-1970*
             (KS); MDS.

3. P_c = implied deflator of consumers' expenditure. Sources: *KS* and
             MDS.

4. Δp_c^e = expected rate of change of consumer prices. Sources: 1965-74,
             Chapter 6; 1952-64, assumed constant, equal to Δp_c.

5. Δp_w^e = expected rate of change of the price at which firms' domestic
             orders are booked. Sources: 1952-63, assumed equal to p_w;
             1964-74, derived from CBI *Industrial Trends Surveys,* using
             the methods of Chapter 6. The series was centred at the begin-
             ning of the year, and was scaled using the responses to the
             Survey question on price changes during the preceding period.

6. Y = gross domestic product at constant factor cost (from expen-
             diture). Sources: *KS, MDS.*

7. B/E = unemployment benefit (including earnings-related supplement)
             payable to a married man with two children who was formerly
             in receipt of the average wage, expressed as a proportion of
             the net-of-tax average wage. Sources: *Annual Abstract of*
             Statistics, Department of Employment Gazette (DEG), ET, and
             Annual Reports of the Department of Health and Social Security

8. U = Wholly unemployed as a percentage of total employees. Sources
             BLSHA, DEG.

9. Q = GDP at constant factor cost ÷ employees in employment.

5 Price determination

Graham W. Smith[1]

I INTRODUCTION

The price-setting decisions of firms have received much less
attention than the proximate determinants of the wage bargain.
However, knowledge of the former is equally important in any
serious attempt to understand inflation and to design appropriate
policies for its control.

The fundamental problem of controlling inflation raises two
basic questions. First, how are price changes affected by variations in excess demand? Secondly, are prices influenced by any
other policy variables, such as moral suasion or direct controls?
The second of these questions is answered only indirectly: the
statistical properties of the estimated equations do not suggest
the omission of an important explanatory variable; since the effort
apparently expended by successive governments in encouraging
voluntary restraint in raising prices, and in designing and enforcing direct controls, varied substantially over the sample period,
the results provide *prima facie* evidence that price inflation is
insensitive to such influences. A similar conclusion would apply
to any other alleged determinants of price inflation which are not
included in this study. The first question is addressed directly
and, indeed, provides the major focus of this chapter.

While the literature on price determination is relatively small,
the question of the relationship between excess demand and price
inflation has, of course, been examined in earlier studies. The
question has usually been posed, however, in a peculiarly narrow
manner: prices are first described as a mark-up over costs, and
at a second stage, if at all, the responsiveness of the mark-up to
variations in excess demand is examined. The disagreement found
in this literature as to whether the price-cost margin should be
related to the level or first difference of excess demand is one
indication that the customary theoretical framework is inadequate
to bear the weight of any firm conclusions. Indeed, the theoretical
framework is seldom made explicit. In a study which constitutes
one of the rare exceptions, Lipsey and Parkin (1970) showed that

the mark-up model of pricing could be readily derived from an identity and some assumed magic constants; a method of deriving the standard mark-up model from recognised behavioural assumptions has not yet been provided. One of the principal objectives of this chapter is, in contrast, to develop a pricing model based on standard economic theory.

Because the act of changing prices involves costs, the individual firm will revise its prices only at discrete intervals. In a model where prices are not changed continuously, the firm's actual costs of production exercise a significant influence on its pricing decisions only through their influence on its expected costs of production. Godley and Nordhaus (1972) make a similar point in their assertion that 'prices move with long-run costs, and do not change because of variations in cost which are thought to be temporary'.[2] While the model derived in this chapter confirms their rejection of actual costs as a direct determinant of prices, it demonstrates that normalisation *per se* is also irrelevant. Moreover, the normal *cost* hypothesis suffers from the additional defect of omitting other variables which should be included.

If the rate of price inflation does respond to variations in excess demand, it becomes essential to determine whether there is a permanent or only a transitory trade-off. The significance of this question for policy purposes, though typically in the context of wage determination, has become so well known as to make further elaboration superfluous.

To summarise, this chapter seeks to derive a model of price determination consistent with economic theory, and to assess its performance when it is confronted with the facts of recent United Kingdom experience. These topics are the subject of Sections 5.III and 5.IV respectively; but first the existing literature is surveyed to justify the contention that the questions set out above have not been answered satisfactorily.

II PREVIOUS STUDIES OF PRICE DETERMINATION

Early studies based on the mark-up hypothesis either did not test the null hypothesis that the mark-up is invariant with respect to demand (e.g. Klein and Ball (1959), Dicks-Mireaux (1961), Godley and Rowe (1964)), or accepted that hypothesis (Neild, 1963). Later work by Rushdy and Lund (1967), who used Neild's data, revealed that if the demand variable was appropriately specified then that variable was a significant determinant of changes in the price of manufacturing output, irrespective of whether actual or normal unit labour costs were used.

Recent empirical work which has estimated mark-up models for United Kingdom manufacturing industry (Godley and Nordhaus

(1972), Pesaran (1973) and Coutts *et al.* (1976b)) considers only
the normal cost hypothesis that 'the mark-up of price over normal
... cost is independent of the conditions of demand in the factor
and product markets ...'. [3] The basic procedure used in testing
the hypothesis is first to remove reversible cyclical effects from
unit labour costs, then impose a distributed lag on the 'normalised'
labour cost and other factor price variables and aggregate the
cost variables to generate a predicted price variable, $\hat{P}$. The
price index is then regressed on the predicted price variable and
a demand series. Consider the model:

$$P = \alpha \hat{P}^\beta . f(X) \tag{5.1}$$

where P is the price of output, X is excess demand and α and β
are parameters. For the normal cost hypothesis not to be rejected,
it is necessary that $\alpha = \beta = 1$ and the estimated coefficient on the
excess-demand variable to be insignificantly different from zero.
The Godley-Nordhaus preferred estimates (t-statistics in brackets) are:

$$\Delta \ln P_t = 0 \cdot 001399 + 0 \cdot 6248 \ \Delta \ \ln \hat{P}_t + 0 \cdot 000238 \ \Delta \ \ln \left[\frac{X}{XN_t}\right] \tag{5.2}$$
$$[1 \cdot 42] \qquad [5 \cdot 36] \qquad\qquad [0 \cdot 66]$$

$$\overline{R}^2 = 0 \cdot 340 \qquad \text{D.W.} = 1 \cdot 83$$

The estimated coefficient on the predicted price variable is
significantly less than unity on the basis of a t-test at the
5 per cent level, and the excess demand variable is insignificantly
different from zero. The former hypothesis test is interpreted
by Laidler and Parkin (1975) as refuting the normal cost hypothesis, whilst the latter test led Godley and Nordhaus to conclude
that 'the normal price hypothesis is correct'. [4] Their lack of
concern about the lower than expected coefficient on the predicted
price variable rests on an appeal to errors of measurement,
which bias that coefficient downwards. On measurement errors,
Lipsey's view is apposite: 'It is, however, always possible to show
that any set of statistics are not perfect or even, by some absolute
standard, that they are downright bad. The relevant question is
not whether the figures are perfect, but whether they are good
enough for the purposes at hand. The question of whether or not
the postulated relation is strong enough to show up in spite of
imperfections in the data, can only be answered by the empirical
results...'. [5] In this instance, the only definite conclusion is that
the postulated relation shows up in a severely attenuated form.
By weakening a hypothesis sufficiently it is always possible to
explain away its rejection by empirical tests, but nothing is gained
from such an exercise. Whether the rejection of the strict form of
the normal cost hypothesis by Godley and Nordhaus is properly

interpreted as no more than a reflection of measurement error cannot be settled by *a priori* reasoning.

Pesaran's study differs from that of Godley and Nordhaus in three important respects: more careful attention is given to the estimation of the set of models used to normalise unit labour costs; the coefficient on the predicted price variable is constrained to be unity (although the hypothesis that the restriction holds is not tested), and lagged values of excess demand are permitted to affect the mark-up. Pesaran finds that a one-quarter lag on excess demand is marginally significant, although the quantitative effect is rather small.

Coutts *et al.* estimate the coefficient on predicted prices to be insignificantly different from unity and find the estimated coefficient on a contemporaneous excess-demand variable to be insignificantly different from zero. However, the unit coefficient may be spurious, for the normalising procedure used by Coutts *et al.* is extremely weak compared with that of Pesaran and even that of Godley and Nordhaus. The procedure of using within-sample conditional predictions to generate normal unit labour costs is violated and, instead of estimating employment—output relationships to calculate normal productivity, a trend rate of growth of productivity is imposed. Their predicted price variable is inconsistent with the definition of the normal value of a variable, on which the set of tests of the normal cost hypothesis currently under discussion is based.

The prominence of mark-up models, whether of the normal or actual cost variety, in the existing literature is surprising in view of their lack of theoretical justification and their questionable empirical performance. There have been a few studies of price formation, notably those of Johnston *et al.* (1964) and McCallum (1970), which have adopted instead the law of supply and demand as a theoretical basis, and which therefore appear to provide a much more appropriate framework for investigating the role of excess demand. However, the derivation of their estimating equations was conducted so informally that the underlying theory was not fully exploited. Accordingly, the next section presents an explicit derivation of the model to be estimated in order to obtain as much prior information as possible.

III AN EXPECTATIONS-AUGMENTED EXCESS-DEMAND MODEL OF PRICE INFLATION

Conventional economic theory predicts that prices will change in response to excess demand.[6] In such disequilibrium situations the firm's price is not exogenous to that firm, which instead is hypothesised to adjust price in response to some measure of the disequilibrium. Moreover, in such theory, that price is not a money price but a real price, or, more generally, the opportunity cost. Friedman (1966, 1968) and Phelps (1965, 1967, 1968) first developed this idea in the context of labour markets. More recently, Phelps and Winter (1970) and Barro (1972) have developed disequilibrium-dynamic models of the optimum price-setting behaviour of firms. Barro, in particular, specifies a model in which the firm faces a stochastic demand function, one of the arguments of which is the firm's own price, and finds that the proportional rate of change of firms' prices is positively related to the current level of excess demand. One drawback of the Phelps—Winter and Barro type of approach is that it is not empirically operational. Parkin *et al.* (1976) have developed a general framework for the analysis of expectations-augmented excess-demand models which, while less adequate than the Phelps—Winter and Barro analyses in that it does not model price-setting as explicitly optimising behaviour, does provide a thorough integration of the roles of excess demand and expectations in a manner which is useful empirically.

In the present context, utilising the framework of Parkin *et al.*, the procedure is first to specify arguments of the firm's supply and demand functions, then to define the level of excess demand and to express the change in the level of excess demand in terms of functions of the arguments of those supply and demand functions. It is then postulated that the firm forms expectations of the exogenous (price) variables, and adjusts its own price such that the change in the level of excess demand offsets some or all of the actual level of excess demand in some previous period. From this relationship, after averaging over firms, a price equation can be derived in which the rate of change of prices is a function of the level of excess demand and expectations of the rate of change of prices and costs.

Postulate:

$$D_i = D_i \left[\frac{P_i}{P_w} , \frac{P_c}{P_w} \right] \quad S_i = S_i \left[\frac{C_i}{P_i} \right] \tag{5.3}$$

where D_i is the quantity flow demanded from the ith firm;

S_i is the quantity flow supplied by the ith firm;

P_i is the price of one unit of the ith firm's output;

P_w is the average price of the output of manufacturing firms with which the ith firm directly competes;

P_c is the price of consumer goods; and

C_i is the average cost of producing one output unit.

The demand function states that the quantity demanded depends on relative prices: the price of the ith firm's output relative to the average price of other firms in manufacturing and the ratio of manufacturing to consumer prices. The first argument may be likened to the demand functions in Chamberlin's model of monopolistic competition. If $P_i = P_w$ then the average price of direct competitors is the same as that of the firm being analysed and the relationship shows the quantity that is demanded from the ith firm at each common price. If $P_i \neq P_w$ then the first argument of the function is analogous to Chamberlin's *dd* relation which shows the quantity demanded from the ith firm at each price when its price differs from that of its competitors.[7] The function may be contrasted with that of Phelps—Winter, in which the rate of change of a firm's sales is a function of its own price relative to the average price in the market in which it operates. The output supply function relates the quantity supplied to the ratio of the ith firm's average cost of one unit of output to its price of one output unit. The sign restrictions on the partial derivatives of the demand and supply functions are:

$D'_{i1} < 0$ The higher the ith firm's price relative to that of its competitors, the less that will be demanded from that firm.

$D'_{i2} > 0$ The greater the price of consumer goods relative to manufactured goods, the greater the demand for the output of the ith firm in manufacturing.

$S'_{i1} < 0$ The higher the cost of producing one unit of the ith firm's output relative to its price, the less the firm wishes to supply.

The question arises as to who sets prices and how they are set. Firms and consumers meet in markets. The individual firm makes output decisions about the very small number of products which it sells in each market. The household chooses the quantities of many commodities which it purchases from many firms. Each firm's share of supply is considerably greater than the individual household's share of demand. Although it is possible in periods of excess demand that consumers offer a higher price to obtain a commodity, it is easier for, and in the interests of, firms to set prices. This is Arrow's view: 'In general ... it is reasonable to suppose that if the selling side of the market is much more concentrated than the buying side, the main force in changing prices will be the monopolistic behavior of the sellers.'[8]

Assume then that firms set prices and that the ith firm adjust its price in an attempt to maintain a cleared market so that, given expectations of prices and costs, the change in excess demand offsets some or all of the actual level of excess demand in some previous period, that is,

$$\Delta X_i = -X_{i0} \tag{5.4}$$

where $X_i \equiv D_i - S_i$ (5.5)

The change in excess demand over a given finite time interval is given by:

$$\Delta X_i \equiv D_i' \left[\frac{\Delta P_i}{P_w} - P_i \cdot \frac{\Delta P_w}{P_w^2} + \frac{\Delta P_c}{P_w} - P_c \cdot \frac{\Delta P_w}{P_w^2} \right]$$
$$- S_i' \left[\frac{\Delta C_i}{P_i} - C_i \cdot \frac{\Delta P_i}{P_i^2} \right] \tag{5.6}$$

or, adding expectational superscripts and simplifying,

$$\Delta X_i \equiv - \alpha_{i1} (\Delta p_i - \Delta p_w^e) + \alpha_{i2} (\Delta p_c^e - \Delta p_w^e)$$
$$+ \beta_i (\Delta c_i^e - \Delta p_i) = -X_{i0} \tag{5.7}$$

where $\Delta z \equiv \Delta Z / Z$

and
$$\left. \begin{array}{l} -\alpha_{i1} = D_{i1}' \cdot D_{i1} < 0 \\ \alpha_{i2} = D_{i2}' \cdot D_{i2} > 0 \\ -\beta_i = S_i' \cdot S_i < 0 \end{array} \right] \tag{5.8}$$

that is, $\alpha_{i1}, \alpha_{i2}, \beta_i > 0$.

A sufficient condition for $\alpha_{i1}, \alpha_{i2}, \beta_i$ to be constant is that the demand and supply functions are semi-logarithmic, since in this form $D_{i1}' \cdot D_{i1}, D_{i2}' \cdot D_{i2}$ and $S_i' \cdot S_i$ are constants. Equation 5.6 can be re-arranged as a price-setting equation for the individual firm:

$$\Delta p_i = \frac{1}{\alpha_{i1} + \beta_i} X_{i0} + \frac{\alpha_{i1} - \alpha_{i2}}{\alpha_{i1} + \beta_i} \Delta p_w^e + \frac{\alpha_{i2}}{\alpha_{i1} + \beta_i} \Delta p_c^e$$
$$+ \frac{\beta_i}{\alpha_{i1} + \beta_i} \Delta c^e \tag{5.9}$$

Finally, aggregating over firms[9] yields the macro price equation

$$\Delta p_w = \alpha_0 X_0 + \beta_1 \Delta p_w^e + \beta_2 \Delta p_c^e + \beta_3 \Delta c^e \tag{5.10}$$

where Δp_w is the proportional rate of change of the price of output of manufacturing firms;

X is the level of excess demand for manufactured goods;

Δp_w^e is the expected rate of change of the prices of firms in manufacturing;

Δp_c^e is the consumers' expected rate of change of prices;

Δc^e is manufacturing firms' expected rate of change of average cost per unit of output; and

$$\alpha_0 \equiv \frac{1}{\alpha_1 + \beta}, \quad \beta_1 \equiv \frac{\alpha_1 - \alpha_2}{\alpha_1 + \beta}, \quad \beta_2 \equiv \frac{\alpha_2}{\alpha_1 + \beta} \text{ and } \beta_3 \equiv \frac{\beta}{\alpha_1 + \beta}$$

The coefficients on $X_0, \Delta p_c^e$ and Δc^e are unambiguously positive while that on Δp_w^e is $\gtreqless 0$ as $\alpha_1 \gtreqless \alpha_2$. It is likely that the effect of

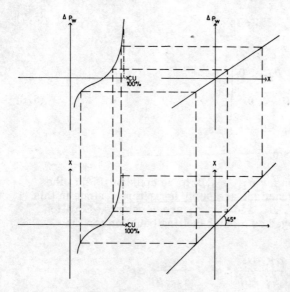

Figure 5.1 The relationship between the rate of change of prices, the level of excess demand for products and the level of capacity utilisation

P_i/P_w on quantity demanded will be greater than that of
P_c/P_w and hence $\alpha_1 > \alpha_2$ and $\beta_1 > 0$. In this model, anticipated
changes in the arguments of the excess-demand function enter
through the expectations variables and unanticipated changes
enter through a non-zero level of excess demand. The coefficients
on the expectational variables, β_1, β_2 and β_3, sum to unity.

Since excess demand for products is not a directly observable
variable, it is proxied by the level of capacity utilisation, CU.
Solow (1969) argues that the relationship between the rate of change
of prices, Δp_w, and the level of capacity utilisation is non-linear;
Δp_w is insensitive to changes in CU around some norm.[10] Given
the usually-assumed linear relationship between price-change and
the level of excess demand, then the non-linearity between Δp_w
and CU arises through the non-linearity between excess demand
and its proxy (Figure 5.1). Substituting a non-linear function of
capacity utilisation for X in equation 5.10 then if, on estimation,
the coefficient on that capacity utilisation variable is significantly
different from zero, there is a short-run relationship between
that variable and the rate of change of prices. Moreover, the
theory predicts that since

$$\beta_1 + \beta_2 + \beta_3 = 1 \tag{5.11}$$

then in the long run, when expected and realised changes are equal,
price change is homogeneous of degree one in all other money
variables:

$$\Delta p_w - (\beta_1 \, \Delta p_w^e + \beta_2 \, \Delta p_c^e + \beta_3 \, \Delta c^e) = 0 \tag{5.12}$$

Therefore, if when the model is estimated the coefficient on
capacity utilisation is significantly greater than zero and if the
sum of the coefficients on the expectional variables is not significantly different from unity, then there is a short-run relationship
between price change and capacity utilisation; but in long-run
equilibrium it is possible to have any rate of change of prices at
a natural, or equilibrium, level of capacity utilisation, CU^N.[11]
If 5.12 holds then CU^N is that level of capacity utilisation
at which $f(CU) = 0$.

The concept of a natural level of capacity utilisation is
analogous to Friedman's concept of a natural rate of unemployment on which he states: 'The "natural rate of unemployment" ...
is the level that would be ground out by the Walrasian system of
general equilibrium equations provided there is imbedded in them
the actual structural characteristics of the labour and commodity
markets ...'[12] Moreover, 'To avoid misunderstanding, let me
emphasize that by using the term "natural" rate of unemployment,
I do not mean to suggest that it is immutable and unchangeable.

On the contrary, many of the market characteristics that determine its level are man-made and policy-made ... I use the term
"natural" ... to try to separate the real forces from monetary
forces.'[13] The equilibrium level of capacity utilisation may not
be constant. This has important implications: specifically, those
coefficients which are associated with the relationship between
excess demand and its proxy may not be constant but may vary
over time. In the empirical section of this chapter, the hypothesis
that the natural level of capacity utilisation is constant is maintained, but an important problem for future research will be to
test that hypothesis directly.

   Given a fixed exchange rate between the small, open, United
Kingdom economy and those with which it trades, then the rate
of change of United Kingdom prices may not be explained by
purely domestic factors. Manufacturing output is internationally
tradeable. With fixed exchange rates, at the theoretical level,
prices of internationally traded goods differ only because of
transport costs and tariffs, although empirically, time lags and
the different weights used in the indices of the price of manufacturing output in different economies may conceal the effect.
However, in an earlier study, Cross and Laidler (1976) found
the distinction between tradeable and non-tradeable goods to be
unhelpful in explaining United Kingdom inflation. They used a
'world' excess-demand variable to explain United Kingdom
tradeable goods prices and found that variable to be no more
successful than a 'domestic' excess-demand variable. This may
however, result from their 'domestic' excess-demand variable
not being totally free from demand forces external to the United
Kingdom economy.

   Forces external to the United Kingdom economy implicitly
enter the above model in two ways. The expected rate of change
of costs includes expectations of the rate of change of costs of
imported materials and an excess demand proxy based on
aggregate real output would encompass output traded in both
domestic and foreign markets. The model may be explicitly
extended to show trade in two distinct markets by including
P_i/P_F, where P_F is the average of all other prices in foreign
markets, as an additional argument in the firm's demand function.
In this case, the expected rate of change of foreign prices would
appear as an additional regressor in the price equation. The sum
of the coefficients on the expectational variables in such a model
would be unity.

IV SOME ESTIMATES

The variable to be explained is the proportional rate of change
of the price of output of the manufacturing sector. The United

Kingdom output price index is especially appropriate for this purpose because it is an index of the price of domestically sold output of manufacturing industry as a whole, measured on a net sector basis: transactions between firms within the manufacturing sector are excluded. The prices used in the construction of the index are exclusive of purchase tax but include any subsidy paid to or duty paid by the firm.

The dependent variable is specified as a proportional, rather than an absolute, change. This specification is more readily interpretable than absolute changes tied to specific levels. However, the model itself gives no clear guidance on the time-span over which to take differences in calculating a proportional rate of change: on quarterly data, for example, should the differencing period be one quarter or should a four-quarter overlapping proportional rate of change be used? Wallis (1971) and others have argued that the latter specification is inappropriate because it tends to improve the fit spuriously and introduce fourth-order serial correlation into the residuals. Furthermore, for a given number of observations computations which use four-quarter overlapping changes leave fewer degrees of freedom. Because of these inadequacies, the dependent variable is specified as:

$$(\ell n \, P_t/P_{t-1}) \cdot 400 \tag{5.13}$$

Using this specification rather than, for example,

$$\left[(P_t - P_{t-1}) / P_{t-1} \right] \cdot 400$$

results in changes being symmetric over consecutive time periods, apart from sign, since

$$ln \, \frac{P_t}{P_{t-1}} = -ln \, \frac{P_{t-1}}{P_t} \tag{5.14}$$

The unobservable excess demand for products is proxied by a Wharton-type capacity utilisation index calculated from seasonally adjusted real output for manufacturing. The procedure used to generate the capacity utilisation variable is fully described in Appendix 5.1. The expectational variables used in this study are derived from sample survey data of households and firms.[15] An important advantage of this method is that it avoids the problem of testing a joint hypothesis.

The particular price-setting theory being used does not specify the lag in adjustment of prices to excess demand, which has to be determined experimentally, although given prior statistical information it is expected to be about one quarter.[16] On the other hand, the model tells us something about the timing of the expectational variables relative to the dependent variable; it indicates that the expectational variables should refer to the time period for which prices are being set. However, there is no information on what that time period actually is. The four-month expectations of firms and the six-month expectations of consumers are those which are used.[17]

The basic model estimated was of the form

$$\Delta p_w = \alpha_1 + \alpha_2 \, g(CU) + \beta_1 \, \Delta p_w^e + \beta_2 \, \Delta p_c^e + \beta_3 \, \Delta c^e$$

$$+ \sum_{j=2}^{4} \gamma_{j-1} \, S_j + u_t \tag{5.15}$$

in which $g(CU)$ is some function of the Wharton-type capacity utilisation index, S_j are quarterly seasonal dummies, included because of (additive) seasonal variation in the capacity utilisation measure and u_t is a random error term. The percentage index, CU, was used for $g(CU)$ and the model estimated by ordinary least squares for United Kingdom manufacturing 1965(1) - 1971(4), twenty-eight quarterly observations, which is the longest time period for which data is available given that exchange rates are 'fixed' and the CBI expectations data is weighted.[18] Alternative lags, up to three quarters, on the capacity utilisation variable were tried. The results are in Table 5.1, equation 5.16.[19] With the preferred lag on capacity utilization, that variable is just significantly different from zero at the 5 per cent level on a two-tailed t-test. The estimated coefficient on Δp_w^e is insignificantly different from zero and the sum of the expectational variables is insignificantly different from unity. The Durbin-Watson statistic is in the inconclusive range.

An alternative and simpler hypothesis was tested. The appropriate price deflator for consumers' nominal prices is the retail price index, and therefore P_i/P_c is the relevant relative price variable to enter into the demand function. Given this, together with the assumption that there is no role for the relative price of wholesale to retail goods in picking up substitution effects between retail and non-retail activities, then firms' product price expectations should be of no importance. The demand function, therefore, was specified as $D_i = D_i \, (P_i/P_c)$ in which the demand for the ith firm's output is expressed directly as the ratio of the price of its output to the consumer price level.

This model was estimated with two excess demand proxies; the percentage capacity utilisation index, CU, and its non-linear transformation, $NLCU$, which was calculated using Solow's method.[20] The results are given in Table 5.1, equations 5.17

Table 5.1

Equation number	Intercept	$\frac{1}{3}\sum_0^2 CU_{t-i}$	$NLCU_{-1}$	Δp^e_w	Δp^e_c	Δc^e	R^2	D.W.
(5.16)	−50·227 [2·243]	0·5251 [2·192]		−0·0868 [0·4353]	0·4180 [2·239]	0·8644 [3·684]	0·9125	2·48
(5.17)	−44·284 [2·574]	0·4621 [2·470]			0·3716 [2·473]	0·7733 [7·420]	0·9120	2·39
(5.18)	−0·2133 [2·622]		18·108 [2·133]		0·3602 [2·320]	0·7835 [7·291]	0·9067	2·47
(5.19)	−41·767 [2·365]	0·4347 [2·298]			0·2276 [—]	0·7724 [7·285]	0·8474	2·11
(5.20)	−0·0794 [2·879]		16·817 [1·967]		0·2169 [—]	0·7831 [7·184]	0·8391	2·22

Note: the dependent variable is Δp_w.

and 5.18. In both models, the estimated coefficients on the capacity utilisation and expectational variables are significantly different from zero at the five per cent level and have their expected sign. Furthermore, the sum of the estimated coefficients on the expectational variables is not significantly different from unity on the basis of a t-test at the five per cent level.[21] The magnitude of the estimated coefficient on the expected costs variable is at least twice that on expected consumer prices, indicating that supply side expectations of costs play a greater role than demand side expectations.[22]

Two further considerations, exchange rate adjustments and export prices, were examined. Dummy variables were added as additional regressors in an attempt to pick up any influence of exchange-rate changes which had not already been reflected in the other explanatory variables. Attempts were made to capture impact and continuation effects.[23] None of these variables was significant.[24] The expected rate of change of export prices was included as an additional regressor and was insignificantly different from zero, indicating international effects to be already captured in the model.[25]

This model was then re-estimated with the restriction that the sum of the coefficients on the expectational variables is unity (Table 5.1: equations 5.19 and 5.20). Imposing the restriction changes the estimated coefficients only slightly and improves the Durbin—Watson statistic. The average value over the estimation period of the natural level of capacity utilisation, CU^N, can be calculated from 5.19 or 5.20.[26] After removing the first quarter seasonal components from the estimated intercepts, estimates of CU^N can be calculated from

$$\hat{\alpha}_1 + \hat{\alpha}_2 \frac{1}{3} \sum_{i=0}^{2} CU_{t-i} = 0 \qquad (5.21)$$

and $\hat{\alpha}_1' + \hat{\alpha}_2' NLCU_{t-1} = 0$ $\qquad (5.22)$[27]

From equation 5.21, CU^N is estimated as 97·7 per cent. Equation 5.22 gives two estimates of CU^N, 97·4 per cent and 93·0 per cent.[28] Clearly, there are no *a priori* grounds for choosing between these estimates. Moreover, they are sensitive to the last few figures in the calculation and so it is probably unwise to choose between them. It is appropriate, however, to point out that the average level of capacity utilisation over the period 1965(1)-1971(4), CU^{AV}, is 96·93 per cent which is close to, but smaller than, two of the point estimates of CU^N.[29] This apparent domestic excess supply accompanying accelerating inflation is not inconsistent with the Phelps-Friedman hypothesis for a small, open, fixed-exchange-rate economy for two reasons. The specification of the capacity utilisation variable may only be an approximation to a true, non-linear, functional form. The higher estimate of CU^N is calculated from the linear capacity utilisation variable whereas with $NLCU$ the higher of the point estimates of CU^N is closer to CU^{AV}. However, this non-linear transformation may be mis-specified because when the variable is significant so is the intercept; with a correctly specified non-linear transformation an intercept would be insignificantly different from zero. Gray and Lipsey (1974) have shown that, in the present context, with a non-linear relationship between excess demand and capacity utilisation, if the level of capacity utilisation is on average at its natural rate but fluctuates about that equilibrium level then inflation will accelerate. In figure 5.2, a non-linear relationship between price change and the level of capacity utilisation, given inflation expectations of a zero rate, is depicted. That level of capacity utilisation at which the function cuts the horizontal axis is a natural level of capacity utilisation, CU^N, if the sum of the coefficients on the expectational variables is unity. In simple terms, if capacity utilisation bounces from CU_L to CU_H then the Gray–Lipsey analysis shows that the level of capacity utilisation which is compatible with a steady rate of inflation, CU^{NN}, is found by adjusting the average level of CU (and hence shifting CU_L and CU_H) until the line joining the points on the inflation-capacity utilisation function at CU_L and CU_H is

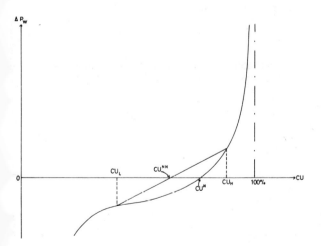

Figure 5.2 The equilibrium rate of capacity utilisation in a cyclical economy

bisected by the horizontal axis. The second reason that we may have domestic excess supply associated with accelerating inflation results from the international character of inflation. With domestic excess supply and assuming expectations are fully adjusted, world excess demand may raise United Kingdom inflation through its effect on price and cost expectations.

V CONCLUSIONS

This chapter has developed a theoretical model of price determination, based on conventional market analysis, in which the determinants of price inflation are excess demand and expectations of price and cost changes. The estimates of the model show that excess demand and expectations, appropriately measured, do indeed affect price inflation. Moreover, there is a trade-off between the rate of change of prices and the level of capacity utilisation in the short run but not in the long run in the United Kingdom manufacturing sector, indicating that in the short run the inflation rate may be changed by demand management policy.

Although this chapter has presented an alternative approach to that usually adopted in previous studies of price determination, there remains much further work to be done. In particular, it is now important that an expectations-augmented excess-demand model of price determination appropriate to a period of flexible exchange rates should be estimated. Moreover, if the natural level of capacity utilisation is not constant, then the factors affecting ' that variable need to be determined.

NOTES TO CHAPTER 5

[1]   I am greatly indebted to the editors of this volume for their helpful guidance, advice and criticisms. The responsibility for any errors is mine.
[2]   Godley and Nordhaus (1972), p. 853.
[3]   *Ibid.*, p. 869.
[4]   *Ibid.*, p. 873.
[5]   Lipsey (1960), p. 3, n. 3.
[6]   Arrow (1959), p. 43.
[7]   Chamberlin (1933), 5th edition, pp. 148-9.
[8]   Arrow (1959), p. 47.
[9]   If α_{i1}, α_{i2} and β_i are constant then the resultant aggregate coefficients are not unique and linear: the requirement of linear supply and demand functions is violated and the micro-coefficients themselves are non-linear transformations of parameters of the supply and demand functions.
[10]   Solow (1969), p. 10.
[11]   If the coefficient on capacity utilisation is significantly greater than zero and if the sum of the estimated coefficients on the expectational variables is significantly less than one, then there is a positive relationship between Δp_w and CU in the short run and in the long run.

12 Friedman (1968), p. 8.

13 *Ibid.*, p. 9.

14 $$\frac{P_t - P_{t-1}}{P_{t-1}} \approx ln \left[1 + \frac{P_t - P_{t-1}}{P_{t-1}} \right] = ln \, \frac{P_t}{P_{t-1}}$$

15 See Chapters Six and Seven respectively.

16 Rushdy and Lund (1967).

17 It is possible to derive expectational variables for alternative lead times from interest rate data, using the well-known Fisher equation, $i = r + \Delta p^e$, where i is the nominal (market) rate of interest, r is the real rate of interest and in which all variables refer to the same future time period, e.g., with three-month interest rates Δp^e is the rate of inflation expected for a three-month future period. A major problem is that the real rate of interest is unobservable and has to be proxied. In work for the United States economy, Gordon (1971) uses a simple macroeconomic model to substitute 'exogenous' components of real per capita aggregate demand, AD, for the real rate of interest and, with the assumption that the only information used in forming price expectations is a weighted average of past actual rates of inflation, estimates a model of the form

$$i_t = AD + \sum_{i=0}^{n} w_i \, \Delta p_{t-i} + u_t$$

using Almon's procedure to estimate the distributed lag on Δp_t. In which case,

$$\Delta p^e = \sum_{i=0}^{n} \hat{w}_i \, \Delta p_{t-i}$$

However, the appropriate price variable to use in this procedure is probably the price deflator of aggregate nominal money balances. This procedure would not be appropriate for deriving separate measures of price expectations for those on both sides of the market, and cost expectations.

18 During this time period, important exchange rate changes occurred on only five dates: 18 November 1967, £ sterling devalued; 8 August 1969, French franc devalued; 14 October 1969, Deutschemark revalued; 7 May 1971, Deutschemark floated; 9 May 1971, Swiss franc and Austrian schilling revalued.

19 The estimated coefficients on the seasonal dummy variables are not reported. The intercepts in Table 5.1 include first-quarter seasonal variation.

20 Solow (1969), pp. 10-11: $NLCU = (CU-\overline{CU})^2/100$, sgn $(CU-\overline{CU})$, where $\overline{CU}$ is the mean of CU. i.e. $NLCU \gtrless 0$ as $CU \gtrless \overline{CU}$.

21 The t-statistics for the test of the null hypothesis that the sum of the estimated coefficients on the expectations variables is unity are 1.33 for 5.17 and 1.28 for 5.18. A t-test is equivalent to an F-test under one restriction because $t_N \equiv \sqrt{F_{(1, N)}}$.

22 Equation 5.17 was re-estimated by maximum likelihood and assuming the error followed a first-order autoregressive scheme. The estimated autoregressive parameter was -0.23 and its asymptotic standard error 0.18, indicating it to be insignificantly different from zero. However, much

weight cannot be attached to this result because the sample is one of only 28 observations.

23   Because of the time taken for the effect of exchange rate changes to appear in published data, a one-period lag on the impact effect was also tried.

24   The fact that dummy variables representing once-and-for-all exchange-rate changes were insignificant does not mean that the model is appropriate to a period of floating exchange rates since under alternative exchange rate regimes the parameter estimates are expected to differ. The dummy variable for the continuation effect of the May 1971 exchange rate changes would also have captured any effect which the CBI voluntary price restraint, introduced 15 July 1971, may have had on prices in 1971.

25    $(\Delta pq^e - \Delta q^e)$ where Δpq^e is the expected rate of change of the value of exports, calculated from CBI surveys, and Δq^e is the expected rate of change of the volume of exports of manufacturing proxied by a distributed lag on Δq, was also tried. The alternative distributed lags used were

$$\sum_{i=0}^{n-i} \frac{2(n-i)}{n(n+1)} \Delta q_{-i} \text{ for } n = 2, \ldots 10$$

and

$$\sum_{i=0}^{\infty} (1-n) n^i \Delta q_{-i} \text{ for } n = 0 \cdot 1, \ldots, 0 \cdot 9$$

both with weights summing to unity. The variables were insignificantly different from zero.

26   CU^N is that value of CU which satisfies $g(CU) = 0$, given that the sum of the coefficients on the expectational variables is unity.

27   For 5.19, $\hat{\alpha}_1 = -42 \cdot 476$ and for 5.20, $\hat{\alpha}_1' = -0 \cdot 825$.

28   Using 5.22, $CU^N = \overline{CU} \pm ([-\hat{\alpha}_1'/\hat{\alpha}_2'] \cdot 100)^{1/2}$, where $\overline{CU}$ is 95·19, the mean of the Wharton-type index over the period 1958(4) - 1971(4).

29   Of course, the natural level of capacity utilisation may not be constant.

APPENDIX 5.1   THE PROCEDURE TO CALCULATE CAPACITY UTILISATION

In this appendix the method used to generate the Wharton-type capacity utilisation index is described. The first step is to inspect the time series of real output of manufacturing industry in order to identify full-capacity peaks. A peak period is defined as one in which output exceeds that of the immediately preceding quarter and of the two succeeding quarters. In the case of output peaks being on a plateau such that output exceeds that of the previous period but is greater than or equal to that of the two following periods, then the first peak is that which is selected. The Wharton school stress that the procedure should be used flexibly in that it is appropriate to use as much information as possible in identifying peaks. Here, the CBI Industrial Trends Survey is useful because included in it is the question: 'What factors are likely to limit your output over the next four months? Please tick the *most* important factor or factors.' The factors are classified as: plant capacity, orders or sales, skilled labour, credit or finance, materials and components, and other. By summing the number of responses over factors, it is possible to obtain some general information as to when capacity is highly utilised. Once identified, the peaks are joined by linear segments. In doing this however, the output index in any period may exceed its interpolated trend value, which implies capacity utilisation greater than 100 per cent, in which case a ray is drawn from the previous peak to the present value of the index, which then becomes an effective peak. The ray is the locus of full-capacity output and the capacity utilisation index at a given point in time is defined as the ratio of actual to full-capacity output.

Such a procedure readily provides a time series of capacity utilisation rates, although some of the assumptions implied by the method are not wholly realistic. It is assumed that plant capacity grows at one constant rate over several observations and then switches to a different constant rate over another period. Moreover, if a peak occurs at a lower level of output than a preceding peak, then that output is below full-capacity relative to the preceding peak yet it may be treated as full capacity. However, this latter problem did not occur in this study.

6   Consumers' price expectations[1]

John A. Carlson and Michael Parkin[2]

This paper shows how an estimate of the expected inflation rate
may be obtained from the qualitative data generated by surveys in
which respondents are asked whether they expect prices to rise,
fall or stay the same; it generates an expected-inflation time
series for the United Kingdom for the period 1961 to 1973 based on
a Gallup Poll monthly survey of the expectations of approximately
one thousand quota-sampled individuals and provides preliminary
tests of a variety of alternative hypotheses about how expectations
of inflation are formed.

The inflationary experience of many countries over the past
few years has served to emphasize the importance of expectations.
The most convincing explanations of the coexistence of high and
increasing unemployment with rapid and accelerating inflation contain an 'expectations hypothesis' that prices rise, in part, because
people expect them to rise. Theoretical discussions of this idea
can be found in Friedman (1968), Phelps (1968), Mortensen (1970)
and Lucas and Rapping (1969b). Empirical studies incorporating
an expectations-of- inflation variable have found it to be one of the
more important determinants of inflation. (See, for example,
Solow (1969), Turnovsky and Wachter (1972), Parkin (1970), Vanderkamp (1972), Andersen and Carlson (1972), Gordon (1972), Nordhaus
(1972b), Lucas and Rapping (1969a).) With the exception of Turnovsky and Wachter, these studies have had no means of independently
measuring expectations. Rather, they have postulated a scheme for
generating expectations in terms of observable variables and used
the hypothesized scheme to eliminate from the analysis the unobserved expected rate of inflation. Thus, two hypotheses have
been tested simultaneously and there has been no way of knowing
whether each sub-hypothesis taken alone would stand up.

It is particularly crucial in this case to avoid simultaneous
hypothesis testing since one of the matters on which information
is sought is the size of the coefficient relating the expected inflation rate to the actual rate. In the absence of money illusion, this
coefficient is predicted to be unity, implying no trade-off between
inflation and the level of economic activity (and the rate of unem-

ployment) in the long run. Using arbitrary weighting schemes to generate an expected inflation rate from past values of actual inflation enables any value to be estimated for that crucial coefficient, thus clouding the issue, at the empirical level, as to the existence or otherwise of a long-run trade-off (Saunders and Nobay, 1972). An independent series for the expected rate of inflation could help disentangle the possible relationships at work and potentially settle that crucial question. Further, it would permit an examination of the process whereby expectations of inflation are themselves generated.

The policy implications of these questions are of crucial importance. If there is no long-run trade-off between inflation and unemployment then policies which are designed to hold the level of unemployment below its equilibrium rate will inevitably lead to accelerating inflation. Further, if the actual inflation rate depends partly on expectations, then means of lowering those expectations are potentially useful devices for controlling inflation. If it turns out that expectations of inflation are determined primarily by previous actual inflationary experience and that other events have at best a transitory effect (as is implicit in the expectations—generating schemes usually used) then the process of stopping or even slowing down inflation becomes a difficult matter. If, alternatively, such devices as wage—price guidelines or exhortation affect expectations in an important and lasting way, then they become useful instruments of inflation control.

There are then three matters which need attention. First, obtaining a time series of the expected rate of inflation; second, a study of the determination of those expectations and third, a study of the role of expectations in generating actual inflation. This paper addresses the first two of these questions (the third question has been examined by Parkin, Sumner and Ward, 1976). In Section 6.I we develop a means for obtaining an expected inflation-rate series. Although we are dealing exclusively with a survey of expected price changes, our approach is general and may prove useful to others who would like to analyse surveys in which each response is classified into one of four categories, such as 'higher', 'lower', 'no change' and 'don't know'. A number of problems associated with deriving our own series for the expected rate of inflation in the United Kingdom are discussed in detail and the series itself is given at the end of the paper. In Section 6.II we provide preliminary tests of alternative hypotheses about the generation of inflation expectations. In particular, we examine error-learning hypotheses and the role of additional information not contained in the past behaviour of the price level.

Broadly our conclusions can be summarised as follows. First, when the inflation rate is high, expected inflation may be viewed as being generated by an error-learning process in which the previous

two errors are important. This suggests that people look at both
the rate of inflation and its rate of change in forming their expectations. Secondly, when inflation rates are modest expectations
seem to be purely autoregressive. Thirdly, the only variable other
than the past behaviour of the inflation rate itself which appears
significantly to influence expectations is the exchange rate. A devaluation has a dramatic impact effect on the expected inflation
rate. Fourthly, such variables as wage—price guidelines, large
highly publicized wage settlements, indirect tax changes and
political factors appear to have no significant effect on expectations of inflation.

I A NEW APPROACH TO QUALITATIVE SURVEY DATA AND MEASUREMENT OF EXPECTED INFLATION

Our first task is to show how *quantitative* information about expected inflation may be obtained from a survey of people's expectations about the *direction* of price change: we use the term
'quantitative' in the sense that the series derived has the same
dimensionality as measures of the actual rate of inflation, namely,
a percentage rate of change per year. Every month since July
1960 the Gallup Poll has interviewed approximately one thousand
people in Great Britain selected on a stratified quota basis and
asked whether they think prices will go up, go down or stay the
same over the next six months. (The exact sample size fluctuated
and dropped below one thousand in some of the early months of
the exercise.) Proportions of the total response in month t have
been computed (rounded to the nearest one per cent) for each of
four categories as follows: 'go up', A_t; 'go down', B_t; 'stay the
same', C_t; 'don't know', D_t. There is evidently a variety of opinion.
Each month more than 50 per cent of the people sampled said that
they expected prices to go up. With the exception of five months
there have always been some who say they expect prices to go
down. There has never been a month in which every respondent
fell into the same category. Thus, our starting point is the set of
data A_t, B_t, C_t, and D_t, with t starting in January 1961 and ending in
December 1973. (The detailed results of the survey are confidential and cannot be reported in this paper. From the published
expected inflation series the reader cannot work back to the $A_t, B_t,$
C_t and D_t data.)

   In order to convert these data into an expected inflation rate
series we need to make some assumptions. We begin by assuming
that, of the people questioned, some fraction α_t are incapable of
developing any view about what will happen to prices, while the
fraction $1 - \alpha_t$ are capable of giving and do in fact give a positive
reaction of some kind.

Those who are incapable of forming a view are assumed consistently to be classified as 'don't know' but not necessarily to exhaust that category, i.e.

$$0 \le \alpha_t \le D_t.$$

Those who are capable of a positive reaction to the question are assumed to behave as follows. First, they suppose they are being asked about the behaviour over the next six months of the price index of their own bundle of commodities. Secondly, each respondent forms his own subjective probability distribution of the percentage change in this index over the next six months. Let x denote the percentage change in the individual's price index over the next six months, and $f_t(x)$ the subjective probability density function of x for a respondent during month t. This subjective distribution may vary across individuals and may change from one month to another. Thirdly, there is a range of price change about zero which the respondent cannot distinguish from zero. This range of imperceptibility is what experimental psychologists have called the difference limen, which is defined as 'the increment in physical stimulus necessary to produce a just noticeable difference in sensation' (Osgood (1953), p. 49). It may be objected that prices are completely unlike the other physical stimuli studied by experimental psychologists and that since prices are discrete variables, an individual can never be in any doubt as to whether one price is higher, lower or the same as some other price. However, it will be recalled that the individual is being asked to consider changes in a price index constructed from a bundle of commodities, some of whose prices may rise, some fall and some remain unchanged. It will at times be difficult for the individual to know whether, on the average, the current or expected future prices of the goods which he buys are higher or lower. Let δ denote the percentage that corresponds to a just perceptible expected price rise and $-\delta$ to a just perceptible expected price fall. Hence, at time t, the range of imperceptibility is $-\delta_t$ to δ_t. Finally, each individual answers the question on the basis of the balance of probabilities; that is on the basis of a fair bet. Specifically, the individual answers as follows: (i) 'up' if more than one half of the distribution $f_t(x)$ exceeds δ_t; (ii) 'down' if more than one half of the distribution $f_t(x)$ is below $-\delta_t$; (iii) 'no change' if more than one half of the distribution $f_t(x)$ lies between $-\delta_t$ and δ_t; (iv) 'don't know' if less than one half of the distribution $f_t(x)$ lies in any of those three ranges. More formally, the responses are:

'prices up' if $m_t \ge \delta_t$

'prices down' if $m_t \le -\delta_t$

'no change' if $-\delta_t < m_t < \delta_t$ and $Pr(-\delta_t < m_t < \delta_t) \geq \frac{1}{2}$

'don't know' if $-\delta_t < m_t < \delta_t$ and $Pr(-\delta_t < m_t < \delta_t) < \frac{1}{2}$

where m_t is the median of $f_t(x)$, i.e. $Pr(x < m_t) = \frac{1}{2}$.

Now consider the population as a whole and define the expected rate of inflation as the mean of the median of each individual's subjective distribution of possible inflation rates during the next six months. We assume that δ_t is common to all individuals. Since the sample size is large, A_t, B_t, C_t and D_t will be treated as good approximations to the true population proportions and substituted for those population values. With these assumptions and definitions we are ready to proceed with the derivation of formulae for the mean and standard deviation of the probability distribution of expected inflation each month.

From our assumptions, it is clear that

$$A_t = (1 - \alpha_t)Pr(m_t \geq \delta_t) \tag{6.1}$$

$$B_t = (1 - \alpha_t)Pr(m_t \leq -\delta_t) \tag{6.2}$$

$$C_t + D_t = (1 - \alpha_t)Pr(-\delta_t < m_t < \delta_t) + \alpha_t \tag{6.3}$$

It is convenient to change m into the variable y with zero mean and unit standard deviation by the transformation $y = (m - \Delta p^e)/\sigma$, whereupon 6.1 and 6.2 become

$$A_t = (1 - \alpha_t)Pr(y_t \geq a_t) \tag{6.4}$$

and

$$B_t = (1 - \alpha_t)Pr(y_t \leq b_t) \tag{6.5}$$

with a_t and b_t given by

$$a_t = \frac{\delta_t - \Delta p_t^e}{\sigma_t} \tag{6.6}$$

and

$$b_t = \frac{-\delta_t - \Delta p_t^e}{\sigma_t} \tag{6.7}$$

Equations 6. 6 and 6. 7 can be 'solved' for p_t^e and σ_t to give

$$\Delta p_t^e = -\delta_t \left(\frac{a_t + b_t}{a_t - b_t}\right) \tag{6.8}$$

$$\sigma_t = 2\delta_t \left(\frac{1}{a_t - b_t}\right) \tag{6.9}$$

To use formula (6. 8) to compute Δp_t^e we need four pieces of information: (i) the survey results A_t, B_t; (ii) the value of α_t; (iii) the form of the distribution of expected inflation across the population; (iv) the value of δ_t. We have the first and must address the problem of obtaining the remaining items.

To obtain a measure of α_t, we begin by postulating that an incapacity to form any view about future price change will be mainly a function of IQ and related variables. Further, since such variables may be presumed to change only slowly over time, we suppose α_t to be a constant, α. Now it is possible that $\alpha = 0$. If this were so, the response 'don't know' (fraction D_t) would differ from the response 'no change' only because of different dispersions of individuals' subjective distributions. In such a case, we might expect to find the relation,

$$D_t = \beta C_t + u_t \qquad \beta > 0$$

where u_t is sampling noise.

If, however, α is not zero, these must be added to the don't know proportion to give,

$$D_t = \alpha + \beta C_t + u_t$$

We maintained this hypothesis and obtained, measuring D_t and C_t as *percentages:*

	α	β	$\overline{R}^2$	d
Coefficient	2·537	0·207	0·58	1·454
t-ratio	9·68	13·55		

The Durbin—Watson statistic, d, indicates the presence of first-order autocorrelation in the residuals of this equation and could be regarded as evidence against our assumption of a constant α. However, in view of the exploratory nature of our study and in the absence of a theory about the determination of α, we simply reestimated the parameters specifying,

$$u_t = \rho u_{t-1} + \epsilon_t$$

and obtained

	α	β	ρ	$\overline{R}^2$
Coefficient	2·539	0·201	0·494	0·61
Ratio of coefficient to asymptotic standard error	3·18	6·70	12·05	

It is clear that α is estimated at 2·5 per cent, which is significant at the 0·05 level, although the significance is artificially enhanced by the first-order autocorrelation in the first-quoted ordinary least squares result. It is interesting to note that 2·5 per cent of the population have (by definition of course) IQs of less than two standard deviations below the mean. The use of $\alpha = 2·5$ raises a problem in that on eight occasions D_t was less than this. In those cases, we took $\alpha_t = D_t$ for computational purposes.

Next we make an assumption about the form of the distribution of inflation expectations across the population. Specifically, we assume this to be normal. Since the investigation is largely an exploratory attempt to obtain a quantitative series for expected inflation, we want a distribution which is computationally easy to handle and which has a mean and variance. Furthermore, since respondents to the survey are exposed to similar information and public prognostications, we would expect at any given time a uni-modal distribution around the 'consensus' rate. With more information than we have available, this assumption would be tested explicitly, as Carlson (1975) has done with other data.

Last we need an estimate of the difference limen, δ_t. Attempts to quantify difference limen experimentally have found a notable regularity known as Weber's Law, which Osgood (1953, p. 75) states as 'The fraction by which a stimulus must be increased (or decreased) in order for the change to be just perceptible is constant regardless of the absolute magnitude of the stimulus'. Osgood goes on to point out that empirically this does not hold precisely for all ranges of stimuli, but that over large ranges, the law is essentially valid. Further, it should be noted that Weber's Law has only previously been applied to 'basic' stimuli such as sound, sight and touch. In contrast to these stimuli, a price index (and its rate of change) is a complex, value-laden stimulus to which different individuals may have a different degree of exposure and for which the time scale is different from the 'basic' stimuli to which the law has been applied. However, mainly for simplicity and partly in the absence of evidence to the contrary, we postulate that, on average, the absolute change in prices that is just noticeable to an observer over a specified time period is proportional to the level of prices. In other words, the percentage change in a price index that is just perceptible to the typical individual may be treated as constant.

This could be studied by experimental techniques, but, until refuted by empirical evidence, we shall accept this hypothesised property, and further, we shall assume that the property holds for expectations about future price changes. There is a range of plus or minus δ per cent that is equivalent to an expectation of no change, and (6. 8) becomes

$$\Delta p_t^e = -\delta \left(\frac{a_t + b_t}{a_t - b_t} \right)$$

with δ now constant. Given the assumptions that we have made about δ and the distribution of expectations across the population and given the A_t, B_t data, the value of $(a_t + b_t)/(a_t - b_t)$ can be computed. Hence, the role of δ is simply to scale Δp_t^e. We achieve this scaling by making the average value of Δp^e over the sample equal to the actual rate of inflation of the retail price index, Δp, over the same period, i.e.,

$$-\hat{\delta} = \sum_{t=1}^{T} \Delta p_t \Big/ \sum_{t=1}^{T} \left(\frac{a_t + b_t}{a_t - b_t} \right)$$

where

$$\Delta p_t = \frac{P_t - P_{t-12}}{P_{t-12}} \times 100$$

and P_t is the retail price index reported for month t. The value of δ̂ obtained by this procedure is 1·764, which at least has the virtue of plausibility.

In their wage studies of the United States, Eckstein and Brinner (1972) use 2·5 per cent as a threshold-expected inflation rate. It could be argued that our method of estimating is only appropriate in a regularly cyclical economy and that one which has a seen a trend in its inflation rate such as the United Kingdom has experienced would have Δp^e lagging behind Δp and hence δ will be biased upwards. As a check on this, we split our sample between January 1961 to June 1967 and July 1967 to December 1973 and obtained

$$\hat{\delta}_1 = 1 \cdot 853 \ (1961 - 67)$$

$$\hat{\delta}_2 = 1 \cdot 719 \ (1967 - 71)$$

Whilst these are not equal to each other, neither are they far from the mean of 1·764 for the entire sample, although a formal test of the equality of the three estimates is difficult, given the way we have defined δ. Also, there is no indication that the different estimates are arising from the fact that the actual inflation rate began to accelerate in the later part of the 1960s. If this were the source of the difference, it would have biased the value of δ_2 upwards above that of δ_1.

There is one final problem. As we remarked when describing the data there are five months in the sample when B_t is zero. With a normal distribution of expectations the probability of this occurrence is zero and hence the normality assumption is apparently called into question. However, the basic A, B data with which we are working are supplied rounded to the nearest integer, hence, $B = 0$ in our data base means that true B is less than 0·5 and not necessarily zero. We could have made some arbitrary assumption about the true value of B in the range $0 < B < 0·5$ but the estimated Δp^e is extremely sensitive to the particular value chosen. Instead of following this procedure we utilised some information contained in the sample but unfortunately not reportable because of the confidential nature of the raw data, concerning the dispersion of expectations. It is clear from equation (6.9) that our assumptions enable us to compute an estimate of the population standard deviation, σ, of inflation expectations (provided $B \neq 0$). If we had an estimate of σ for those months in which $B = 0$ we could compute Δp_t^e as

$$\Delta p_t^e = \delta - a_t \sigma_t$$

Inspection of σ_t showed that, on either side of a month in which $B = 0$ the standard deviation was approximately equal except in one case. In the case where the standard deviation changed, it rose sharply, the month in question being November 1967 during which sterling was devalued. It seemed plausible to us that the devaluation brought an increase in inflation expectations but also an increase in confusion and hence disagreement. We therefore assumed that the higher post-devaluation standard deviation applied to the month of devaluation as well. Although from an arithmetic point of view it makes virtually no difference in the other cases, we assumed the higher of the two adjacent standard deviations to apply to those months also and used the above formula to compute Δp^e.

This completes the discussion of the mechanics of obtaining our expected inflation series. The results are given in Appendix 6.1 and plotted in Figure 6.1 alongside the actual rate of inflation of the retail price index. The series clearly has some interesting features. First, it is apparently noisier than the actual inflation rate. This could well be arising from sampling fluctuations. Secondly, the series in broad terms seems to correspond well with

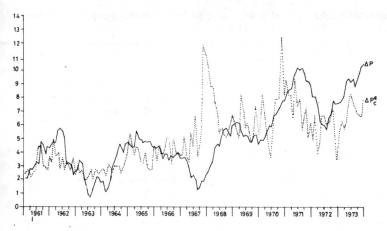

Figure 6.1 Actual and expected rate of inflation, 1961-73

the actual inflation rate. Through the two cycles from 1961 to 1967, the expected inflation rate follows the actual rate but with a cycle which has a smaller amplitude. Also, through the second of these cycles the expected rate seems to be at the beginning of a trend increase which, with some notable departures, is continued to the end of 1970. The most notable of these departures occurs in the final months of 1967 when the expected rate shoots up to 11 per cent. Throughout 1971, even while the actual inflation rate was increasing, the expected rate began to decline. It would be possible to discuss possible explanations for these movements in an impressionistic manner. Rather than do this, we attempt, in the next section, a systematic analysis of the forces at work.

II THE DETERMINANTS OF EXPECTED INFLATION

Now that we have obtained a series for the expected inflation rate we want to deal with the question: how are expectations formed? More precisely, can we 'explain' variations in the expected inflation rate? The work reported in this section should be regarded as illustrative of the use to which the newly available expectations data may be put rather than a comprehensive attempt to answer the above questions.

Possibly the most commonly used hypothesis about inflation expectations is that they adjust in proportion to the last recorded error—the adaptive expectations hypothesis. Writing Δp_t^e as the expectation formed at t for $t + 1$ and Δp_t as the actual rate of inflation at t, this may be written

$$\Delta p_t^e - \Delta p_{t-1}^e = \lambda(\Delta p_t - \Delta p_{t-1}^e). \tag{6.10}$$

A slightly more sophisticated error-learning mechanism would take account of both the recent rate of inflation and its rate of change. This could be captured by postulating that people adapt to the size of the previous two errors, i.e.

$$\Delta p_t^e - \Delta p_{t-1}^e = \lambda_0(\Delta p_t - \Delta p_{t-1}^e) + \lambda_1(\Delta p_{t-1} - \Delta p_{t-2}^e) \tag{6.11}$$

This formulation is suggested by the work of Rose (1972). In an experimental study of sales forecasts, Carlson (1967) found that subjects soon became aware of second-order adjustments in the sales series being forecasted. Each of these error-learning hypotheses can be reformulated to show that current expectations are a distributed lag function of past actual inflation and independent of other variables.

However, it may be the case that other variables are also important determinants of inflation expectations. Further, if expectations are to be influenced independently of previous inflation then other variables which are capable of independent control must be shown to have an effect. Two considerations suggest other variables whose influence deserves examination. First, economic theory indicates variables which might affect a rational person's expectation of inflation. Secondly, government policy aimed at controlling inflation via expectations suggests variables which, rightly or wrongly, may be believed to influence actual (and hence expected) inflation. In the former category are changes in the foreign exchange rate and changes in the political party in power. Exchange rate changes will affect expectations of inflation independently of the recent inflationary history provided that individuals are rational, and provided that previous inflation did not lead them to anticipate the exchange rate change. Changes in the political party in power will affect expectations independently of the recent inflation history if people believe one party to be less concerned to control inflation than the other. In the second category are wage—price controls, voluntary price restraint, large and highly publicised wage increases and changes in indirect taxes. It is clearly of some importance to establish whether or not any of these variables have had an effect on inflationary expectations since government policy has relied on each of them at various times in recent years and repeatedly espouses the first.

We conducted a large number of experiments measuring each of the above six factors with a variety of qualitative and quantitative dummy variables designed to capture their impact and con-

Table 6.1 Estimates of the determinants of expected inflation

Equation	Time period	Constant	Δp_t	Δp_{t-1}	Δp_{t-1}^e	Δp_{t-2}^e	D	$\bar{R}^2$	h	F
6.12	'Entire' March 1961–Dec.1973	0·618 (2·57)	0·132 (2·92)		0·745 (15·14)		6·340 (5·69)	0·75	−3·159	
6.13		0·560 (2·32)	0·300 (1·62)	−0·201 (1·10)	0·597 (8·08)	0·191 (2·56)	6·527 (5·95)	0·76	−2·372	
6.14	'Low inflation' March 1961–June 1967	1·005 (2·67)	0·038 (0·24)	0·043 (0·26)	0·390 (3·30)	0·237 (1·87)		0·35		3·73
6.15	'High inflation' July 1967–Dec.1973	2·472 (3·33)	0·755 (2·20)	−0·719 (2·11)	0·544 (5·31)	0·040 (0·38)	5·759 (4·33)	0·48	−0·847	
6.16			0·340 (3·50)	−0·196 (2·03)	0·660	0·196	6·583 (4·77)	0·48	−0·625	4·28

Note: The dependent variable in all equations is Δp_t^e, D is the devaluation dummy variable taking the value 1 in November 1967 and zero elsewhere, t-ratios are given in parentheses, and h is Durbin's (1970) test statistic for autocorrelation when lagged dependent variables are present, which could not be calculated in one case. The F statistic for lines 3 and 4 provides a test of the hypothesis of common regression coefficients for the two sub-samples, and that in line 5 tests the hypothesis that the restrictions implied by the error-learning formulation (6.11) are true: the corresponding critical values at the 0·05 level are 2·21 and 2·74 respectively.

tinuing effects on expectations. We attempted to discover such
effects both as the only set of factors affecting expectations and as
factors augmenting an error-learning process. We also examined
the pure error-learning processes 6.10 and 6.11. We restrict our-
selves here to reporting only in general terms the experiments
with other variables which turned out to be negative, but we discuss
our results on error-learning mechanisms and one positive finding
concerning the role of devaluation more fully.

Our principal negative results on the role of the six factors
listed above are as follows (see Appendix 6.2 for full details).
First, the political party in power, wage—price controls, highly
publicised wage settlements, and changes in indirect taxes all
appear to have trivial and totally insignificant effects on expectations. Secondly, we found an insignificant two per cent point reduction in the expected rate of inflation in July 1970 which might
be attributed to the election campaign of that year during which the
newly elected Prime Minister had promised to cut prices 'at a
stroke'. Thirdly, following the Confederation of British Industry's
voluntary price restraint introduced in July 1971, there was an
almost significant one per cent point reduction in expectations
which continued through the rest of 1971.

In contrast, the sterling devaluation of November 1967 had a
strong and significant impact effect (but no discernible continuing
effect) on the expected rate of inflation. We take this into account
therefore in our discussion of the performance of the various
error-learning hypotheses.

A selection of our results is presented in Table 6.1. The first
equation is an unconstrained formulation of the first-order error-
learning hypothesis 6.10. Both the actual and previous expected
rate of inflation enter this equation with coefficients which have
t-ratios greater than two and which sum to $0 \cdot 877$ (as compared
with unity in the *a priori* specification). However, the h statistic
indicates the presence of negative autocorrelation and hence
leaves us unable to make firm inferences about the coefficients in
this model. (It is possible that the source of this negative autocorrelation is the sampling error in the p^e series, which is ignored
in these regression estimates.) An unconstrained version of the
second-order error-learning model is presented in line 2. It is
apparent that in this case the negative autocorrelation is less
troublesome although it still cannot be rejected at the 5 per cent
level. Here the coefficients on the previous actual inflation rate
fade out and the purely autoregressive structure of inflation expectations dominates. The next two equations consider the second-
order error-learning hypothesis but split the sample between the
first half which had very gentle inflation and the second half in
which inflation became much higher. It is clear that these two sub-
samples are different from each other. In the first half when in-

flation rates were low (line 3), expectations were apparently dominated by an autoregressive process. However, during the second half (when inflation rates were high) the behaviour of the actual rate of inflation apparently had a significant effect on expectations. For this 'high inflation' sub-sample we thought it interesting to test explicitly the error-learning restrictions embodied in 6.11. The result of this is given in line 5. It is clear that, for this sub-period, those restrictions are rejected. However, expectations are significantly influenced by current actual inflation.

The effect of the sterling devaluation of November 1967 is shown by the coefficient of D. It is clear that this effect comes out at approximately six per cent regardless of the specification employed.

To summarise, these results suggest that when inflation is rapid, expectations approximate a second-order error-learning process, whilst when inflation is mild, expectations approximate an autoregressive scheme. In the sample period the only additional variable to have had any significant impact on the expected inflation rate is the devaluation of the exchange rate. Here we get a well-determined and robust estimate that the 1967 devaluation raised the expected inflation rate by 6 per cent at an annual rate.

The policy implication of these results, if correct, is an unwelcome one. To reduce the expected rate of inflation it is necessary to reduce the actual rate of inflation. Such a reduction would lower inflationary expectations through the error-learning process and, eventually perhaps, by permitting (forcing) an up-valuation of the currency. None of the other factors we have studied, with the possible exception of voluntary price restraint, seems to have a measurable effect; hence manipulating them will be of little or even no value.

NOTES TO CHAPTER 6

[1]   This paper was originally published in *Economica* (NS), vol. 42, May 1975, pp. 123-38. Appendix 6.2 has not been published previously.
[2]   We are grateful to the Social Science Research Council for financial support and to the Gallup Poll for making available the results of their monthly consumer attitude surveys. Work on this paper was begun while Carlson was Research Fellow in Economic Statistics at the University of Manchester and continued while Parkin was visiting Professor of Economics at Brown University. Both authors gratefully acknowledge the facilities provided by their respective hosts. Earlier versions of the paper have been given at too many seminars to list, and helpful comments given by too many people to name. We would, however, like to thank especially our colleagues in the Manchester Inflation Workshop, Malcolm Gray, David Rose, Gene Savin, Michael Sumner and also the referees and editors of *Economica*. We would also like to thank Nigel Duck, Clive Stones and Robert Ward who have provided assistance with data handling and computing.

APPENDIX 6.1 The actual and expected inflation series

		Δp	Δp^e			Δp	Δp^e
1961:	Jan.	2·184	2·422	*1965:*	Jan.	4·585	5·446
	Feb.	2·184	2·601		Feb.	4·485	4·433
	Mar.	2·735	2·372		Mar.	4·468	3·855
	Apr.	2·720	2·405		Apr.	5·561	4·433
	May	2·992	2·789		May	5·047	4·244
	June	3·336	3·372		June	4·935	3·372
	July	3·150	4·433		July	4·935	3·226
	Aug.	4·801	4·433		Aug.	4·731	3·904
	Sept.	4·525	3·020		Sept.	4·824	2·874
	Oct.	3·860	2·916		Oct.	4·819	2·708
	Nov.	4·468	2·736		Nov.	4·412	2·736
	Dec.	4·367	3·600		Dec.	4·487	4·445
1962:	Jan.	4·630	3·342	*1966:*	Jan.	4·384	3·305
	Feb.	4·735	4·904		Feb.	4·475	4·577
	Mar.	4·780	3·742		Mar.	4·277	3·904
	Apr.	5·677	3·904		Apr.	3·571	3·925
	May	5·709	2·823		May	3·915	4·489
	June	5·504	3·547		June	3·904	5·210
	July	5·094	2·736		July	3·461	4·904
	Aug.	3·181	3·386		Aug.	3·897	3·203
	Sept.	3·258	2·961		Sept.	3·628	5·013
	Oct.	2·978	2·708		Oct.	3·802	3·904
	Nov.	2·322	3·519		Nov.	3·961	3·925
	Dec.	2·649	2·422		Dec.	3·681	3·756
1963:	Jan.	2·700	3·026	*1967:*	Jan.	3·675	3·897
	Feb.	3·497	2·563		Feb.	3·671	5·210
	Mar.	3·184	2·709		Mar.	3·490	3·600
	Apr.	2·061	2·084		Apr.	3·017	3·372
	May	1·663	2·084		May	2·226	5·446
	June	0·972	2·296		June	2·391	4·489
	July	0·780	2·789		July	2·230	6·655
	Aug.	1·378	2·041		Aug.	1·364	3·782
	Sept.	1·773	2·789		Sept.	1·452	4·506
	Oct.	2·268	2·736		Oct.	1·959	6·261
	Nov.	2·161	2·496		Nov.	1·948	11·877
	Dec.	1·857	2·632		Dec.	2·451	11·093
1964:	Jan.	1·947	2·736	*1968:*	Jan.	2·616	10·240
	Feb.	1·158	2·281		Feb.	3·035	8·807
	Mar.	1·446	3·135		Mar.	3·373	8·807
	Apr.	2·019	2·918		Apr.	4·435	7·821
	May	2·984	2·563		May	4·606	7·088
	June	3·369	3·014		June	4·587	5·471
	July	3·969	3·014		July	5·285	5·791
	Aug.	4·660	3·056		Aug.	5·719	5·471
	Sept.	4·356	2·496		Sept.	5·892	5·161
	Oct.	4·050	2·961		Oct.	5·597	5·446
	Nov.	4·615	3·411		Nov.	5·233	5·835
	Dec.	4·798	4·082		Dec.	5·941	6·784

Appendix 6.1—continued

		Δp	Δp^e			Δp	Δp^e
1969:	Jan.	6·168	6·261	*1972:*	Jan.	8·163	4·913
	Feb.	6·219	5·835		Feb.	8·119	6·756
	Mar.	6·281	5·161		Mar.	7·584	3·844
	Apr.	5·529	8·290		Apr.	6·307	4·756
	May	5·284	7·150		May	6·136	6·712
	June	5·343	5·835		June	6·092	6·756
	July	5·259	6·261		July	5·799	6·049
	Aug.	4·853	5·471		Aug.	6·568	6·209
	Sept.	5·087	4·881		Sept.	7·010	6·809
	Oct.	5·380	5·471		Oct.	7·864	7·275
	Nov.	5·367	7·446		Nov.	7·629	4·934
	Dec.	4·673	5·471		Dec.	7·653	3·544
1970:	Jan.	4·957	6·784	*1973:*	Jan.	7·736	5·698
	Feb.	4·931	8·290		Feb.	7·885	6·280
	Mar.	5·142	6·784		Mar.	8·172	5·886
	Apr.	5·619	5·471		Apr.	9·209	6·209
	May	6·084	5·471		May	9·471	7·241
	June	5·905	3·697		June	9·285	8·336
	July	6·662	6·185		July	9·440	7·938
	Aug.	6·829	7·911		Aug.	8·882	7·479
	Sept.	7·035	7·911		Sept.	9·255	6·828
	Oct.	7·357	11·201		Oct.	9·899	6·711
	Nov.	7·865	12·400		Nov.	10·337	6·711
	Dec.	7·887	8·290		Dec.	10·576	7·885
1971:	Jan.	8·487	9·320				
	Feb.	8·517	8·290				
	Mar.	8·759	8·290				
	Apr.	9·418	6·655				
	May	9·821	9·470				
	June	10·293	7·446				
	July	10·149	7·908				
	Aug.	10·298	5·716				
	Sept.	9·894	6·655				
	Oct.	9·371	7·446				
	Nov.	9·236	5·161				
	Dec.	9·034	6·261				

APPENDIX 6.2 The influence of other variables on inflation expectations

(a) Introduction

In this appendix we report the results of an investigation of the effects of variables other than the past history of the actual inflation rate on inflation expectations.

Two considerations have guided our choice of other variables. First, economic theory suggests variables which might affect actual inflation and, hence, which might affect a rational person's expectation of it. Secondly, government policy aimed at controlling inflation via expectations suggests variables which, rightly or wrongly, may be believed to influence actual (and hence expected) inflation.

In the former category are:

(i)   changes in the foreign exchange rate;

(ii) changes in the political party in power.

Exchange rate changes will affect expectations of inflation independently of the recent inflationary history provided that individuals are rational, and provided that the previous inflation did not lead them to anticipate the exchange rate change. Changes in the political party in power will affect expectations independently of the recent inflation history if people believe one party to be less concerned to control inflation and more inclined to create an excess money supply and fiscal deficit than the other.

In the second category are:

(iii) wage-price controls/guidelines (or norms);

(iv) voluntary price restraint;

(v)   large and highly publicised wage increases;

(vi) changes in indirect taxes.

It is clearly of some importance to establish whether or not any of these variables have an effect on inflationary expectations. Government policy has relied on each of them at various times in recent years and repeatedly espouses the first. Wage-price guidelines/controls presumably could work (in principle) by reducing people's expectations of inflation and thereby reducing the actual wage and price increases implemented. We can, with our expected inflation series, test whether or not such policies do, in fact, have any effect on expectations. Voluntary price restraint has not been common but a recent pledge by the CBI to limit price rises to not more than five per cent in any one year was widely acclaimed as a contributor to the fall in the inflation rate in the United Kingdom through the latter part of 1971 and early 1972. The anti-inflation policy of the Conservative government elected in June 1970, before it too was converted to a belief in the efficacy of wage-price controls, concentrated on the last two factors to be considered. The belief that inflation was being caused by the inflationary expectations set up by large and highly publicised wage increases (especially in the public sector) led to the policy of what came to be known as 'union bashing'. This involved heavy government pressure on employers (mainly public sector employers where the pressure could take the form of real threats) to resist claims for increases which exceeded some target rate chosen so as gradually to reduce the actual inflation rate. The final variable, indirect tax changes, featured very heavily in the 1970 election campaign and is presumably what the then leader of the opposition had in mind when he promised to 'cut inflation at a stroke'. Do any of these variables have an effect on the expected inflation rate?

In order to test whether any of the six variables have any effect we must first decide how to measure the variables and second choose some appropriate form in which to look for any effects. First, we discuss the measurement problem.

(i) Exchange-rate changes. For the period with which we are working, January 1961 to December 1971, there was only one exchange-rate change, a devaluation of 14·7 per cent on 18 November 1967. We characterise the devaluation with two dummy variables,

D_1 = 1 for November 1967

= 0 elsewhere

and

D_2 = 0 to, and including November 1967

= 1 from, and including, December 1967.

This construction will enable us to examine whether the event of devaluation (D_1) had any impact on the expected inflation rate and also whether expectations were different after the event than before it (D_2).

(ii) Change in political party in power. We again used binary dummy variables to represent elections and changes in the party in power. These took the form:

E_{1i} = 1 for the month following a general election

= 0 elsewhere

i = 1 for 1964 election

= 2 for 1966 election

= 3 for 1970 election

E_2 = 1 when a Labour government is in office

= 0 when a Conservative government in office

(iii) Incomes policy/wage–price controls and guidelines. Incomes policies vary in a number of potentially important dimensions. Some are statutory, some voluntary but with varying degrees of 'moral suasion'. Some involve wages alone, some prices alone and some both. Some aim to reduce the inflation rate by a large margin and others by a little. A qualitative consideration of the various phases of incomes policy in our sample period led us to conclude that there were five sub-periods, sufficiently different from each other to be treated as different policies. These were:

1. July 1961 to March 1962 (Selwyn Lloyd's 'pay pause')

2. April 1962 to March 1963 (2·5 per cent for wage increases)

3. April 1963 to June 1966 (3·5 per cent 'guiding light')

4. July 1966 to December 1966 ('Freeze')

5. January 1967 and November 1969 ('severe restraint')

Each sub-period was characterised by two dummy variables:

I_{i1} = 1 for month in which new policy was introduced

= 0 elsewhere

I_{i2} = 0 up to, and including, month in which new policy was introduced

= 1 from month after new policy was introduced

i $= 1$ (1961-62 phase)

   $= 2$ (1962-63 phase)

   $= 3$ (1963-66 phase)

   $= 4$ (1966-67 phase)

   $= 5$ (1967-69 phase)

Additionally, we thought it worthwhile attempting to measure incomes policies in quantitative terms. To do this we use the variable:

$\Delta w^* =$ wage change 'norm' (or guideline)

For periods when an official 'norm' was in force, Δw^* took that value. When a range was in force we used the mid point. 'Freeze' and 'Pause' were taken to imply $\Delta w^* = 0$. When no norm was announced, Δw^* took the value of the actual rate of change of the index of weekly wage rates. There is room for disagreement about the period after December 1969. We decided to treat it as if the last Labour government's incomes policy ended at that time. In addition, we define two variables designed to allow for the possibility that the effects of incomes policies depend on the extent to which the norm (guideline) departs from the current actual rate of wage change.

One measures the impact effect and the other the continuing effect. They are:

$z_1 = \Delta w^* - \Delta w$ for the month following the introduction of a new Δw^*

  $= 0$ elsewhere

$z_2 = \Delta w^* - \Delta w$ from the second month following the introduction of a new Δw^* until its abandonment or modification.

  $= 0$ elsewhere

       and where Δw is the change in the index of weekly wage rates

With these thirteen incomes policy variables we can attempt to estimate the effects of the norm, Δw^*; the effects of the gap between the norm and the current actual wage change rate, z_1 and z_2; and finally the effects arising from the non-quantifiable, more detailed institutional and legal characteristics of the different phases of policy l_{i1} and l_{i2}.

(iv) Voluntary price restraint. There was only one phase of voluntary price restraint in our sample period. This was the voluntary initiative taken by the CBI on 15 July 1971. We characterise this with the two dummy variables,

  $CBI_1 = 1$ in July 1971

     $= 0$ elsewhere

  $CBI_2 = 1$ from August 1971 onwards

     $= 0$ elsewhere

CBI_i will measure the impact effect and CBI_2 the continuing effect of this restraint.

(v) *Large and highly publicised wage increases.* What constitutes 'large and highly publicised wage increases' is, of course, not precisely definable. We felt that we should, ideally, regard any wage increase thought sufficiently important to be featured, say, on television newscasts and on the front pages of the leading popular newspapers as fitting our category. However, the resource cost of obtaining enough information deterred us from using that as an operational criterion. Instead we decided to consider as 'large and highly publicised' any wage rises thought important enough to be recorded in the 'Calendar of economic events' compiled by the National Institute for Economic and Social Research and published each quarter in its *Economic Review*.

We constructed the series so that it treated the wage increases as if they would apply to the whole economy by giving them weights which were fractions of the number of settlements reached in the period in question, i.e.

$$\Delta \overline{w} = \sum \frac{n_i}{N} \Delta \overline{w}_i$$

where

Δw = percentage (per annum equivalent) rate of wage change in the *i*th sector as recorded in the NIER 'Calendar of economic events'

n_i = number of workers involved

N = Σn_i total number involved in settlements in the month

(vi) *Changes in indirect taxes.* We use here a variable which measures changes in the rate of purchase tax on consumer durables, i.e.,

PT = the percentage change in the rates of purchase tax on consumer durables in the month a change is announced

= 0 elsewhere

This completes our definition and measurement of variables which may be considered to have an effect on the expected rate of inflation. We now turn to an examination of those effects.

(b) *Estimating the effects of 'other variables' on Δp^e*

As an alternative to the error-learning models reported in the preceding chapter, we used the hypothesis that

$$\Delta p_t^e = \gamma_0 + \sum_{i=1}^{k} \gamma_i x_{it} + u_t \tag{6.17}$$

where the x_i variables are the twenty-three defined above, $D_1, D_2, E_{11}, E_{12}, E_{13}, E_2, I_{11}, I_{12}, I_{21}, I_{22}, I_{31}, I_{32}, I_{41}, I_{51}, I_{52}, \Delta w^*, z_1, z_2, CBI_1, CBI_2, \Delta w$ and PT, and the γ_i are parameters to be estimated.

Table 6.2 sets out the result of this estimation. The impression given by these results is as follows,

1. The 1967 devaluation had a large and significant impact and continuing effect.

Table 6.2 Effects of devaluation, political factors, incomes policy, voluntary price restraint, large and publicised wage claims, and purchase tax changes on the expected rate of inflation ($\overline{R}^2 = 0.75$; D.W. = 1.32).

Symbol	Brief description of variable	Coefficient	t-statistic
D_1	Impact effect of devaluation: November 1967	6.558	5.854
D_2	Continuing effect of devaluation: November 1967	1.668	4.174
E_{11}	Impact effect of General Election: Sept. 1964	−0.718	0.649
E_{12}	Impact effect of General Election: Sept. 1966	−1.188	0.936
E_{13}	Impact effect of General Election: July 1970	−3.142	2.784
E_2	Effect of Labour Party being in power	0.829	2.575
I_{11}	Impact effect of 'Pay pause' July 1961	0.924	0.540
I_{12}	Continuing effect of 'Pay pause' to March 1962	0.275	1.682
I_{21}	Impact effect of 2.5 norm April 1962	2.448	1.748
I_{22}	Continuing effect of 2.5 norm to March 1963	0.575	0.997
I_{31}	Impact effect of 3.5 'Guiding light' April '63	−2.632	1.538
I_{32}	Continuing effect of 3.5 'Guiding light' to June 1966	−1.487	2.104
I_{41}	Impact effect of 'Freeze' July 1966	−0.080	0.065
I_{42}	Continuing effect of 'Freeze' to December 1966	0.766	0.928
I_{51}	Impact effect of 'Severe restraint' Jan. 1967	0.532	0.429
I_{52}	Continuing effect of 'Severe restraint' to Nov. 1969	1.454	0.975
Δw^*	Effect of wage change 'norm'	0.446	5.850
z_1	Impact effect of difference between norm and actual wage change.	−0.434	1.578
z_2	Continuing effect of difference between norm and actual wage change	−0.325	2.121
CBI_1	Impact effect of CBI voluntary price restraint	0.740	0.498
CBI_2	Continuing effect of CBI voluntary price restraint	−2.116	3.740
$\Delta \overline{w}$	Effect of large and publicised wage settlements	−0.009	0.333
PT	Effect of changes in purchase tax rates	0.337	1.656
	Constant	0.731	1.039

2. The impact of electing a Conservative government in 1970 reduced inflationary expectations by 3 per cent while a Conservative government has the lasting effect of reducing inflationary expectations by almost 1 per cent.

3. Incomes policies have had significant effects in three ways:

   (i) the 3·5 per cent 'Guiding Light' period was one in which expected inflation was reduced by about one and a half per cent.

   (ii) a change in the wage norm, Δw^*, changes expectations by approximately one half the norm change provided that the actual rate of wage change adjusts to keep the gap between the actual and norm constant, i.e. z_2, constant.

   (iii) a change in the wage norm with no accompanying change in the actual wage inflation rate reduces expectations by only one eighth of one per cent.

4. The CBI voluntary restraint had no impact effect but had a continuing effect which reduced expectations by 2 per cent.

5. The remaining variables had insignificant effects.

It may be objected that the apparent insignificance of most of the incomes policy variables arises from multicolinearity. As a partial check on this we inspected the zero order correlation matrix for the thirteen incomes policy variables. This is set out in Table 6.3.

It is immediately apparent that there are no high correlations except Δw^* and z_1. This correlation is, of course, entirely to be expected since the definition of z_2 is the difference between Δw^* and the actual rate of wage change. What is important is the lack of correlation between the qualitative dummies I_{ij} and the quantitative variables.

The overall goodness of fit of the equation reported in Table 6.2, $\overline{R}^2 = 0·75$, is larger than that on the second-order error-learning scheme. However, the Durbin-Watson statistic, 1·32, is in the region which indicates bias in the estimated standard errors and t-ratios. This means, of course, that we cannot regard the impression given by Table 6.2 as reliable.

If it was necessary to choose between the results given in Table 6.2 and the second-order adaptive scheme given above, it would be difficult to make the choice. From a statistical point of view, the adaptive scheme has residuals which are more random and has reliable standard errors while the equation in Table 6.2 has a doubtful residual error pattern and hence doubtful standard errors. From a policy point of view, the two results tell a very different story and have dramatically different implications. The adaptive expectations scheme implies that inflationary expectations can only be reduced by reducing the actual inflation rate while the Table 6.2 results suggest a wide variety of measures which could reduce the expected inflation rate. Thus, from a policy point of view, it is crucial that we should sort out which of the two processes is the more important.

Fortunately, there is no reason why we should regard the two approaches to expectations formation as mutually exclusive. It is possible that there is an error-learning process at work which is modified and augmented by the information such as that contained in the results in Table 6.2. We now examine such a possibility.

Table 6.3 Zero order correlations between incomes policy variables

	I_{11}	I_{12}	I_{21}	I_{22}	I_{31}	I_{32}	I_{41}	I_{42}	I_{51}	I_{52}	Δw^*	z_1
I_{11}												
I_{12}	−0·023											
I_{21}	−0·008	−0·023										
I_{22}	−0·027	−0·078	−0·027									
I_{31}	−0·008	−0·023	−0·008	−0·027								
I_{32}	−0·053	−0·155	−0·053	−0·185	−0·053							
I_{41}	−0·008	−0·023	−0·008	−0·027	−0·008	−0·053						
I_{42}	−0·016	−0·046	−0·016	−0·054	−0·016	−0·108	−0·016					
I_{51}	−0·008	−0·023	−0·008	−0·027	−0·008	−0·053	−0·008	−0·016				
I_{52}	−0·052	−0·152	−0·052	−0·181	−0·052	−0·361	−0·052	−0·016	−0·052			
Δw^*	−0·075	−0·219	−0·022	−0·077	−0·001	−0·009	−0·075	−0·016	−0·075	−0·508		
z_1	−0·479	0·000	0·363	0·000	0·543	0·000	0·000	0·000	0·000	0·000	−0·302	
z_2	0·139	−0·065	−0·022	0·329	0·095	−0·555	−0·045	−0·090	−0·045	0·048	−0·162	0·677

(c) Estimates of an error-learning process augmented by other information

As a starting point we combined the second order error-learning hypothesis with the twenty-three additional variables to give:

$$\Delta p_t^e - \Delta p_{t-1}^e = \lambda_0(\Delta p_{t-1} - \Delta p_{t-1}^e) + \lambda_1(\Delta p_{t-2} - \Delta p_{t-2}^e) + \sum_{i=1}^{23} \gamma_i x_{it} + u_t$$

$$(6.18)$$

The estimated model is set out in Table 6.4. It is immediately apparent that the goodness of fit has not improved over that in Table 6.2, but the Durbin—Watson statistic has moved into the region which indicates a rejection of the hypothesis of first-order autocorrelation. The second-order error-learning parameters are significant and have magnitudes similar to those estimated in the pure error-learning model. Of the other variables only the impact effect of the devaluation, D_1, and the continuing effect of the CBI voluntary price restraint, CBI_2, retain their significance. All the remaining variables now appear to be insignificant. It is noteworthy, however, that the incomes policy dummy variables are predominantly negative, although none were significantly non-zero. The two variables which the Conservative Government emphasised, purchase tax changes and large, highly publicised wage claims are both totally insignificant and small.

The 'other variables' were originally formulated without explicit reference to the expectations series itself so that we would not be tempted to insert variables just for the purpose of improving the fit. In view of the acknowledged shortcomings of many of our constructs, it is surprising, perhaps, that the results reported in Table 6.2 are as good as they are. In view of the instability of so many of the coefficients when we augment the model with the error-learning variables, however (Table 6.4), the good fit may be largely spurious. While differently defined other variables may prove to have better statistical properties, we believe the preferred explanatory model, with our data, should definitely include the last two errors, or at least the two terms Δp_{t-1}^e and Δp_{t-2}^e.

Table 6.4 Effects of devaluation, political factors, incomes policy, voluntary price restraint, large and publicised wage claims, and purchase tax changes on the expected rate of inflation with a second-order error-learning process ($\overline{R}^2 = 0.75$; D.W. = 2.206).

Symbol	Brief description of variable	Coefficient	t-statistic
D_1	Impact effect of devaluation, November 1967	5.873	5.378
D_2	Continuing effect of devaluation	−0.391	1.013
E_{11}	Impact effect of General Election, September 1964	0.313	0.292
E_{12}	Impact effect of General Election, September 1964	−0.655	0.534
E_{13}	Impact effect of General Election, July 1970	−2.008	1.918

Table 6.4—continued

Symbol	Brief description of variable	Coefficient	t-statistic
E_2	Effect of Labour Party being in power	−0·186	0·613
I_{11}	Impact effect of 'Pay pause' July 1961	0·127	0·081
I_{12}	Continuing effect of 'Pay pause' to March 1962	−0·733	1·133
I_{21}	Impact effect of 2·5% norm April 1962	−0·380	0·276
I_{22}	Continuing effect of 2·5% norm to March 1963	−0·505	1·415
I_{31}	Impact effect of 3·5% 'Guiding light' April, 1963	−1·362	0·825
I_{32}	Continuing effect of 3·5% 'Guiding light' to June 1966	−0·642	0·939
I_{41}	Impact effect of 'Freeze' July 1966	−1·897	0·619
I_{42}	Continuing effect of 'Freeze' to December 1966	−0·127	0·168
I_{51}	Impact effect of 'Severe restraint' January, 1967	−0·152	0·130
I_{52}	Continuing effect of 'Severe restraint' to November 1969	0·185	0·275
Δw^*	Effect of wage change 'norm'	0·013	0·296
z_1	Impact effect of difference between norm and actual wage change	−0·177	0·653
z_2	Continuing effect of difference between norm and actual wage change	−0·085	0·673
CBI_1	Impact effect of CBI voluntary price restraint	−0·031	0·021
CBI_2	Continuing effect of CBI voluntary price restraint	−1·178	2·033
$\Delta \overline{w}$	Effect of large and publicised wage settlements	0·028	1·050
PT	Effect of changes in purchase tax rates	0·129	0·651
$(\Delta p - \Delta p^e_{-1})$	Latest error	0·402	4·836
$(\Delta p_{-1} - \Delta p^e_{-2})$	Previous error	−0·181	2·183

In view of the non-significance of all but two of the 'other variables' we thought it worth while re-estimating the model with only those two additional variables. This yields results as in Table 6.5.

Table 6.5

Variable	Coefficient	t-statistic
D_1	6·194	6·071
CBI_2	−0·910	1·903
$\Delta p - \Delta p^e_{-1}$	0·358	4·795
$\Delta p - \Delta p^e_{-2}$	−0·194	2·593
$\overline{R}^2 = 0·77$		D.W. = 2·227

The coefficients on the error-learning variables are about as well determined as before, that on the devaluation is now better determined, but the
CBI_2 variable just falls below the 0·05 level of significance. There is,
therefore, some doubt about the effectiveness of the CBI restraint although
a strong hint that it may have made a contribution.

Finally, in view of the non-significance of the CBI_2 variable, we estimated the second-order error-learning model with the addition simply of
the devaluation impact dummy. This was also estimated for two sub-
samples: (i) early 1960s, (ii) late 1960s. These results are reported in
the main text above.

APPENDIX 6.3 Data on 'other' variables

		$\Delta \overline{w}$	PT	Δw^*	z_1	z_2
1961:	Mar.	0·00	0	4·202	0	0
	Apr.	4·00	0	3·846	0	0
	May	0·00	0	3·920	0	0
	June	5·50	0	4·254	0	0
	July	0·00	2·000	0	−4·163	0
	Aug.	0·00	0	0	0	−4·163
	Sept.	0·00	0	0	0	−4·163
	Oct.	0·00	0	0	0	−4·163
	Nov.	11·00	0	0	0	−4·163
	Dec.	0·00	0	0	0	−4·163
1962:	Jan.	0·00	0	0	0	−4·163
	Feb.	0·00	0	0	0	−4·163
	Mar.	3·48	0	0	0	−4·163
	Apr.	3·29	−1·961	2·500	3·040	−4·163
	May	3·52	0	2·500	0	−1·123
	June	4·54	0	2·500	0	−1·123
	July	3·37	0	2·500	0	−1·123
	Aug.	2·96	0	2·500	0	−1·123
	Sept.	5·63	0	2·500	0	−1·123
	Oct.	4·51	0	2·500	0	−1·123
	Nov.	6·00	0	2·500	0	−1·123
	Dec.	5·90	0	2·500	0	−1·123

APPENDIX 6.3—continued

		$\Delta \bar{w}$	PT	Δw^*	z_1	z_2
1963:	Jan.	2·25	0	2·500	0	−1·123
	Feb.	5·65	0	2·500	0	−1·123
	Mar.	4·45	0	2·500	0	−1·123
	Apr.	5·99	0	3·500	−4·546	−1·123
	May	3·80	0	3·500	0	−5·669
	June	4·55	0	3·500	0	−5·669
	July	0·00	0	3·500	0	−5·669
	Aug.	8·71	0	3·500	0	−5·669
	Sept.	5·55	0	3·500	0	−5·669
	Oct.	3·65	0	3·500	0	−5·669
	Nov.	6·53	0	3·500	0	−5·669
	Dec.	5·00	0	3·500	0	−5·669
1964:	Jan.	4·96	0	3·500	0	−5·669
	Feb.	5·00	0	3·500	0	−5·669
	Mar.	0·00	0	3·500	0	−5·669
	Apr.	0·00	0	3·500	0	−5·669
	May	0·00	0	3·500	0	−5·669
	June	8·50	0	3·500	0	−5·669
	July	6·50	0	3·500	0	−5·669
	Aug.	4·00	0	3·500	0	−5·669
	Sept.	0·00	0	3·500	0	−5·669
	Oct.	0·00	0	3·500	0	−5·669
	Nov.	7·30	0	3·500	0	−5·669
	Dec.	0·00	0	3·500	0	−5·669
1965:	Jan.	0·00	0	3·500	0	−5·669
	Feb.	6·00	0	3·500	0	−5·669
	Mar.	0·00	0	3·500	0	−5·669
	Apr.	0·00	0	3·500	0	−5·669
	May	2·50	0	3·500	0	−5·669
	June	11·00	0	3·500	0	−5·669
	July	0·00	0	3·500	0	−5·669
	Aug.	12·99	0	3·500	0	−5·669
	Sept.	5·00	0	3·500	0	−5·669
	Oct.	13·00	0	3·500	0	−5·669
	Nov.	7·48	0	3·500	0	−5·669
	Dec.	0·00	0	3·500	0	−5·669
1966:	Jan.	19·33	0	3·500	0	−5·669
	Feb.	5·51	0	3·500	0	−5·669
	Mar.	3·95	0	3·500	0	−5·669
	Apr.	13·00	0	3·500	0	−5·669
	May	5·77	0	3·500	0	−5·669
	June	5·67	0	3·500	0	−5·669
	July	4·39	2·000	0	0·926	−5·669
	Aug.	4·00	0	0	0	−4·743
	Sept.	0·00	0	0	0	−4·743
	Oct.	0·00	0	0	0	−4·743
	Nov.	0·00	0	0	0	−4·743
	Dec.	0·00	0	0	0	−4·743

APPENDIX 6. 3—continued

		$\Delta\overline{w}$	PT	Δw^*	z_1	z_2
1967:	Jan.	0·00	0	0	0	−4·743
	Feb.	2·90	0	0	0	−4·743
	Mar.	0·00	0	0	0	−4·743
	Apr.	5·64	0	0	0	−4·743
	May	0·00	0	0	0	−4·743
	June	9·81	0	0	0	−4·743
	July	7·22	0	0	0	−4·743
	Aug.	6·79	0	0	0	−4·743
	Sept.	0·00	0	0	0	−4·743
	Oct.	4·50	0	0	0	−4·743
	Nov.	4·31	0	0	0	−4·743
	Dec.	6·09	0	0	0	−4·743
1968:	Jan.	2·43	0	0	0	−4·743
	Feb.	25·00	0	0	0	−4·743
	Mar.	0·00	4·575	0	0	−4·743
	Apr.	8·98	0	0	0	−4·743
	May	10·24	0	0	0	−4·743
	June	7·78	0	0	0	−4·743
	July	3·54	0	0	0	−4·743
	Aug.	8·50	0	0	0	−4·743
	Sept.	6·00	0	0	0	−4·743
	Oct.	8·31	0	0	0	−4·743
	Nov.	6·48	2·500	0	0	−4·743
	Dec.	5·35	0	0	0	−4·743
1969:	Jan.	3·77	0	0	0	−4·743
	Feb.	7·13	0	0	0	−4·743
	Mar.	0·00	0	0	0	−4·743
	Apr.	9·05	0	0	0	−4·743
	May	0·00	0	0	0	−4·743
	June	3·10	0	0	0	−4·743
	July	8·60	0	0	0	−4·743
	Aug.	0·00	0	0	0	−4·743
	Sept.	6·00	0	0	0	−4·743
	Oct.	0·00	0	0	0	−4·743
	Nov.	8·00	0	0	0	−4·743
	Dec.	0·00	0	5·758	4·743	−4·743
1970:	Jan.	18·18	0	6·136	0	0
	Feb.	15·84	0	7·252	0	0
	Mar.	10·80	0	7·919	0	0
	Apr.	10·46	0	8·197	0	0
	May	12·65	0	9·317	0	0
	June	20·00	0	9·797	0	0
	July	15·88	0	10·208	0	0
	Aug.	19·93	0	11·018	0	0
	Sept.	10·00	0	10·827	0	0
	Oct.	10·00	0	11·487	0	0
	Nov.	16·66	0	13·484	0	0
	Dec.	11·09	0	13·531	0	0

APPENDIX 6. 3—continued

1971:	Jan.	8·33	0	14·454	0	0
	Feb.	9·88	0	13·048	0	0
	Mar.	11·35	0	12·474	0	0
	Apr.	10·60	0	12·692	0	0
	May	9·22	0	13·068	0	0
	June	13·02	0	13·333	0	0
	July	10·34	−4·878	13·384	0	0
	Aug.	9·89	0	12·897	0	0
	Sept.	16·90	0	12·876	0	0
	Oct.	11·99	0	12·444	0	0
	Nov.	8·50	0	12·658	0	0
	Dec.	7·50	0	12·346	0	0

7 Producers' price and cost expectations

Graham W. Smith[1]

I INTRODUCTION

In this chapter, the Carlson-Parkin technique described in Chapter 6 is used to generate time series of firms' expectations of the proportional rates of change of their product prices, Δp_w^e, export prices, Δp_f^e, and average costs per unit of output, Δc^e.

Hypotheses on the determinants of these expectational variables are also tested.[2] These expectations series are needed for two principal purposes. First, in empirical studies of wage determination it is necessary to incorporate expectational variables from both the supply and demand sides of the labour market. The Gallup Poll data used by Carlson and Parkin provide the appropriate supply-side expectational variable and the data generated here provide the missing demand-side variables. Secondly, for studies of the determination of prices in product markets, expectational data on costs and on other firms' prices are required.

   An additional set of questions can be analysed with the aid of the data generated in this chapter. They concern the information used by producers in order to reformulate and modify their expectations. Knowledge of this process will make it possible to establish whether or not there are forces at work bringing expectations into equality with actual inflation and, further, whether or not governments can intervene directly in influencing inflationary expectations.

   Four possible types of information may be distinguished on which price expectations may be based. The information usually assumed to be used is that on recent actual rates of inflation and on previous expectations. So far as the individual firm or household is concerned, its own expectations-formation scheme might include its own previous expectations of the rate of inflation and information about the recent experience of the actual rate of inflation of the prices of the goods which it produces or consumes. Secondly, economic theory suggests variables which may be relevant to the inflationary process and so may influence the price

expectations of a rational individual. Thirdly, specific policies to
control inflation may be believed to be effective and hence the
adoption of such policies, which may not reduce the actual rate of
inflation directly, may reduce it indirectly by influencing individuals' expectations of inflation so that they are revised downwards,
with a resultant reduction in the actual rate of inflation. Fourthly,
price expectations may be influenced by events which could be
considered to be primarily non-economic in nature. For example,
a particular government might be believed (correctly or incorrectly) to be more concerned about controlling inflation than some
other, and so it might be the case that price expectations might be
influenced by the result of a general election (an impact effect) or
by the political party in power (a continuation effect).

It should be stressed, however, that these four classifications
are not necessarily distinct. For example, to the extent that individuals base price expectations on the appropriate economic
determinants of actual price changes and have correct knowledge
about the effectiveness or otherwise of government policies and
non-economic factors on the actual rate of inflation, then this
information is present in the past history of actual price changes.
What is relevant is whether economic variables, policy variables
and non-economic factors are important proximate determinants
of price expectations, in addition to previous actual rates of change
of prices.

In the next section, the sample survey data on firms' expectations is discussed and transformed using the Carlson-Parkin
method. In Section 7. III, the main expectations-formation hypotheses are examined and in Section 7. IV preliminary tests of the
alternative hypotheses are presented. Conclusions appear in
Section 7. V.

II THE SAMPLE SURVEY DATA AND ITS TRANSFORMATION

Since February 1958 the Confederation of British Industry (CBI)
(until June 1965 the Federation of British Industry (FBI)), has
carried out surveys of industrial trends in manufacturing industry.
Up to June 1971 the surveys were thrice yearly and the results,
published in February, June and October, indicated expectations
held during the last week of the preceding month. From January
1972 onwards, surveys were taken quarterly and the results indicate expectations held in the middle of January, April, July and
October.[3] The average number of respondents in the earlier
surveys, until February 1965, was 640 and since then it has been
approximately 1, 350. Until and including February 1964, the
survey results were unweighted, which would bias the results
towards small firms although, with the FBI having the reputation

of being a 'large firm club' with few small firms as members, this may not introduce serious bias. Later surveys are weighted. The last two surveys of 1964 have employment weights, the response of individual firms being weighted by the number of employees of that firm. From February 1965 output weights are used for questions referring to the domestic economy, and weights based on the value of the firm's exports are used for the export questions.

The FBI/CBI surveys are extremely detailed and cover a wide set of questions. Those relevant here are:

Excluding seasonal variations ... what are the expected trends for the next four months with regard to:

Average costs per unit of output?[4]

Average selling prices?[5]

Average prices at which export orders are booked?[6]

In general, over time, the trend in the proportion answering 'up' has been positive and the trends in those classified as 'down', 'same' and 'not answered' negative. In contrast to the Gallup survey (Chapter 6) a much larger proportion, often over 70 per cent until the late 1960s, have replied 'same'. Over the period 1958(J)-1971(J), which is that used in this preliminary empirical investigation, there have been no occasions on which the proportion of respondents answering 'down' has been less than 0·5 per cent for any of the variables.[7]

The basic assumption underlying the Carlson-Parkin procedure is that inflation expectations are normally distributed across the population.[8] Such a distribution is presented in Figure 7.1.[9] A proportion, α, of economic agents are assumed to be incapable of formulating inflation expectations. Moreover there is a threshold around zero, indicated by the two vertical lines in Figure 7.1, such that within this band firms are not able to predict a change in prices. The proportion of firms which expect prices to rise are in the large area, A; the proportion which expect prices

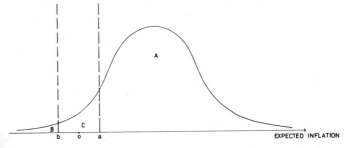

Figure 7.1 Probability density function of respondents

to fall are in the small area, B, and those which either don't know or expect there will be no change are in the area C. The expected rate of inflation is defined to be the average of this distribution which can be measured given (i) the survey results, (ii) the value of α, and (iii) the value of the threshold, δ.[10]

Following Carlson and Parkin and assuming that when firms do not answer a question this is because they 'don't know', then these 'don't knows' were regressed on an intercept and 'stay the same' for the periods 1958(J)-1971(J), 1958(J)-1964(F) and 1965(F)-1971(J) to find the proportion of firms, α, not in a position to answer the question through lack of adequate forecasting procedures. The choice of the time periods is based on data characterists; 1958(J)-1971(J) is the full time period on thrice yearly observations, for 1958(J)-1964(F) the data are unweighted and for 1965(F)-1971(J) they have output weights.[11] The models were estimated by OLS (and also for the period 1958(J)-1971(J) by maximum likelihood with the assumption that the error followed a first-order autogressive scheme) but no stable relationship was found for any of the three price series for any time period.

In such a case, how can the 'don't knows' be dealt with? Two alternatives were tried. The first was to assume that the 'don't knows' do not form expectations because the costs of forming them are too great; the 'don't knows' behave as if 'no change' in which case $\alpha=0$, and so 'up' 'down' and 'same' are A, B and $(C + D)$ respectively. The second alternative is based on the assumption that firms do not answer because they are not interested in the question. Assuming such responses are distributed independently of the other responses in the population then they can be considered purely random. In the case, 'up', 'down' and 'same' become $A/(1-(D/100))$, $B/(1-(D/100))$ and $C/(1-(D/100))$ respectively. All three series were transformed to the unscaled expectations series using both approaches.

The next step is to calculate scaling factors for each of the expectational variables. In the Carlson-Parkin study the scaling factor is assumed constant and is the difference limen. In this chapter, a similar procedure is used.[12] For scaling expected average costs, an index of average unit costs was calculated as:

$$(\beta_1 . MF + \beta_2 BWR . L_{op})/X$$

where MF is the price of materials and fuel,

BWR is basic weekly wage rates,

L_{op} is employment of operatives,

X is real output,

β_1, β_2 are appropriate weights,[13]

and in which all the indices are for United Kingdom manufacturing and have a common base.[14] For scaling the series calculated from responses to the questions on average selling prices and export prices, indices of the price of manufacturing output and of the unit value of manufacturing exports were used. In cases where the actual and/or expected rates of change variables take negative values, the type of scaling factor used by Carlson and Parkin is inappropriate. The scaling factor is, therefore, defined as the ratio of the mean of the moduli of the actual rates of change to the mean of the moduli of the unscaled series. This is merely a minor modification to the Carlson-Parkin definition, with which it is equivalent when the actual and expected rates of change are always positive. The rates of change variables are defined as $(lnP_t/P_{t-1}).300$. The scaling factors are given in Table 7.1.

Table 7.1 Scaling factors

Variable	Treatment of 'don't knows'	
	$\alpha = 0$	$\alpha \neq 0$
Average unit costs	5·8070	5·1354
Output prices	9·4672	8·8756
Export prices	12·8481	12·4829

The most noticeable feature when the scaling factors for the CBI variables are compared with those for the Gallup data is that the former are much greater in magnitude.[15] Firms set output and export prices and to them costs are exogenous. In deciding whether or not to change prices, firms consider the costs and benefits of such changes, the cost of change being greater for export than domestic prices and zero for costs. Firms change their product and export prices discretely because there are costs to the firm of changing such prices. However, the frequency with which export prices are changed will depend on the prevailing exchange-rate regime. With fixed exchange rates, export prices will be changed much less frequently than with flexible exchange rates. Costs, however, which are exogenous to the firm, are more likely to be changing continuously. This explains the ranking of the scaling factors. However, their magnitude is large but not inconsistent with other statistical information. Glynn (1969), in a questionnaire on the questionnaire undertaken in June 1967 asked firms the most narrow range of movement over four months within which they would reply 'same'. Glynn's results are presented in Table 7.2.

Table 7.2

	Number of firms answering within each range		
	<3%	3%-5%	5%-10%
Average unit cost	14	14	5
Output prices	15	14	5
Export prices	11	14	5

Using the mid-point in each of these ranges, taking a weighted average (the weights being the proportion of firms answering within a given range) and converting to annual percentage rates of change, Glynn's results imply scaling factors of 10·4, 10·2 and 13·8 for average costs, output prices and export prices respectively. Whilst great importance cannot be attached to the results because of the small sample, it is apparent that they are not inconsistent with the scaling factors calculated by the modified Carlson-Parkin method.

Graphs of the expected and actual rates of change of average costs, output prices and export prices are given in Figures 7.2 to 7.4 for the period ending June 1971.[16] The graphs are set up so that the actual rate of change is aligned with its expectation formed in the previous period. The rate of change of actual unit costs is much noisier than that of the expectational variable and

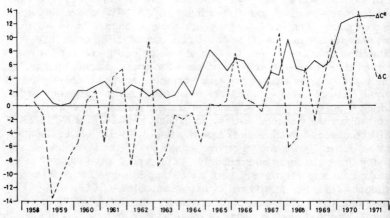

Figure 7.2 Actual and expected rates of change of average unit costs, 1958-71

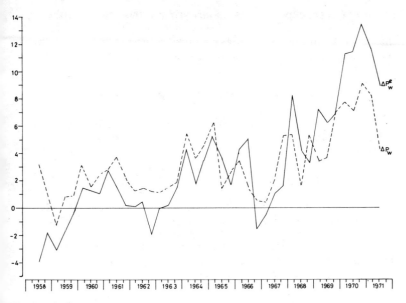

Figure 7.3 Actual and expected rates of change of firms' output prices, 1958-71

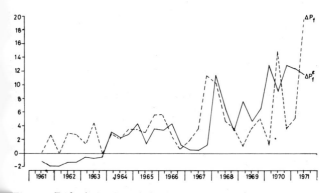

Figure 7.4 Actual and expected rates of change of firms' export prices, 1961-71

in the period before 1965 turning points are poorly forecast. The situation is not as bad in the later period when the trends correspond reasonably.[17] The expected and actual rates of change of output prices correspond much more closely: both turning points and trends are predicted well. In the early part of the period, characterised by low rates of inflation and for which the data are unweighted, expectations underestimate the rate of inflation, and for the more recent period they overestimate it. The rate of change of export prices corresponds with the actual rate of change reasonably well, especially since the mid 1960s.

III HYPOTHESES OF EXPECTATIONS FORMATION

The expectations formation schemes which will be investigated fall into two broad groups: error learning and extrapolative models.

(a) Error-learning models

(i) *First-order error learning* is often referred to as 'adaptive expectations'. To quote Cagan: 'The expected rate of change of prices is revised per period of time in proportion to the difference between the actual rate of change in prices and the rate of change that was expected.'[18] Cagan's original formulation was in continuous time. In discrete time adaptive expectations may be written as

$$\Delta p_t^e - \Delta p_{t-1}^e = \mu(\Delta p_t - \Delta p_{t-1}^e),\ 0 < \mu < 1 \qquad (7.1)$$

in which

Δp_t^e is the expectation formed at t of the rate of inflation at time $t + 1$;

Δp_t is the actual rate of inflation at time t;

μ is the proportion of the error by which expectations are revised; and

$(\Delta p_t - \Delta p_{t-1}^e)$ is the most recent error.

The expected rate of change of prices may be written as an infinite distributed lag of previous actual rates of inflation, the lag distribution having geometrically declining weights summing to unity; since

$$\Delta p_t^e = \mu \Delta p_t + (1 - \mu)\ \Delta p_{t-1}^e \qquad (7.2)$$

define $\lambda \equiv 1 - \mu$, hence,

$$\Delta p_t^e = (1 - \lambda) \sum_{j=0}^{\infty} \lambda^j\ \Delta p_{t-j},\ 0 < \lambda < 1 \qquad (7.3)[1]$$

From 7.1:

If $\mu = 0$, $\Delta p^e_t = \Delta p^e_{t-1}$, that is, expectations are never revised. The expected rate of inflation does not depend on observations of the actual rate of inflation.

If $\mu = 1$, $\Delta p^e_t = \Delta p_t$. The expected rate of inflation equals the actual rate of inflation at the time at which the expectation was formed.

When $0 < \mu < 1$, the larger the value of μ, the greater the weight given to the most recent actual rate of inflation.

Turnovsky (1969) has used Bayesian analysis to derive a model of the form of 7.1, but in which the adjustment parameter is not constant and varies with the subjective variance of the expected rate of change of prices. Turnovsky shows that if the subjective variance at the time the expectation is formed is infinite, that is, the individual forming expectations believes there to be no precision whatsoever in his previous forecast of the inflation rate, then $\mu = 1$ and $\Delta p^e_t = \Delta p_t$. More generally, $\mu = f(\sigma^2 \Delta p^e_{t-1}), f' > 0$, where $\sigma^2 \Delta p^e_{t-1}$ is the variance of the most recent expectation.

Moreover, Turnovsky shows that for the error-adjustment to be constant in a Bayesian context it is necessary for the individual forming expectations to sample such that his subjective variance decreases geometrically over time.

(*ii*) *Higher-order error-learning*. Rose (1972) shows that for error-learning to be optimal (in the sense of yielding minimum-mean-square error forecasts) all past errors must be considered.[20] With second-order learning it is hypothesised that expectations are revised by proportions, which are usually assumed to be different, of the two previous errors:

$$\Delta p^e_t - \Delta p^e_{t-1} = \mu_1 (\Delta p_t - \Delta p^e_{t-1}) + \mu_2 (\Delta p_{t-1} - \Delta p^e_{t-2}) \quad (7.4)[21]$$

This is equivalent to postulating that the change in expectations depends on the most recent error and the change in the most recent error:

$$\Delta p^e_t - \Delta p^e_{t-1} = (\mu_1 + \mu_2)(\Delta p_t - \Delta p^e_{t-1}) - \mu_2 (\Delta p_t - \Delta p^e_{t-1}$$

$$- \{\Delta p_{t-1} - \Delta p^e_{t-2}\}) \quad (7.5)$$

More generally, error-learning schemes may be written as

$$\Delta p_t^e - \Delta p_{t-1}^e = \sum_{i=0}^{\infty} \mu_i \, (\Delta p_{t-i} - \Delta p_{t-i-1}^e) \tag{7.6}$$

(b) *Extrapolative models*

Early formulations of the extrapolative expectations hypothesis by Hicks (1946) and Goodwin (1947) were cast in terms of price levels rather than in terms of rates of change. Turnovsky (1970) has advocated a model of extrapolative expectations where the most recent actual rate of inflation is adjusted by a proportion of the most recent change in the inflation rate, to give the expected rate of inflation:

$$\Delta p_t^e = \Delta p_t + \gamma \, (\Delta p_t - \Delta p_{t-1}) \tag{7.7}$$

If $\gamma < 0$, the most recent change in the rate of inflation signalled a downturn and expectations are said to be regressive.

If $\gamma = 0$, $\Delta p_t^e = \Delta p_t$, which is the same as $\mu = 1$ in the above formulation of adaptive expectations.

If $\gamma > 0$, inflation is believed to be accelerating and the recent trend is extrapolated.

Equation 7.7 can be written as

$$\Delta p_t^e - \Delta p_{t-1}^e = \Delta p_t - \Delta p_{t-1} + \gamma \, (\{\Delta p_t - \Delta p_{t-1}\} - \{\Delta p_{t-1} - \Delta p_{t-2}\}) \tag{7.8}$$

which states that expectations are revised by the change in the actual rate of inflation adjusted by some proportion of the change in the acceleration of inflation, that is, some proportion of the third derivative of prices with respect to time.

Equation 7.7 may be interpreted another way. Since

$$\Delta p_t^e = (1 + \gamma) \, \Delta p_t - \gamma \, \Delta p_{t-1} \tag{7.9}$$

the expected rate of inflation in $t+1$ formed at t is equal to a weighted average of the two most recent actual rates of inflation with weights summing to unity.

More generally, extrapolative expectations may be written as

$$\Delta p^e_t = \gamma_0 + \sum_{i=1}^{\infty} \gamma_i \, \Delta p_{t-i+1} \qquad (7.10)$$

IV PRELIMINARY ESTIMATES OF THE DETERMINANTS OF FIRMS' INFLATION EXPECTATIONS

In this section, the expectations hypotheses previously examined are tested for each of three variables: firms' expected rates of change of output prices, Δp^e_w, export prices, Δp^e_f, and average unit costs, Δc^e, and the possible influence of other variables is investigated. The basic models to be estimated are given below.

The unrestricted form of the first-order error-learning model is

$$\Delta p^e_t = \alpha_0 + \alpha_1 \, \Delta p_t + \alpha_2 \, \Delta p^e_{t-1} \qquad (7.11)$$

Imposing the restrictions $\alpha_0 = 0$ and $\alpha_2 = (1 - \alpha_1)$ then $\alpha_1 = \mu$ and this gives equation 7.1.

The unrestricted form of the second-order error-learning model is

$$\Delta p^e_t = \beta_0 + \beta_1 \, \Delta p_t + \beta_2 \, \Delta p_{t-1} + \beta_3 \, \Delta p^e_{t-1} + \beta_4 \, \Delta p^e_{t-2} \qquad (7.12)$$

With the restrictions $\beta_0 = 0, \beta_3 = (1 - \beta_1)$ and $\beta_4 = -\beta_2$ imposed then $\beta_1 = \mu_1$ and $\beta_2 = \mu_2$ which is equation 7.4.

The third-order error-learning model without constraints may be written as:

$$\Delta p^e_t = \delta_0 + \delta_1 \, \Delta p_t + \delta_2 \, \Delta p_{t-1} + \delta_3 \, \Delta p_{t-2} + \delta_4 \, \Delta p^e_{t-1} + \delta_5 \, \Delta p^e_{t-2}$$

$$+ \delta_6 \, \Delta p^e_{t-3} \qquad (7.13)$$

and the restrictions are $\delta_0 = 0, \delta_4 = 1 - \delta_1, \delta_5 = -\delta_2$ and $\delta_6 = -\delta_3$ hence $\delta_1 = \mu_1, \delta_2 = \mu_2$ and $\delta_3 = \mu_3$.

In the absence of constraints, Turnovsky's model may be written as

$$\Delta p^e_t = \epsilon_0 + \epsilon_1 \, \Delta p_t + \epsilon_2 \, \Delta p_{t-1} \qquad (7.14)$$

and imposing the restrictions $\epsilon_0 = 0, \epsilon_1 = 1 - \epsilon_2$ then $-\epsilon_2 = \gamma$ and the model of 7.9.

The more general extrapolative model is:

$$\Delta p_t^e = \gamma_0 + \sum_{i=1}^{n} \gamma_i \, \Delta p_{t-i+1} \qquad (7.15)$$

with $n = 3$ for the four-monthly data.

The strategy adopted here is to estimate first-, second- and third-order error-learning models and the extrapolative models for the entire time period and periods of 'low' and 'high' inflation.[2] The possible additional influence of variables other than past prices and previous expectations is then investigated. Finally some simple tests of whether the adjustment parameter varies with the variance of the expectational variable are presented.

For firms' expectations of output prices and average unit costs the entire period is 1959(J)-1971(J) (thirty-seven four-monthly observations) and for their export price expectations 1962(J)-1971(J) (twenty-eight four-monthly observations). These are the longest estimation periods on four-monthly data after allowing for the time lags explicit in third-order error-learning models.. For the output price and average cost expectational variables the models were also estimated for two sub-periods, 1959(J)-1964(F) and 1966(F)-1971(J) and for export price expectations for the more recent sub-period only.[24] These periods are those for which the expectational variables were generally below and above 4 per cent per annum respectively. Moreover, for the earlier period all the CBI survey data is unweighted whereas for the more recent period it has output weights.

A random error term was added to each of the models. The presence of lagged dependent variables in the error-learning models results in estimation problems. Specifically, if OLS is applied to such a model and if the lagged dependent variable is contemporaneously uncorrelated with the error term then the estimated coefficient on the lagged dependent variable will be biased (downwards) but consistent. If, however, the estimated residuals are serially correlated then the estimated coefficient on the lagged dependent variable will be biased and inconsistent. However, there are only thirty-seven observations on the expectational variables and for the periods of 'low' and 'high' inflation fifteen and seventeen observations respectively. Clearly, with so few observations, neither Durbin's h statistic nor the estimation of a first-order autogressive scheme will be a very useful test against first-order serial correlation in the residuals with a lagged dependent variable. Moreover, in the extrapolative models estimated for data on firms' expectations, the power of the Durbin Watson test is low. The procedure used here for the error-learning models is to estimate by OLS. In those regressions where Durbin's h statistic rejects the null hypothesis of no serial correlation in the residuals, or could not be calculated, then those models are re-estimated by maximum likelihood assuming the error follows a first-order autogressive scheme. If that first-order autogressive parameter is insignificantly different from zero, the OLS estimates are used.[25]

Some general results can be stated briefly. For all expectational variables, the error-learning models out-performed the extrapolative models, the simple model used by Turnovsky being superior to the more general formulation. Nowhere was the third error important. For the 'low' inflation period the expectational variables are autogressive. The residuals of the models estimated for the entire time period and for the period of 'low' inflation, with the exception of firms' export price expectations, are heteroscedastic.[26] In the more detailed discussion of the results for the separate expectational variable which follows, it is clearly of little help to report all the regressions which were run. Since the basic choice seems to be between error-learning and extrapolative models, the best error-learning and best extrapolative models are reported for each of the expectational variables.[27]

Firm's output price expectations are best characterised by a first-order error-learning process. These results are given in Table 7.3.[28] The residuals of the second-order error-learning and extrapolative models exhibited significant positive serial correlation. For the first-order model, first-order autocorrelation only occurs for the period of 'low' inflation. The restrictions, however, are rejected for the 'high' inflation period on the basis of an F-test at the 5 per cent level.[29]

Firms' export price expectations are also most appropriately modelled by adaptive expectations, the results for which are given in Table 7.4. When a second error was included, in unrestricted or constrained models, that error was always insignificant. In the first-order error-learning models the residuals exhibit neither first-order serial correlation nor heteroscedasticity and the restrictions are not rejected on the basis of F-tests at the five per cent level.[30]

For firms' expectations of their average unit costs the second-order error-learning model is the most appropriate (Table 7.5). Although the residuals for neither first- nor second-order models were autocorrelated, when the constraints were imposed on the first-order model for the period of 'high' inflation, the error became insignificantly different from zero. When the second error was included, it was always insignificantly different from zero in free estimation and, when the restrictions were imposed, for the 'high' inflation period. However, the inclusion of the second error resulted in the first error becoming significant for the more recent time-period and with the restrictions imposed.

Table 7.3 Output price expectations

Equation	Estimation period	Dependent variable	Intercept	$\Delta p_{w,t}$	$\Delta p^e_{w,t-1}$	$\Delta p_{w,t} - \Delta p^e_{w,t-1}$	ρ	R^2	BLUS	Optimal basis
7.16	Entire	$\Delta p^e_{w,t}$	−0·5609 (0·933)	0·9385 (3·427)	0·3287 (1·957)			0·768	$F_{(17,17)} = 2·30$	18-20
7.17	'Low' inflation	$\Delta p^e_{w,t}$	1·304 (1·554)	−0·4921 (0·874)	1·014 (2·172)		0·14 (2·25)	0·458	$F_{(6,6)} = 4·63$	7-9
7.18	'High' inflation	$\Delta p^e_{w,t}$	−0·5830 (0·6321)	1·593 (4·752)	−0·0574 (0·284)			0·838	$F_{(7,7)} = 2·21$	8-10
7.19	'High' inflation	$\Delta p^e_{w,t} - \Delta p^e_{w,t-1}$				0·5933 (2·646)		0·304	$F_{(8,8)} = 1·05$	9

Notes to Table 7.3

1. *F*-statistic for the test of the constraints for the 'high' inflation sub-period, $F_{(2,14)} = 7·88$.
2. *t*-statistics are given in parentheses.

Table 7.4 Export price expectations

Equation	Estimation period	Dependent variable	Intercept	$\Delta p_{f,t}$	$\Delta p^e_{f,t-1}$	$\Delta p_{f,t} - \Delta p^e_{f,t-1}$	R^2	BLUS	Optimal basis
7.20	Entire	$\Delta p^e_{f,t}$	−0·0375 (0·044)	0·4864 (2·776)	0·6320 (4·959)		0·664	$F_{(13,\,12)}$ = 3·80	13–15
7.21	Entire	$\Delta p^e_{f,t} - \Delta p^e_{f,t-1}$				0·4024 (3·443)	0·305 (0·306)	$F_{(13,\,14)}$ = 2·97	15
7.22	'High' inflation	$\Delta p^e_{f,t}$	0·2949 (0·184)	0·5249 (2·342)	0·578 (3·127)		0·573	$F_{(7,\,7)}$ = 1·37	8–10
7.23	'High' inflation	$\Delta p^e_{f,t} - \Delta p^e_{f,t-1}$				0·4379 (2·930)	0·349	$F_{(8,\,8)}$ = 1·68	9

Note: F-statistics for tests of constraints: entire period, $F_{(2,\,25)}$ = 0·54; 'high' inflation sub-period, $F_{(2,\,14)}$ = 0·58.

Table 7.5 Average unit cost expectations

Equation	Estimation period	Dependent variable	Intercept	Δc_t	Δc_{t-1}^e	Δc_{t-1}	Δc_{t-2}^e	$\Delta c_t - \Delta c_{t-1}^e$	$\Delta c_{t-1} - \Delta c_{t-2}^e$	R^2	BLUS	Optimal basis
7.24	Entire	Δc_t^e	1·255 (1·932)	0·1444 (2·676)	0·7508 (4·327)	−0·0209 (0·355)	0·0651 (0·381)			0·800	$F_{(16,16)} = 2·62$	17-21
7.25	'Low' inflation	Δc_t^e	1·791 (2·553)	0·0856 (2·560)	0·8221 (3·032)	−0·0172 (0·475)	−0·4997 (2·044)			0·715	$F_{(5,5)} = 2·76$	6-10
7.26	'High' inflation	Δc_t^e	1·409 (1·067)	0·2676 (2·808)	0·5676 (1·972)	0·0322 (0·261)	0·1842 (0·0699)			0·770	$F_{(6,6)} = 1·01$	7-11
7.27	'High' inflation	$\Delta c_t^e \Delta c_{t-1}^e$						0·1642 (2·163)	−0·1240 (1·656)	0·290	$F_{(8,7)} = 1·13$	8-9

Note: F-statistic for the test of the constraints for the 'high' inflation sub-period, $F_{(3, 12)} = 1·38$.

Table 7.6 Models of extrapolative expectations

Equation	Expectations	Estimation period	Dependent variable	Intercept	Δz_t	Δz_{t-1}	R^2	D.W.	BLUS	Optimal basis
7.28	Firms' output price	Entire	$\Delta p^e_{w,t}$	−1·234 (2·049)	1·266 (6·622)	0·2140 (1·063)	0·750	1·11	$F_{(17,17)} = 2\cdot83$	18-20
7.29	Firms' export price	Entire	$\Delta p^e_{f,t}$	−0·1190 (0·0907)	0·7534 (3·428)	0·3684 (1·675)	0·400	0·74	$F_{(13,12)} = 4\cdot39$	13-15
7.30	Firms' average unit costs	Entire	Δc^e_t	5·264 (11·46)	0·3103 (4·177)	0·2007 (2·629)	0·488	0·72	$F_{(17,17)} = 2\cdot29$	18-20

Note: Δz is the rate of change of the corresponding realised variable.

The constraints are not rejected on the basis of an F-test at the five per cent level.[31]

Results for the extrapolative model preferred by Turnovsky in his study, which utilised the Livingston sample survey data for the United States, are given in Table 7. 6. The estimates reported are those for all expectational variables over the entire period, without constraints. The null hypothesis of no first-order serial correlation in the residuals is rejected for all of the extrapolative models and those models exhibit less explanatory power than the error-learning formulations.[32]

The evidence so far suggests that when the rate of inflation is 'low' then price expectations are autogressive and independent of the actual rate of change variables. When inflation is 'high', firms' expectations of their domestic output prices and their export prices are approximately characterised by adaptive expectations, and expectations of their average cost per unit of output by a second-order error-learning process. With a constant error then the proportions by which this error is adjusted over four months for the 'high' inflation periods are, for output prices 0· 60, export prices 0· 44 and average costs 0· 04.

Following Carlson and Parkin, variables which may affect the actual rate of inflation may influence rational individuals' expectations of it, and on these grounds additional variables (economic variables and variables designed to pick up the effects, if any, of government policy and non-economic factors) were tried. Many variables were used—all those of Carlson and Parkin together with dummy variables for the impact and continuation effects of Selective Employment Tax and the introduction of the Import Deposit Scheme in 1968. The additional variables were tried in error-learning models for the 'high' inflation period. However, the estimates of these models should be treated with caution. Whereas with monthly data (used by Carlson and Parkin) it is possible to align quite accurately a dummy variable for a specific point in time, this is not the case with the four-monthly data. Suppose an event, for example a general election, occurs in the first month of the four month time period. A dummy variable covering the whole of the four-month period will register the average of the impact and continuation effects over that period, *ceteris paribus*. In the case of possible effects which span two or more consecutive time periods, but which do not occupy the whole of the two end periods, a choice has to be made between either including the outside observations with the same weight as the others or assuming the effect over an end observation is some proportion of the average effect over the other observations.[33] Because of the small sample of only seventeen observations it was not possible to include all of the additional variables in one regression. The strategy adopted was to include each variable in turn and then to include all those variables that were significant at the five per cent level on a two-tailed test in one regression. These estimates are presented below.

Firms' export price expectations

$$\Delta p^e_{f,t} - \Delta p^e_{f,t-1} = \underset{[3 \cdot 603]}{0 \cdot 4649} \ (\Delta p_{f,t} - \Delta p^e_{f,t-1}) + \underset{[2 \cdot 41]}{6 \cdot 55D} - \underset{[2 \cdot 04]}{4 \cdot 49 \ SET}$$

$$\underset{[1 \cdot 27]}{-0 \cdot 14 \Delta \bar{w}} + \underset{[3 \cdot 00]}{0 \cdot 39 \Delta w^*}, \ R^2 = 0 \cdot 8045, \ F_{(5, 11)} = 9 \cdot 05 \qquad (7.31)$$

Firms' average cost expectations

$$\Delta c^e_t = \underset{[1 \cdot 842]}{1 \cdot 148} + \underset{[4 \cdot 618]}{0 \cdot 2246} \ \Delta c_t + \underset{[2 \cdot 457]}{0 \cdot 2700} \ \Delta c^e_{t-1} + \underset{[5 \cdot 84]}{0 \cdot 55 \Delta \bar{w}},$$

$$R^2 = 0 \cdot 9340, \ F_{(3, 13)} = 61 \cdot 32 \qquad (7.32)$$

where

D = Impact effect of sterling devaluation, 1967

SET = Impact effect of Selective Employment Tax, 1966(O)

$\Delta \bar{w}$ = Large and highly publicised wage settlements

$\Delta \bar{w}$ $= \Sigma \dfrac{n_{it}}{N_t} \ w_{it}$

> where w_i is the ith sector's annual percentage change in weekly wage rates, n_i is the number of men involved in the ith sector's settlements and N_t is the total number of men receiving settlements in period t.

Δw^* = Effect of wage-change norm. Takes the value of the official norm but where there was no norm takes the value of the annual percentage rate of change of basic weekly wage rates.[34]

None of the additional variables was significant in the model for firms' output price expectations.

Although three additional variables significantly influence firms' expectations of their export prices, their inclusion does not affect the point estimate of the error-learning adjustment parameter nor the constraints.[35] The average effect of the sterling devaluation in 1967 was to raise firms' export price expectations by an average of approximately 6·5 percentage points over the period from December 1967 to March 1968. The selective employment tax dummy variable, which is significant at the ten per cent level on a two-tailed test, suggests that firms' export price expectations fell, on average, approximately 4 percentage points over the period August to December 1966. It seems possible that this variable may be picking-up the effect of the statutory 'freeze' (of prices and money incomes in the latter half of that year) on the expectational variable. The wage-change norm, however, appears to have had a perverse effect on firms' export price expectations, raising those expectations by approximately two-fifths of the norm.

The only additional variable which affected firms' expectations of their average unit costs is one reflecting large and highly pub-licised wage changes. There was neither heteroscedasticity nor autocorrelation in the cost-expectations models, but with the addition of this further variable the influence of the second error is rejected on the basis of an F-test[36] and in the first-order error-learning model the constraints are rejected.[37]

Finally, following Turnovsky's theoretical work, which suggests there is a positive relationship between the adjustment para-meter and the variance of the most recent expected rate of change at the time the next expectation was formed, the above models were re-estimated with the adjustment parameter permitted to vary with the appropriate variance.

A simple linear formulation was used:

$$\mu = \alpha + \beta(\sigma^2 \Delta p^e_{t-1}) \tag{7.33}$$

where $\sigma^2 \Delta p^e_{t-1}$ is the variance of Δp^e_{t-1}. With first-order error-learning, the model becomes:

$$\Delta p^e_t - \Delta p^e_{t-1} = \alpha(\Delta p_t - \Delta p^e_{t-1}) + \beta(\Delta p_t \cdot \sigma^2 \Delta p^e_{t-1} - \Delta p^e_{t-1} \cdot \sigma^2 \Delta p^e_{t-1})$$

$$+ u_t \tag{7.34}$$

For all models, the inclusion of the variance term was rejected by the appropriate F-test.[38] The results for firms' output price expectations, which are typical, are presented below.

$$\Delta p^e_{w,t} = -1 \cdot 096 + 1 \cdot 835 \, \Delta p_{w,t} + 0 \cdot 4625 \, \Delta p^e_{w,t-1}$$
$$[0 \cdot 896] \quad [0 \cdot 508] \qquad\quad [0 \cdot 194]$$

$$- \, 0 \cdot 018 \, \Delta p_{w,t} \cdot \sigma^2 \Delta p^e_{t-1} - 0 \cdot 049 \, \Delta p^e_{t-1} \, \sigma^2 \Delta p^e_{t-1}, R^2 = 0 \cdot 847$$
$$[0 \cdot 042] \qquad\qquad\qquad [0 \cdot 169]$$

$$\tag{7.35}$$

There is extensive multicollinearity amongst the regressors. None of the explanatory variables is significantly different from zero on the basis of individual t-tests although the regression as a whole is significant, $F_{(4, 12)} = 16 \cdot 66$, which is greater than the 5 per cent critical value of $3 \cdot 26$.

In summary, none of these attempts to augment the error-learning model of expectations formation changed the initial results appreciably.

V CONCLUSIONS

The results of this chapter indicate that firms' expectations-formation may be characterised by error-learning models, at least for periods of 'high' inflation. When the rate of inflation is 'low' expectations are autogressive. Firms' expectations of domestic output prices, export prices and average costs may be characterised by adaptive expectations; only for firms' export price expectations are the constraints not rejected. With the exception of firms' output price expectations, expectations are affected by factors other than past prices and previous expectations. Firms' export price expectations were affected by the sterling devaluation of 1967 and possibly incomes policies; average cost expectations were influenced by large and highly publicised wage increases. The empirical evidence rejects the hypothesis that the error-learning adjustment parameter varies with the variance of the previous expected rate of change of prices.

These results may be compared with those of other investigators who have tested expectations-formation schemes using expectational variables derived from sample survey data. Previous empirical work for the United Kingdom by Carlson and Parkin (1975) (see Chapter 6) found that the determinants of consumers' inflation expectations differed according to whether the actual rate of inflation was 'high' or 'low'. For 'high' rates of inflation they found that the expectations formation process approximates a second-order error-learning scheme although the sterling devaluation of November 1967 had an impact affect on price expectations of approximately six percentage points. Using quarterly data, Parkin *et al.* (1976) found that firms' expected rates of change of output and export prices both approximate adaptive expectations, the latter also being affected by the sterling devaluation of 1967 and the Deutschemark revaluation of October 1969, both of which had an impact effect on export price expectations of approximately eight per cent. These results may be contrasted with those of Turnovsky (1970) and Knöbl (1974). Turnovsky, using the Livingston price expectations series for the United States, found the expectations formation process to be characterised by the extrapolative model. Knöbl, in a study of inflation expectations in Germany over the period 1965(1)-1972(4) reported that the extra-polative model was superior to adaptive expectations. However, although Knöbl does not report his estimated adaptive expectations model, his estimates of the extrapolative models exhibit significant positive first-order serial correlation in the residuals and 'imply that the inflation rate is expected to fall whenever the current actual inflation rate has increased by 100 per cent or less compared with the previous period' (Sumner, 1976). However, Paunio and Suvanto (1977) in a study of the determinants of inflation expectations for Finland, 1963-74, using monthly expectations data based on yield differentials between indexed and non-indexed bonds, rejected the extrapolative model in favour of an adaptive expectations model, augmented by a devaluation dummy for 1967 and a shift dummy for the period April 1968 to December 1974, which approximates to Carlson and Parkin's 'high' inflation period. In a study of the determinants of inflation expectations in Australia using sample survey data transformed by the Carlson-Parkin method, Danes (1975) found that, generally, error-learning models were superior to extrapolative ones. It seems, therefore, that the results of this chapter are broadly consistent with the bulk of the available evidence in supporting some version of the error-learning hypothesis as an explanation of the determinants of inflation expectations. Few of the additional variables examined made a significant contribution to the results.

The policy implications of the results are clear. To reduce firms' expectations of the rates of change of output prices, export prices and average costs, it is necessary to reduce the actual rates of change of those variables. For firms' output prices, none of the additional factors studied seemed to have any effect. Firms' expected export price changes might be reduced by an exchange-rate change or, possibly, by particular incomes policies. Not surprisingly, firms' expectations of the rate of change of their average costs may fall as a result of a reduction in large and highly publicised wage settlements.

NOTES TO CHAPTER 7

[1]   I am indebted to the editors of this volume and members of the former SSRC-University of Manchester Inflation Workshop for helpful comments on an earlier draft. Of course, they are not responsible for any errors which may be present.
[2]   See Appendix 6.2 for a similar exercise concerning the determinants of consumers' price expectations.
[3]   The last survey in 1964 was postponed until November because of the general election; the last one in 1971 was held in September in preparation for the introduction of quarterly surveys and that to be held in February 1971 was cancelled because of the Post Office workers' strike.

4   Whereas the Gallup question is concerned with changes in levels, the CBI question asks about changes in trends. This suggests that for the latter sample survey data, the appropriate scaling factor should be the acceleration of inflation, and the resulting series would be a measure of the expected change in the inflation rate. This was investigated but, in the light of comparisons of the expectational variables with the actual variables, the results were most implausible and highly inconsistent. Because of this, the un-scaled expectational series were scaled against the proportional first derivative with respect to time of the appropriate price variable.

5   From and including October 1970, this question referred to average prices at which domestic orders are booked.

6   This question was introduced in June 1961.

7   J ≡ June, F ≡ February and O ≡ October.

8   The reader is referred to Chapter 6 for a complete discussion of the procedure.

9   The assumption of normality for the distribution of inflation expectations across the population at a given point in time is justified on simplicity criteria: the normal distribution is easy to handle empirically and has a mean and variance. This assumption cannot be tested for the data available for the United Kingdom, but has been tested for the Livingston data of United States price expectations. Carlson (1975) finds that the normal distribution is not entirely appropriate for such a series, a distribution skewed towards higher rates of inflation being superior. However, Carlson comments, 'In most cases it appears that one or two outlying predictions were entirely responsible [for the inadequacy of the normal distribution]' (p. 753). This is not particularly disconcerting for studies based on United Kingdom data. The Livingston data for the United States are known to be a small and unrepresentative sample.

10   The mathematics of the procedure is given in Chapter 6 to which the reader is referred.

11   The observation for February 1971 was linearly interpolated. The exclusion of this one interpolated observation does not affect the results.

12   Since the CBI also ask firms 'what has been the trend over the past four months?', it is also possible to derive a variable scaling factor by calculating a time series for firms' actual price changes from CBI surveys, scaling that variable against data from the *Monthly Digest of Statistics* and using the resultant scaling factor for the expectations series.

13   The source of the weights is the *Report of the Census of Production, 1968,* Summary Tables, Industry Analysis U.K. Table 1, p. 156.

14   Clearly this definition of average unit cost is narrow; some costs are excluded and the labour cost component is not comprehensive. However, including further cost components would require interpolation for the variable to be centred correctly and would introduce autocorrelation, the presence of which would otherwise be a helpful guide to the existence of specification errors. For the period from 1963, data from the New Earnings Survey was tried instead of basic weekly rates. The resultant scaling factor was almost identical with that presented here and graphs of the two actual average cost series had similar characteristics.

15   The scaling factor used by Carlson and Parkin was 1·764.

16   The graphs of the expectational variables are those for which 'same' and 'don't know' are grouped together. The graphs of the expectational variables in which the 'don't knows' were treated according to the second method are very similar, even at extreme values.

[17]   Similar characteristics were observed when data from the New Earnings Survey were used in deriving the labour cost component of average cost.

[18]   Cagan (1956), p. 37.

[19]   The aggregation of adaptive expectations models over individual economic units had been discussed by Bierwag and Grove (1966) who show that a necessary condition for such a distributed lag function to exist at the macro level is that all the micro adjustment parameters be equal. If this is not the case then the aggregate distributed lag function is a member of the general class of Pascal functions.

[20]   Rose (1972), p. 18.

[21]   For higher-order error-learning, $0 < \mu_1 < 2$ (Rose (1972), p. 19).

[22]   If $\gamma = -1$, $\Delta p_t^e = \Delta p_{t-1}$. The most recent observation of the actual rate of inflation is ignored, as it would be if there was believed to be excessive noise in the most recent observation of the actual rate of change of prices.

[23]   Any distinction between 'low' and 'high' inflation is, of course, arbitrary. For example a rate of inflation for the United Kingdom of five per cent was considered 'high' in the mid 1960s whereas a decade later such a figure would be regarded as 'low'. However, it seems appropriate to classify a period as one over which the rate of inflation was high if at that time it was so considered.

[24]   Since 1962(J)-1964(F) is only six observations on four-monthly data.

[25]   This particular procedure uses considerably less computer time than one of estimating all models by maximum likelihood. Moreover, the small sample bias of Durbin's h statistic is such that it tends to reject the null hypothesis when it is true (Spencer, 1975). The approach adopted here results in a further check when a type one error might be committed.

[26]   Consequently the models are mis-specified. It is not possible to test whether the constraints in such models hold since the usual tests are invalid.

[27]   'Best' in the sense of models having the most plausible estimated coefficients and more appropriate statistical credentials.

[28]   The results for all the variables based on CBI data are the same irrespective of whether 'don't knows' and 'stay the sames' are grouped together or 'don't knows' are allocated proportionately among 'up', 'down' and 'stay the same'. Those presented are those for which 'same' and 'don't know' are grouped together.

[29] $F_{(2, 14)} = 7 \cdot 88$; the five per cent critical value is $3 \cdot 74$.

[30]   The observed values for the entire and 'high' inflation periods are $F_{(2, 25)} = 0 \cdot 54$ and $F_{(2, 14)} = 0 \cdot 58$ respectively. The corresponding critical values at the $0 \cdot 05$ level are $3 \cdot 38$ and $3 \cdot 74$.

[31] $F_{(3, 12)} = 1 \cdot 38$, which is less than the critical value at the five per cent level of $3 \cdot 49$.

[32]   For expected average unit costs, $\bar{R}^2$ is $0 \cdot 458$ for the extrapolative model and $0 \cdot 775$ for the second-order error-learning model estimated over the same time period.

[33]   This can be done by letting a dummy variable take the value 'one' for periods over which the full effect was continuous and, for example, '$\frac{1}{2}$' for the observation where half of the full effect is believed to be appropriate.

[34]   The variables $\Delta \bar{w}$ and Δw^* are fully described in Appendix 6.2.

[35] $F_{(2, 10)} = 1 \cdot 35$, which is less than the five per cent critical value of $4 \cdot 10$.

36    $F_{(2, 11)} = 2 \cdot 32$, which is less than the five per cent critical value of $3 \cdot 98$.

37    $F_{(3. 13)} = 19 \cdot 91$, which is greater than the five per cent critical value of $3 \cdot 41$.

38   Firms' output price expectations, $F_{(2, 12)} = 0 \cdot 39$. The five per cent critical value is $3 \cdot 88$. Firms' expected average costs, $F_{(2, 11)} = 0 \cdot 17$. The five per cent critical value is $3 \cdot 98$. Firms' export price expectations, $F_{(1, 11)} = 0 \cdot 94$. The five per cent critical value is $4 \cdot 84$.

Bibliography

Allen, R. G. D. (1975), 'The immediate contributors to inflation', *Economic Journal*, 85, pp. 607-11.

Anderson, L. C. and K. M. Carlson (1972), 'An econometric analysis of the relation of monetary variables to the behavior of prices and unemployment', in *The Econometrics of Price Determination Conference* (O. Eckstein, ed.).

Archibald, G. C. (1969), 'The Phillips curve and the distribution of unemployment', *American Economic Review* (Papers and Proceedings), 59, pp. 124-34.

Arrow, K. J. (1959), 'Towards a theory of price adjustment', in *The Allocation of Economic Resources* (M. Abramovitz, ed.) Stanford: Stanford University Press.

Artis, M. J. and M. K. Lewis (1976), 'The demand for money in the U.K.: 1963-73', *Manchester School*, 54, pp. 147-81

Artis, M. J. and A. R. Nobay (1969), 'Two aspects of the monetary debate', *National Institute Economic Review*, 49, pp. 33-42.

Ball, R. J. and T. Burns (1976), 'The inflationary mechanism in the U.K. economy', *American Economic Review*, 66, pp. 467-84.

Ball, R. J. and M. Duffy (1972), 'Price formation in European countries', in *The Econometrics of Price Determination Conference* (O. Eckstein, ed.).

Bank of England (1970a), 'The importance of money', *Bank of England Quarterly Bulletin*, 10, pp. 159-98.

—— (1970b), 'Timing relationships between movements of monetary and national income variables', *Bank of England Quarterly Bulletin*, 10, pp. 459-68.

Barro, R. J. (1972), 'A theory of monopolistic price adjustment', *Review of Economic Studies*, 39, pp. 17-26.

Barro, R. J. and H. I. Grossman (1976), *Money, Employment and Inflation*. Cambridge: Cambridge University Press.

Bierwag, G. O. and M. A. Grove (1966), 'Aggregate Koyck functions', *Econometrica*, 34, pp. 820-32.

Bishop, R. L. (1963), 'Game theoretic analyses of bargaining', *Quarterly Journal of Economics*, 77, pp. 559-602.

Bispham, J. A. (1975), 'The new Cambridge and monetarist criticisms of conventional economic policy-making', *National Institute Economic Review*, 74, pp. 39-55.

Bowers, J. K., P. C. Cheshire and A. E. Webb (1970), 'The change in the relationship between unemployment and earnings increases: a review of some possible explanations', *National Institute Economic Review,* 54, pp. 44-63.

Bowers, J. K., P. C. Cheshire, A. E. Webb and R. Weedon (1972), 'Some aspects of unemployment and the labour market 1966-71', *National Institute Economic Review,* 62, pp. 75-88.

Box, G. E. P. and G. M. Jenkins (1970), *Time Series Analysis: Forecasting and Control.* San Francisco: Holden-Day.

Brechling, F. P. R. (1972), 'Some empirical evidence on the effectiveness of prices and incomes policies', in *Incomes Policy and Inflation* (M. Parkin and M. T. Sumner, eds.).

Brittan, S. (1975), *Second Thoughts on Full Employment Policy.* London: Centre for Policy Studies.

Brown, A. J. (1939), 'Interest, prices and the demand for idle money', *Oxford Economic Papers,* 2, pp. 46-69.

Bruce, C. J. (1975), 'The wage-tax spiral: Canada 1953-1970', *Economic Journal,* 85, pp. 372-6.

Cagan, P. (1956), 'The monetary dynamics of hyperinflation', in *Studies in the Quantity Theory of Money* (M. Friedman, ed.). Chicago, Ill.: Chicago University Press.

Carlson, J. A. (1967), 'The classroom economy: rules, results, reflections', Purdue University Institute Paper No. 166.

—— (1972), 'Elusive passage to the non-Walrasian continent', University of Manchester (mimeo).

—— (1975), 'Are price expectations normally distributed?' *Journal of the American Statistical Association,* 70, Applications Section, pp. 749-54.

Carlson, J. A. and M. Parkin (1975), 'Inflation expectations', *Economica,* N.S. 42, pp. 123-38.

Chamberlin, R. H. (1933), *The Theory of Monopolistic Competition.* Cambridge, Mass.: Harvard University Press.

Coddington, A. (1966), 'A theory of the bargaining process: comment', *American Economic Review,* 56, pp. 522-30.

—— (1968), *Theories of the Bargaining Process.* London: Allen & Unwin.

Coutts, K., R. Tarling and F. Wilkinson (1976a), 'Wage bargaining and the inflation process', *Economic Policy Review,* 2, pp. 20-7. University of Cambridge, Department of Applied Economics.

—— (1976b), 'Costs and prices 1974-1976', *Economic Policy Review*, 2, pp. 28-34. University of Cambridge, Department of Applied Economics.

Cross, J. G. (1965), 'A theory of the bargaining process', *American Economic Review*, 55, pp. 67-94.

—— (1966), 'A theory of the bargaining process—reply', *American Economic Review*, 56, pp. 630-3.

Cross, R. B. and D. E. W. Laidler (1976), 'Inflation, excess demand and expectations in fixed exchange rate open economies: some preliminary empirical results', in *Inflation in the World Economy* (M. Parkin and G. Zis, eds.).

Danes, M (1975), 'The measurement and explanation of inflationary expectations in Australia', *Australian Economic Papers*, 19, pp. 75-87.

de Menil, G. (1971), *Bargaining: Monopoly Power-versus Union Power*. Cambridge, Mass.: MIT Press.

de Menil, G. and S. Bhalla (1975), 'Direct measurement of popular price expectations', *American Economic Review*, 65, pp. 169-80.

Dicks-Mireaux, L. A. (1961), 'The interrelationship between cost and price changes, 1945-59: a study of inflation in post-war Britain', *Oxford Economic Papers*, 13, pp. 267-92.

Duck, N., M. Parkin, D. Rose and G. Zis, 'The determination of the rate of change of wages and prices in the fixed exchange rate world economy, 1956-71', in *Inflation in the World Economy* (M. Parkin and G. Zis, eds.).

Durbin, J. (1970), 'Testing for serial correlation in least-squares regression when some of the regressors are lagged dependent variables', *Econometrica*, 37, pp. 410-21.

Eckstein, O. (ed.) (1972), *The Econometrics of Price Determination Conference*. Washington, D.C.: Board of Governors of the Federal Reserve System and SSRC

Eckstein, O. and R. Brinner (1972), 'The inflation process in the United States', a study prepared for the use of the *Joint Economic Committee, 92nd Congress, 2nd Session*. Washington, D.C.

Eckstein, O. and T. A. Wilson (1962), 'Determination of money wages in American industry', *Quarterly Journal of Economics*, 76, pp. 379-414.

Edgren, G., K. O. Faxén and G. E. Odhner (1969), 'Wages, growth and the distribution of income', *Swedish Journal of Economics*, 71, pp. 133-60.

Fisher, D. (1968), 'The demand for money in Britain: quarterly results 1951-67', *Manchester School,* 38, pp. 327-51.

Foldes, L. (1964), 'A determinate model of bilateral monopoly', *Economica,* N.S. 31, pp. 117-31.

Foster, J. I. (1973), 'The behaviour of unemployment and unfilled vacancies in Great Britain, 1958-71: a comment', *Economic Journal,* 83, pp. 192-201.

—— (1974), 'The relationship between unemployment and vacancies in Great Britain, 1958-72: some further evidence', in *Inflation and Labour Markets* (D. E. W. Laidler and D. L. Purdy, eds.).

Friedman, M. (1966), 'What price guideposts?' in *Guidelines, Informal Controls and the Market Place* (G. P. Schultz and R. Z. Aliber, eds.). Chicago, Ill.: University of Chicago Press.

—— (1968), 'The role of monetary policy', *American Economic Review,* 58, pp. 1-17.

Friedman, M. and A. J. Schwartz (1963), *A Monetary History of the United States, 1867-1960.* Princeton, N.J.: Princeton University Press for NBER.

Glynn, D. A. (1969), 'The CBI industrial trends survey', *Applied Economics,* 1, pp. 183-96.

Godfrey, L. G. (1971), 'The Phillips curve: incomes policy and trade union effects', in *The Current Inflation* (H. G. Johnson and A. R. Nobay, eds.). Abridged and amended version in *Incomes Policy and Inflation* (M. Parkin and M. T. Sumner, eds.).

Godley, W. A. H. and W. D. Nordhaus, (1972), 'Pricing in the trade cycle', *Economic Journal,* 82, pp. 853-82.

Godley, W. A. H. and D. A. Rowe (1964), 'Retail and consumer prices, 1953-1963', *National Institute Economic Review,* 27, pp. 44-57.

Goodwin, R. M. (1947), 'Dynamic coupling with especial reference to markets having production lags', *Econometrica,* 15, pp. 181-204.

Gordon, R. J. (1971), 'Inflation in recession and recovery', *Brookings Papers on Economic Activity,* 2, pp. 105-58.

—— (1972), 'Wage-price controls and the shifting Phillips curve', *Brookings Papers on Economic Activity,* 3, pp. 385-421.

—— (1975), 'The supply of and demand for inflation', *Journal of Law and Economics,* 18, pp. 807-36.

Gray, M. R. and R. G. Lipsey (1974), 'Is the natural rate of unemployment the appropriate policy target for maintaining a stable rate of inflation?', University of Manchester—SSRC Inflation Workshop Discussion Paper.

Gray, M. R. and M. Parkin (1976), 'Discriminating between alternative explanations of inflation', in the *Proceedings of the Conference on Bank Credit, Money and Inflation in Open Economies* (M. Fratianni and K. Tavernier, eds.). Leuven, Belgium.

Gujarati, D. (1972), 'The behaviour of unemployment and unfilled vacancies: Great Britain, 1958-1971', *Economic Journal*, 82, pp. 195-204.

Harrod, R. (1972), 'The issues: five views', in *Inflation as a Global Problem* (R. Hinshaw, ed.). London: Johns Hopkins University Press.

Harsanyi, J. C. (1956), 'Approaches to the bargaining problem before and after the theory of games: a critical discussion on Zeuthen's, Hicks's and Nash's theories', *Econometrica*, 24, pp. 144-57.

Henry, S. G. B., M. C. Sawyer and P. Smith (1976), 'Models of inflation in the United Kingdom: an evaluation', *National Institute Economic Review*, 77, pp. 60-71.

Hicks, J. R. (1932), *The Theory of Wages*. London: Macmillan.

—— (1946), *Value and Capital* (2nd ed.). Oxford: Oxford University Press.

—— (1955), 'Economic foundations of wages policy', *Economic Journal*, 65, pp. 389-404.

—— (1974), *The Crisis in Keynesian Economics*. Oxford: Blackwell.

—— (1975), 'What is wrong with monetarism', *Lloyds Bank Review*, 118, pp. 1-13.

Hines, A. G. (1964), 'Trade unions and wage inflation in the United Kingdom, 1893-1961', *Review of Economic Studies*, 31, pp. 221-52.

—— (1968), 'Unemployment and the rate of change of money wage rates in the United Kingdom, 1862-1963: a reappraisal', *Review of Economics and Statistics*, 50, pp. 60-7.

—— (1969), 'Wage inflation in the United Kingdom, 1948-62: a disaggregated study', *Economic Journal*, 79, pp. 66-89.

—— (1971), 'The determinants of the rate of change of money wage rates and the effectiveness of incomes policy', in *The Current Inflation* (H. G. Johnson and A. R. Nobay, eds.).

Holt, C. C. (1969), 'Improving the labor market trade-off between inflation and unemployment', *American Economic Review* (Papers and Proceedings), 59, pp. 135-46.

—— (1970), 'Job search, Phillips' wage relation, and union influence: theory and evidence', in *Microeconomic Foundations of Employment and Inflation Theory* (E. S. Phelps, ed.).

House of Commons (1974), *Ninth Report from the Expenditure Committee, Session 1974-75, Public Expenditure, Inflation and the Balance of Payments*. London: HMSO.

—— (1975), *First Report from the Expenditure Committee, Session 1975-76, The Financing of Public Expenditure, 1*. London: HMSO.

Johnson, H. G. (1972), *Inflation and the Monetarist Controversy*. Amsterdam: North-Holland.

Johnson, H. G. and A. R. Nobay (eds.) (1971), *The Current Inflation*. London: Macmillan.

Johnston, J. (1972), 'A model of wage determination under bilateral monopoly', *Economic Journal*, 82, pp. 837-52. Reprinted in *Inflation and Labour Markets* (D. E. W. Laidler and D. L. Purdy, eds.).

Johnston, J. and M. C. Timbrell (1973), 'Empirical tests of a bargaining theory of wage rate determination', *Manchester School*, 41, pp. 141-67. Reprinted in *Inflation and Labour Markets* (D. E. W. Laidler and D. L. Purdy, eds.).

Johnston, J., D. D. Bugg and P. J. Lund (1964), 'Some econometrics of inflation in the U.K.', in *Econometric Analysis for National Economic Planning* (P. E. Hart, G. Mills and J. K. Whitaker, eds.). London: Butterworth.

Jones, A. (1972), *The New Inflation: The Politics of Prices and Incomes*. London: Penguin Books and Andre Deutsch.

Jonson, P. D. and H. I. Kierzkowski (1975), 'The balance of payments: an analytic exercise', *Manchester School*, 43, pp. 105-33.

Kahn, Lord (1976), 'Inflation: a Keynesian view', *Scottish Journal of Political Economy*, 23, pp. 11-16.

Kavanagh, N. J. and A. A. Walters (1966), 'The demand for money in the United Kingdom 1877-1961: preliminary findings', *Bulletin of the Oxford Institute of Economics and Statistics*, 28, pp. 93-116.

Khusro, A. M. (1952), 'An investigation of liquidity preference', *Yorkshire Bulletin of Economic and Social Research,* 4, pp. 1-20.

Klein, L. R. and R. J. Ball (1959), 'Some econometrics of the determination of the absolute level of wages and prices', *Economic Journal,* 69, pp. 465-82.

Knöbl, A. (1974), 'Price expectations and actual price behaviour in Germany', *IMF Staff Papers,* 21, pp. 83-100.

Laidler, D. E. W. (1975), *Essays on Money and Inflation.* Manchester and Chicago, Ill.: Manchester University Press and Chicago University Press.

—— (1976), 'Inflation: alternative explanations of and policy tests on data drawn from six countries', in *Institutions, Policies and Economic Performance,* Carnegie-Rochester Conference Series on Public Policy, 4 (K. Brunner and A. H. Meltzer, eds.). Amsterdam: North-Holland.

Laidler, D. E. W. and M. Parkin (1970), 'The demand for money in the United Kingdom, 1955-1967: preliminary estimates', *Manchester School,* 38, pp. 187-208.

—— (1975), 'Inflation: a survey', *Economic Journal,* 85, pp. 741-809.

Laidler, D. E. W. and D. L. Purdy (eds.) (1974), *Inflation and Labour Markets.* Manchester and Toronto: Manchester University Press and University of Toronto Press.

Lipsey, R. G. (1960), 'The relation between unemployment and the rate of change of money wage rates in the United Kingdom, 1862-1957: a further analysis', *Economica,* N.S. 27, pp. 1-31.

Lipsey, R. G. and M. Parkin (1970), 'Incomes policy: a re-appraisal', *Economica,* N.S. 37, pp. 115-38. Reprinted in *Incomes Policy and Inflation* (M. Parkin and M. T. Sumner, eds.).

Lucas, R. E. Jr. (1972), 'Econometric testing of the natural rate hypothesis', in *The Econometrics of Price Determination Conference* (O. Eckstein, ed.).

Lucas, R. E. Jr. and L. A. Rapping (1969a), 'Price expectations and the Phillips curve', *American Economic Review,* 59, pp. 342-50.

—— (1969b), 'Real wages, employment and inflation', *Journal of Political Economy,* 77, pp. 721-54.

McCallum, B. T. (1970), 'The effect of demand on prices in British manufacturing: another view', *Review of Economic Studies,* 37, pp. 147-55.

—— (1974), 'Wage rate changes and the excess demand for labour: an alternative formulation', *Economica,* N.S., 41, pp. 269-77.

—— (1975), 'Rational expectations and the natural rate hypothesis: some evidence for the United Kingdom', *Manchester School*, 43, pp. 56-67.

McGuire, T. W. (1976), 'Price change expectations and the Phillips curve', in *The Economics of Price and Wage Controls*, Carnegie-Rochester Conference Series on Public Policy, 2 (K. Brunner and A. H. Meltzer, eds.). Amsterdam: North-Holland.

MacKay, D. I. and R A. Hart (1974), 'Wage inflation and the Phillips relationship', *Manchester School*, 42, pp. 131-61.

Maki, D. and Z. A. Spindler (1975), 'The effect of unemployment compensation on the rate of unemployment in Great Britain', *Oxford Economic Papers*, N.S. 27, pp. 440-55.

Marris, S (1972), 'World inflation—panel discussion', in *Stabilisation Policies in Interdependent Economies* (E. Claassen and P. Salin, eds.). Amsterdam: North-Holland.

Miller, M. H. (1976), 'Can a rise in import prices be inflationary and deflationary? Economists and U.K. inflation, 1973-74', *American Economic Review*, 66, pp. 501-19.

Mortensen, D T. (1970), 'A theory of wage and employment dynamics', in *Microeconomic Foundations of Employment and Inflation Theory* (E. S. Phelps, ed.).

Mundell, R. A. (1971), *Monetary Theory, Inflation, Interest and Growth in the World Economy*. California: Goodyear Publishing.

Muth, J. F. (1961), 'Rational expectations and the theory of price movements', *Econometrica*, 29, pp. 315-35.

Nash, J. F. Jr. (1950), 'The bargaining problem', *Econometrica*, 18, pp. 155-62.

—— (1953), 'Two person co-operative games', *Econometrica*, 21, pp. 128-40.

Neild, R. R. (1963), *Pricing and Employment in the Trade Cycle*. London: Cambridge University Press.

Nordhaus, W. D. (1972a), 'Recent developments in price dynamics', in *The Econometrics of Price Determination Conference* (O Eckstein, ed.).

—— (1972b), 'The worldwide wage explosion', *Brookings Papers on Economic Activity*, 2, pp. 431-64.

Okun, A. (1962), 'Potential G.N.P.: its measurements and significance', *Proceedings of the Business and Economic Statistics Section of the American Statistical Association*, Section 7, pp. 98-104.

Osgood, C. E. (1953), *Method and Theory in Experimental Psychology*. New York: Oxford University Press.

Parkin, M. (1970), 'Incomes policy: some further results on the determination of the rate of change of money wages', *Economica*, N.S 37, pp. 386-401.

―― (1975a), 'Inflation, the balance of payments, domestic credit expansion and exchange rate adjustment', in *National Monetary Policies and the International Financial System* (R. Aliber, ed.). Chicago, Ill.: University of Chicago Press.

―― (1975b), 'The politics of inflation', *Government and Opposition*, 10, pp. 189-202.

Parkin, M. and M. T. Sumner (eds.) (1972), *Incomes Policy and Inflation*. Manchester: Manchester University Press.

Parkin, M. and A. K Swoboda (1977), 'Inflation: a review of the issues', in *Inflation Theory and Anti-Inflation Policy* (E. Lundberg, ed.). London: Macmillan for International Economic Association.

Parkin, M. and G. Zis (eds.) (1976a), *Inflation in the World Economy*. Manchester and Toronto: Manchester University Press and University of Toronto Press.

―― (1976b), *Inflation in Open Economies*. Manchester and Toronto: Manchester University Press and University of Toronto Press.

Parkin, M., M. T. Sumner and R. A. Jones (1972), 'A survey of the econometric evidence on the effects of incomes policy on the rate of inflation', in *Incomes Policy and Inflation* (M. Parkin and M. T. Sumner, eds.).

Parkin, M., M. T. Sumner and R. Ward (1976), 'The effects of excess demand, generalized expectations and wage-price controls on wage inflation in the U.K.: 1956-71', in *The Economics of Price and Wage Controls*, Carnegie-Rochester Conference Series on Public Policy, 2 (K. Brunner and A. H. Meltzer, eds.). Amsterdam: North-Holland.

Patinkin, D. (1956), *Money, Interest and Prices*. Evanston, Ill.: Row, Peterson.

Paunio, J. J. and A. Suvanto (1977), 'Changes in price expectations: some tests using data on indexed and non-indexed bonds', *Economica*, N.S. 44, pp. 37-45.

Perry, G. L. (1966), *Unemployment, Money Wage Rates and Inflation*. Cambridge, Mass.: MIT Press.

—— (1975), 'Determinants of wage inflation around the world', *Brookings Papers on Economic Activity*, 6, pp. 403-35.

Pesaran, H (1972), 'A dynamic inter-industry model of price determination: a test of the normal price hypothesis', *Quarterly Journal of Economic Research*, 9, pp. 88-123.

Phelps, E S. (1965), 'Anticipated inflation and economic welfare', *Journal of Political Economy*, 73, pp 1-17.

—— (1967), 'Phillips curves, expectations of inflation and optimal unemployment over time', *Economica*, N.S. 34, pp. 254-81.

—— (1968), 'Money-wage dynamics and labor-market equilibrium', *Journal of Political Economy*, 76, pp. 678-711.

—— (ed.) (1970), *Microeconomic Foundations of Employment and Inflation Theory*. New York: Norton.

—— (1972), *Inflation Policy and Unemployment Theory*. New York: Norton.

Phelps, E. S. and S. G. Winter (1970), 'Optimal price policy under atomistic competition', in *Microeconomic Foundations of Employment and Inflation Theory* (E. S. Phelps, ed.).

Phelps-Brown, Sir E. H. (1975), 'A non-monetarist view of the pay explosion', *Three Banks Review*, 106, pp. 183-91.

Phillips, A. W. (1958), 'The relationship between unemployment and the rate of change of money wage rates in the U.K., 1861-1957', *Economica*, N.S. 25, pp. 283-99.

Pissarides, C. A. (1972), 'A model of British macroeconomic policy, 1955-69', *Manchester School*, 40, pp. 245-59.

Purdy, D. L. and G. Zis (1973), 'Trade unions and wage inflation in the U.K.: a re-appraisal', in *Essays in Modern Economics* (M. Parkin, ed.). London: Longman. Reprinted in *Inflation and Labour Markets* (D. E. W. Laidler and D. L. Purdy, eds.).

—— (1974), 'On the concept and measurement of union militancy', in *Inflation and Labour Markets* (D. E. W. Laidler and D. L. Purdy, eds.).

—— (1976), 'Trade unions and wage inflation in the U.K.: a reply to Dogas and Hines', *Applied Economics*, 8, pp. 249-65.

Radcliffe Committee (Committee on the Working of the Monetary System) (1959), *Report, Principal Memoranda of Evidence, Minutes of Evidence*. London: HMSO.

Raiffa, H. (1953), 'Arbitration schemes for generalized two-person games', in *Contributions to the Theory of Games II* (H. W.

Kuhn and A.W. Tucker, eds.). Princeton, N.J.: Princeton University Press.

Rose, D. E. (1972), 'A general error-learning model of expectations formation', paper presented to European Meeting of the Econometric Society, Budapest. University of Manchester-SSRC Inflation Workshop Discussion Paper.

Rushdy, F. and P. J. Lund (1967), 'The effect of demand on prices in British manufacturing industry', *Review of Economic Studies,* 34, pp. 361-71.

Sargan, J. D. (1971), 'A study of wages and prices in the U.K., 1949-68', in *The Current Inflation* (H. G. Johnson and A. R. Nobay, eds.).

Sargent, T. J. (1972), 'Anticipated inflation and the nominal rate of interest', *Quarterly Journal of Economics,* 86, pp. 313-25.

—— (1973), 'Rational expectations, the real rate of interest, and the natural rate of unemployment', *Brookings Papers on Economic Activity,* 4, pp. 429-72.

Saunders, P. G. and A. R. Nobay (1972), 'Price expectations, the Phillips curve and incomes policy', in *Incomes Policy and Inflation* (M. Parkin and M. T. Sumner, eds.).

Smith, D. C. (1968), 'Incomes policy', in *Britain's Economic Prospects* (R. E. Caves, ed.). Washington, D.C.: The Brookings Institution. Abridged version reprinted in *Incomes Policy and Inflation* (M. Parkin and M. T. Sumner, eds.).

Smith, G. W. (1976), 'The price equation: an econometric investigation', unpublished Ph.D. thesis, University of Manchester.

Solow, R. M. (1969), *Price Expectations and the Behavior of the Price Level.* Manchester: Manchester University Press.

Spencer, B. G. (1975), 'The small sample bias of Durbin's test for serial correlation when one of the regressors is a lagged dependent variable and the null hypothesis is true', *Journal of Econometrics,* 3, pp. 249-54.

Sumner, M. T. (1976), 'European Monetary union and the control of Europe's inflation rate', in *Inflation in the World Economy* (M. Parkin and G. Zis, eds.).

Taylor, J. (1972), 'Incomes policy, the structure of unemployment and the Phillips curve: the United Kingdom experience, 1953-70', in *Incomes Policy and Inflation* (M. Parkin and M. T. Sumner, eds.).

—— (1975), 'Wage inflation, unemployment, and the organised pressure for higher wages in the U.K., 1961-71', in *Contem-*

porary Issues in Economics (M. Parkin and A. R. Nobay, eds.).
Manchester: Manchester University Press.

Tobin, J. (1965), 'The monetary interpretation of history',
American Economic Review, 55, pp. 464-85.

Turnovsky, S. J. (1969), 'A Bayesian approach to the theory of
expectations', *Journal of Economic Theory*, 1, pp. 220-7.

—— (1970), 'Empirical evidence on the formation of price expectations', *Journal of the American Statistical Association*, 65,
pp. 1441-54.

Turnovsky, S. J. and M. L. Wachter (1972), 'A test of the 'expectations hypothesis' using directly observed wage and price
expectations', *Review of Economics and Statistics*, 54,
pp. 47-54.

Vanderkamp. J. (1972), 'Wage adjustment, productivity and price
change expectations', *Review of Economic Studies*, 39,
pp. 61-72.

Wallis, K. F. (1971), 'Wages, prices and incomes policies: some
comments', *Economica*, N.S. 38, pp. 304-10. Reprinted in
Incomes Policy and Inflation (M. Parkin and M. T. Sumner, eds.).

Walters, A. A. (1969), *Money in Boom and Slump*, Hobart Paper 44.
London: Institute of Economic Affairs.

Ward, R. and G. Zis (1974), 'Trade union militancy as an explanation
of inflation: an international comparison', *Manchester School*,
42, pp. 46-65.

Wiles, P. J. (1973), 'Cost inflation and the state of economic theory',
Economic Journal, 83, pp. 377-98.

Williamson, J. and G. E. Wood (1976), 'The British inflation:
indigenous or imported', *American Economic Review*, 66,
pp. 520-31.

Zeuthen, F. (1930), *Problems of Monopoly and Economic Warfare*.
London: Routledge.

Zis, G. (1977), 'On the role of strikes variables in U.K. wage
equations', *Scottish Journal of Political Economy*, 24,
pp. 43-55.

Index of names